How Now
Shall We Live?

© Copyright 1999 • LifeWay Press
Third printing, July 2001
All rights reserved

ISBN 0-7673-3177-X

Dewey Decimal Classification: 248.84
Subject Heading: CHRISTIAN LIFE

This book is the text for course CG-0555 in the study area Personal Life
in the Christian Growth Study Plan.

Unless otherwise noted, Scripture quotations are from the Holy Bible,
New International Version, copyright © 1973, 1978, 1984
by International Bible Society.

To order additional copies of this resource: WRITE LifeWay Church Resources Customer Service;
127 Ninth Avenue, North; Nashville, TN 37234-0113; FAX order to (615) 251-5933;
PHONE 1-800-458-2772; EMAIL to *customerservice@lifeway.com;*
ONLINE at *www.lifeway.com;* or visit the LifeWay Christian Store serving you.

Editor : Dale McCleskey
Art Direction and Design : Edward Crawford
Cover and Theme Illustration : Richard Tuschman
Assistant Editor : Joyce McGregor
Manuscript Assistant : Rhonda Porter Delph

Printed in the United States of America

☩

LifeWay Press
127 Ninth Avenue, North
Nashville, Tennessee 37234-0151

*As God works through us, we will help people and churches know Jesus Christ and seek His kingdom
by providing biblical solutions that spiritually transform individuals and cultures.*

How Now Shall We Live?

Charles Colson
and Nancy Pearcey

LifeWay Press
Nashville, Tennessee

Contents

Introduction

Centuries ago, when the Jews were in exile, in the depths of despair, they cried out to God, "How should we then live?" (Ezek. 33:10 KJV).

The same question still rings down through the ages. How shall we live—today?

The new millennium marks an extraordinary opportunity for the church. After two thousand years, the birth of the son of God still remains the defining moment of history. Jesus founded a church that could not be destroyed—not by his own crucifixion or by his followers' deaths in the Colosseum, not by the barbarian hoards or by mighty Turkish emperors, not by modern tyrants or by the power of sophisticated ideologies.

After two thousand years, we can affirm that Jesus Christ is indeed the same yesterday, today, and forever. This alone should make the opening decade of the millennium cause for jubilation, a time when Christians boldly and confidently recommit themselves to engage contemporary culture with a fresh vision of hope. Yet my sense is that most Christians are anything but jubilant, and for good reason.

We live in a culture that is at best morally indifferent. A culture in which Judeo-Christian values are mocked and where immorality in high places is not only ignored but even rewarded in the voting booth. A culture in which violence, banality, meanness, and disintegrating personal behavior are destroying civility and endangering the very life of our communities. A culture in which the most profound moral dilemmas are addressed by the cold logic of utilitarianism.

What's more, when Christians do make good-faith efforts to halt this slide into barbarism, we are maligned as intolerant or bigoted. Small wonder that many people have concluded that the "culture war" is over—and that we lost. Battle weary, we are tempted to withdraw into the safety of our sanctuaries, hoping to keep ourselves and our children safe from the coming desolation.

Right after signing the contract for this book, and while still plagued by writer's remorse (was I really convinced that this book needed to be written?), my wife, Patty, and I visited old friends for a weekend and attended their local evangelical church, which is well known for its biblical preaching. I found the message solidly scriptural and well delivered. That is, until the pastor reminded the congregation of what he sees as the church's mission: to prepare for Jesus' return through prayer, Bible study, worship, fellowship, and witnessing. In that instant, all lingering doubts about whether I should write this book evaporated.

Don't get me wrong. We need prayer, Bible study, worship, fellowship, and witnessing. But if we focus exclusively on these disciplines and in the process ignore our responsibility to redeem the surrounding culture, our Christianity will remain private and marginal.

Turning our backs on the culture is a betrayal of our biblical mandate and our own heritage because it denies God's sovereignty over all of life. Nothing could be more ill-timed or more deadly for the church. Furthermore, to abandon the battlefield now is to desert the cause just when we are seeing the first signs that historic Christianity may be on the verge of a great breakthrough. The process of secularization begun in the Enlightenment is grinding to a halt. All the ideologies, all the utopian promises that have marked this century have proven utterly bankrupt.

Americans have achieved what modernism presented as life's great shining purpose: individual autonomy, the right to do what one chooses. Yet this has not produced the promised freedom; we have discovered that we cannot live with the chaos that inevitably results from choice divorced from morality. As a result, Americans are groping for something that will restore the shattered bonds of family and community, something that will make sense of life. If the church turns inward now, if we focus only on our own needs, we will miss the opportunity to provide answers at a time when people are sensing a deep longing for meaning and order.

It is not enough to focus exclusively on the spiritual, on Bible studies and evangelistic campaigns, while turning a blind eye to the distinctive tensions of contemporary life. We must show the world that Christianity is more than a private belief, more than personal salvation. We must show that it is a comprehensive life system that answers all of humanity's age-old questions: Where did I come from? Why am I here? Where am I going? Does life have any meaning and purpose?

As we will argue in these pages, Christianity offers the only viable, rationally defensible answers to these questions. Only Christianity offers a way to understand the physical and moral order. Only Christianity offers a comprehensive worldview that covers all areas of life and thought, every aspect of creation. Only Christianity offers a way to live in response to these realities.

God exists. He has spoken. He is revealed in Christ, the Alpha and the Omega. He is sovereign over all creation, but if Christians are going to carry this life-giving message to the world, we must first understand it and live it ourselves. We must understand that God's revelation is the source of all truth, a comprehensive framework for all of reality.

The church's singular failure in recent decades has been the failure to see Christianity as a life system, or worldview, that governs every area of existence and speaks to both the moral and the physical order of the universe.

This failure has been crippling in many ways. For one thing, we cannot answer the questions our children bring home from school, so we are incapable of preparing them to answer the challenges they face. For ourselves, we cannot explain to our friends and neighbors why we believe, and we often cannot defend our faith when we are challenged.

We do not know how to organize our lives correctly. We live in the dark, allowing our lives to be shaped by the world around us. What's more, by failing to see Christian truth in every aspect of life, we miss so much beauty and meaning in our own lives: the thrill of seeing God's splendor in the intricacies of nature or hearing his voice in the performance of a great symphony or detecting his character in the harmony of a well-ordered community.

Most of all, our failure to see Christianity as a comprehensive framework of truth has crippled our efforts to have a redemptive effect on the surrounding culture. At its most fundamental level, the so-called "culture war" is a clash of belief systems. It is, as Kuyper put it, a clash of principle against principle, of worldview against worldview. Only when we see this can we effectively evangelize a post-Christian culture, bringing God's righteousness to bear in the world around us.

That is why Nancy Pearcey and I felt compelled to write this book. We want to present Christianity as a total worldview and life system. We have a passion to help believers discover the truth of the biblical worldview and live accordingly. We must be involved in the task of equipping believers to communicate the great truths of the faith. We must seize the opportunity of the new millennium.

We have the opportunity to be nothing less than God's agents in building a new Christian culture. Can such a vision make a difference? Is there yet time in this epic moment, at the dawn of the third millennium, for Christians to bring fresh hope to the church and bear witness to the immutable truth of biblical revelation? Can a culture be rebuilt, and can all the world see in its splendor and glory the contours of God's kingdom? Emphatically yes.

In this study we will see how the beliefs that have shaped modern society are in disarray. The old "isms" have shown themselves to be not only false but disasters. People are searching for answers that can make sense of the world. We have an opportunity to present the gospel in these days and see a new revival of Christianity throughout the world.

For that to happen, however, we must first listen to the answer God gave his people when they cried out, "How now shall we live?" Through the prophet Ezekiel, God told his people to repent and turn to him, to reject the culture that was mocking him, and to show their neighbors that their hope was in him, in his justice and righteousness.

God's word to us today is precisely the same. And to see what that means for us, we begin our journey in an unlikely place, among unlikely people, where you will first descend into hell and later catch a glimpse of heaven. This unlikely place is a microcosm in which we see the pattern by which we must redeem the world around us.

Sola Deo Gloria
Charles W. Colson
Nancy Pearcey
January, 1999
Washington, D.C.

Tyndale House Publishers is pleased to partner with LifeWay to produce this study material which contains excerpts from the longer hardback version of *How Now Shall We Live?* Copies of the hardback version may be obtained wherever Christian books are sold.

How We See Our World

Most people do not know what a worldview is, much less know how to critique worldviews. This unit will introduce worldview, show the importance of ideas, and get you into the study.

A Journey from Hell to Heaven

Dr. Jorge Crespo de Toral is the chairman of Prison Fellowship in Ecuador. Before Crespo began his work, the García Moreno Prison was a monument to human depravity. Now, through Crespo's work, the Prison Fellowship side of the facility has been turned into a testimony of the power of Christ. The prison is a place where two forces vying for allegiance in the human heart become dramatically visible. It represents an allegory of good and evil, heaven and hell.

In December 1995 I went to Quito to visit the deteriorating prison, one wing of which had been turned over to Prison Fellowship. I will never forget the prison. The sights and smells are seared indelibly into my memory. The prison sits on a steep, narrow street. The front entrance is a small doorway at the top of a few steps. On each side of the steps I saw huge mounds of garbage decaying in the heat, and the putrid odor was nearly overpowering. The uneven steps were slippery in places, the top step splattered with fresh blood.

"Someone was beaten and then dragged over the threshold," said Crespo, shaking his head. As we passed from the sun-drenched street into the unlighted, narrow passageways in the first section of the prison, known as the Detainees Pavilion, Crespo pointed out several black, cell-like holes in the concrete walls. These had been the notorious torture chambers. They were no longer used—thanks to his work—but still they gaped there, grotesque evidence of their bloody history.

As we descended into darkness, we came to a series of cells that were still in use. Twelve inmates shared each cell, meaning that the men had to sleep in shifts or stretch out on the floor, thick with grime and spilled sewage. There was no plumbing, and the smell was fetid. Water was brought into the cells in buckets; when empty, these same buckets were filled with waste and hauled back out.

I was stunned. I've been in more than 600 prisons in 40 countries, yet these were some of the worst conditions I had ever seen. Worse than one of the most notorious in the Soviet Gulags. Worse than prisons in the remotest reaches of India, Sri Lanka, and Zambia, or the wretched Luringancho Prison in Peru. But what was more startling was the fact that these men had not even been convicted of any crime. The cells in the Detainees Pavilion were used for men awaiting trial. Truly this was a kingdom of evil. Hell on earth.

After ministering in the Detainees Pavilion, we proceeded to the area that had been turned over to Prison Fellowship. All at once, we stepped out of the darkness into a radiant burst of light.

"This is Pavilion C," Crespo said proudly with a wide smile. Gathered in an open area more than two hundred inmates were singing and applauding. All were glowing with joy and enthusiasm. In Pavilion C, Prison Fellowship volunteers and inmate leaders provided rigorous instruction in Christian faith and character development to inmates. This was a holy community, a church like none I had ever seen.

Yet Jorge Crespo was quick to point out that Pavilion C was only a stop on the way, a place of preparation. The ultimate destination was Casa de San Pablo (St. Paul's House), a prison wing in which those who had been received into full Christian fellowship lived, worked, and ministered to the rest of the prisoners. Like Pavilion C, Casa de San Pablo was spotlessly clean, with the added beauty of tiled floors and separate dormitories, warmly furnished with wooden bunks made by inmates. Pictures of Christ and other religious symbols were everywhere, and I momentarily forgot that we were in a prison.

By living out the reality of being a new creation in Christ, Jorge Crespo has helped to create a whole new world for others. Crespo saw the battered inmates of García Moreno as potential citizens of the kingdom of God, and he helped create a corner of that kingdom even in a dark prison.

These two prisons in one represent the clash of two worldviews we will study. The evil forces that created the hell of the Detainees Pavilion are the same forces that ravage families, cities, and whole cultures around the globe. Conversely, the divine force that brought new life to dejected inmates is the same divine force that can renew people anywhere. How does this happen? Renewal can occur when Christians are committed to living out their faith, seeing the world as God sees it, viewing reality through the lens of divine revelation.

In this study we will examine the forces that shape our world. We will contrast the worldview that creates places like the Detainees Pavilion with the worldview that can make human society into a foretaste of heaven. Whether heaven-on-earth or the opposite, it all starts with ideas—the ideas that determine how we see the world.

DAY ONE
The Power of Ideas

"For as he thinketh in his heart, so is he."–Proverbs 23:7, KJV

The writer of Proverbs was describing a specific type of person, but his words form a banner for understanding the power of belief systems. As people think, so they are. Our most basic core beliefs determine our identity and our destiny. Those central ideas control how we perceive the world around us.

Our modern world abounds with both positive and negative illustrations of the principle. Jorge Crespo's God-given concept of prison reform transformed the lives of hundreds of men. Similarly, a false idea can have incredibly destructive power. A gun or bomb may kill a few people in one place and time; but an idea can murder millions. An idea can stretch across national boundaries, oceans, and centuries to continue either to bless or to destroy.

The following paragraph describes the origin of an idea that led to the death of millions. When you guess what movement resulted from the idea, led by what leader, write the names here.

_____
_____
_____
_____

In the nineteenth century, German philosopher Friedrich Nietzsche declared the death of God. He etched out what that would mean: the death of morality. Nietzsche, one of the most powerful influences on fascism, dismissed sin as nothing but a ruse invented by a wretched band of "ascetic priest[s]," Old Testament shamans who had achieved a magical hold over men

Different life systems compete for our minds. Unless we consciously and consistently choose a biblical system for seeing all of life, we will be influenced by destructive worldviews around us.

Handwritten notes (top margin): 1960's–1980's declared "God is dead" + emphasized power as the real motivator + explanation FOR people's actions · revealed new ways to challenge totalitarianism

Handwritten notes (left margin): http://plato.stanford.edu/entries/nietzsche/#7 · deep influence in 20th century + continental Europe + accepted ideas + explanations for commonly accepted animal instincts + explanation for morality dealing w/ animal psychoanalysis + others referred to Sigmund Freud's various views + so crucial to interpret to resemble various ways to interpret war, capitalism + domination + racial self-glorification + nationalism + racial self-glorification · passage for the dated nationalism

Friedrich Nietzsche (1844-1900)

Nietzsche was born on October 15, 1844, in Röcken, Prussia. His father, a Lutheran minister, died when Nietzsche was four, and he was raised by his mother. He was convinced that traditional values represented a "slave morality," a morality created by weak and resentful individuals who encouraged such behavior as gentleness and kindness because the behavior served their interests. Nietzsche claimed that new values could be created to replace the old ones.

and women by playing the "ravishing music" of guilt in their souls.[1]

Nietzsche denounced Christian morality as a morality for slaves. Kindness, forgiveness, humility, obedience, and self-denial were the characteristics of weak, repressed slaves who had rejected the joy of life. In Nietzsche's mind, the biblical ethic was nothing less than a pathology, a life-killing prudery. He looked forward to the evolution of a race of superhumans imbued with an ethic of power—exactly what the Nazis hoped to create from the Aryan race.

Nietzsche never flew a Nazi flag. He never commanded a Panzer division, but his ideas gave birth to the Nazis. Hitler simply translated Nietzsche's ideas into actions and cost the lives of fifty million people in World War II. Amazingly, Nietzsche's ideas continue their swath of destruction today.

The Power of an Idea

A few years ago home-grown terrorists motivated by a twisted view of the world exploded a bomb outside the federal building in Oklahoma City. As this study was being prepared our nation once again found itself gripped by trauma over yet another school-shooting tragedy. Young men once again carried a false set of beliefs to its tragic conclusion.

How can these things be? Though many factors contribute, you can trace the cause to ideas. In this study you will learn about some of those ideas. You will examine the direct links from the thinkers and ideas to the practical results. You will also see how only Jesus Christ and a biblical worldview can supply the solutions to transform people and entire societies.

You may be unaccustomed to the term "worldview". What do you think of when you see the term?

❑ I have no idea what the term means.
❑ I think of the basic beliefs that shape how we see the world.

❑ It sounds like a term used only by college professors.
❑ My definition of a worldview is:

_____
_____
_____

The word *worldview* may sound abstract or philosophical, a topic discussed by pipe-smoking, tweed-jacketed professors in academic settings. Actually a person's worldview is intensely practical. It is simply the sum total of our beliefs about the world, the "big picture" that directs our daily decisions and actions. What we assume or believe becomes the lens through which we then see everything around us.

If we asked you to describe your worldview, how difficult would it be to put it into words?

EASY   VERY DIFFICULT

Most of us would initially have considerable difficulty explaining our worldview. We don't know where to start. We need a framework, some way to explain and evaluate the core of our belief system. In this study we want to help you become adept at just such a framework. You will have the opportunity to become skillful at expressing your belief system.

The Three-Part Evaluation

Understanding what a worldview is and how it works gives us a way to make sense of the ideas all around us. Every worldview can be analyzed by the way it answers three basic questions:

1. Where did we come from and who are we?
2. What has gone wrong with the world?
3. What can we do to fix it?

These three questions form a grid we can use to break down the inner logic of every belief system or philosophy we encounter. Any philosophy, from the textbooks in our classrooms to the unspoken belief system that shapes the message we hear on a television talk show, can be tested by these three questions.

The questions are universal. Every philosophy and religion recognizes that we came from somewhere, that something is wrong with our world, and that we must do something about it. By using the three questions, we can evaluate any belief system. We will show you how to apply the three-part grid to critique nonbiblical worldviews, while at the same time framing a biblical worldview on any subject, from family life to education, from politics to science, from art to popular culture.

Now consider the ease or difficulty of explaining your worldview again. Briefly state your worldview by completing the sentences in the three areas.

1. I believe we came from _God created us for a purpose_

2. I believe what has gone wrong with the world is _Sin and man's desire to satisfy natural desires_

3. I believe what we must do to fix what has gone wrong is _Change in morality, behavior & thus society/won't happen until we all turn to God_

You have just stated the core of your worldview. Your worldview is the most basic level of your faith—the core of your beliefs about the world. It is the "big picture" that directs your daily decisions and your actions.

We will picture the three parts of a worldview as follows:

| Where We Came From | What Has Gone Wrong | The Solution |

You could note several relationships between the three parts of the worldview grid. Particularly notice that part 3, what needs to be done to fix the world, depends on part 2, what has gone wrong.

Look back to the story of Fredrich Nietzsche on pages 11-12. Write what Nietzsche thought had gone wrong with the world in the formula below.

We came from… _Not answered_

weakness from traditional animal habits

What has gone wrong… _believes morality is a weakness and robs us of joy._

Then write Nietzsche's proposed solution in the third space below.

The solution… _rejected values of gentleness, kindness, forgiveness, humility, obedience + self denial (fruits of the spirit) in exchange for values that empowered_

Nietzsche believed religion or Christian morality was the problem. He considered it a "life-killing prudery." He believed in an ethic of power, including doing away with religion as the solution.

Worldview Controls What We See

Our worldview serves as the lens through which we see circumstances and events. We have all observed occasions when people see the same event very differently. One reason is worldview. Our worldview con-

frame of reference

philosophy \fe-'la-se-fe\ (14C) *n.* **4 a :** the most general beliefs, concepts, and attitudes of an individual or group. (Webster's)

How We See Our World

"We demolish arguments and every pretension that sets itself up against the knowl-edge of God, and we take captive every thought to make it obedient to Christ" (2 Cor. 10:5).

Today's Prayer
Many of us have compartmentalized our Christianity and separated God from the "real" world. If the Holy Spirit is bringing conviction of this to you, pray today for God's direc-tion in developing a perspective that covers all aspects of the world.

trols the media of our minds. It filters infor-mation and colors what we perceive.

Here's an assignment requiring some thought. Think of an analogy to explain how worldview automatically shapes our percep-tion. I'll give you an example. One person said worldview controls and interprets what we see and hear like a teacher in a classroom, presenting the information to the students. Now write your own analogy.

A worldview is like…

when one person walks into a party and makes assumptions about the people that may be different from a person standing next to him.

"Do not conform any longer to the pattern of this world, but be transformed by the renew-ing of your mind" (Rom. 12:2).

How do you suppose the challenge of Romans 12:2 relates to the subject of worldview? Have you ever wondered how, in a practical sense, "the renewing of your mind" takes place? What does it mean to be "conformed" to the pattern of this world?

Don is a photographer. When his Bible-study group discussed Romans 12:2 and worldviews, he said, "I can change the ap-pearance of a picture using filters. The filter screens out certain wavelengths of light, thus altering the look of the finished photo. I see that a person's worldview does the same thing. I can make a photograph show what I want the viewer to see rather than what is real. That's what the world does to us. It warps our vision, conforms us to its pattern, and seeks to make us think its way."

We want to suggest that several different worldviews exist. These different life sys-tems each compete for our minds. Unless we consciously and consistently choose a biblical system for seeing all of life, we will

be influenced by the destructive world-views around us. We will be conformed to the pattern of this world.

Some of the information and concepts in this study may not be easy; however, we urge you to do this intellectual and spiri-tual work. God has given us a commission to impact society. Jesus said we are the salt and light to transform a world rotting in its own filth (Matt. 5:13-14). The apostle Paul passed along God's command that we con-front the ideas of our day.

Read 2 Corinthians 10:5 in the margin. What arguments or beliefs can you think of that set themselves up "against the knowledge of God" in our world today?

_____
_____
_____
_____
_____
_____
_____
_____
_____

We have a commission to understand and effectively combat the false ideas that compete for hearts and lives. I believe every Christian can do just that. We dare not hide our heads in the sand and leave the battle to others.

PRAYER Father,
Thank You for including us in the great task of presenting You to a needy world. I recognize that You have commanded us to take every thought captive and demolish the arguments that oppose the knowledge of You. I want to learn to think "Christianly." I want my world-view to be based totally on the truth that is perfectly revealed in Jesus Christ. Please give me the leadership of Your Spirit and the encouragement I need to learn and understand.

The Two Worldviews

"He who is not with me is against me, and he who does not gather with me scatters."—Matthew 12:30

Distinguished Harvard scholar Samuel Huntington argued that the world is divided not so much by geographic boundaries as by religious and cultural traditions, by people's most deeply-held beliefs, and by worldviews. We agree.

Political scientist James Kurth contends that the most significant clash is between those who adhere to a Judeo-Christian framework and those who favor postmodernism and multiculturalism. Postmodernism is a system of thought that denies all truth claims. Multiculturalism considers all cultures to be equal since it excludes the idea that one value can be better than another. We will examine postmodernism and multiculturalism more thoroughly later, but first we need to consider the worldview from which they have grown. They are expressions of the worldview called naturalism.

The following paragraph contains descriptions of a naturalistic and biblical worldview. Underline words or phrases that are part of a biblical worldview.

STATEMENT The conflict of our day is between the biblical worldview and the naturalist worldview. The biblical worldview presents a transcendent God who created the universe; naturalism claims that natural causes alone are sufficient to explain everything that exists. The conflict voices itself in foundational questions. Is ultimate reality God or the cosmos? Is there a supernatural realm, or is nature all that exists? Has God spoken and revealed His truth to us, or is truth something we have to find, even invent, for ourselves? Is there a purpose to our lives, or are we cosmic accidents emerging from the slime?

With just what you now know, how do you suppose that the worldview called naturalism would complete the first part of the three-part evaluation?

1. We came from *evolution*

Naturalism has one absolute answer to the question where we came from, but many answers to the second and third parts of a worldview. According to naturalism, we came from natural processes working over immense periods of time—evolution.

Now let's consider the second and third questions of a worldview as they apply to naturalism:

- Depending on which advocate of naturalism you ask, you may get any of a bewildering array of ideas of what has gone wrong with the world. The list could include human beings, Europeans, the wealthy, males, the private ownership of property, sexual repression, ignorance, religion, democracy, or many other proposed evils.
- Each sub-group within the naturalist worldview has its own idea of what must

nat·u·ral·ism
\'na-che-re-li-zem\
n (ca. 1641)
2 : a theory denying that an event or object has a supernatural significance; *specif* : the doctrine that scientific laws are adequate to account for all phenomena. (Webster's)

be done to fix our problems. Some believe life's ills come from ignorance and can be solved by more learning and a growing technical competence. Karl Marx believed the division of labor and private ownership of property caused the evils of life. Therefore, state control in a communist system was his proposed solution. Some radical animal-rights activists believe that the elimination of humanity would solve the planet's basic problem. What you believe must be done to fix our world depends on which opinion you hold about what has gone wrong.

Absolute Opposites

These two major systems—Naturalism and Christianity— are utterly opposed. If we are going to defend the truth effectively, we must grasp the full implications of the differences.

- *Naturalism* is the idea that nature is all that exists, that life arose from a chance collision of atoms, evolving eventually into human life as we know it today. In its broadest sense, naturalism can even include certain forms of religion—those in which the spiritual is considered part of nature, such as neo-pagan and New Age religions.
- By contrast, *Christianity* teaches that a transcendent God existed before the world and that God is the ultimate origin of everything. The universe is dependent at every moment on His providential governance and care.

You may have noticed that the Bible speaks directly to the three parts of a worldview. Complete the three statements below with a word we use to describe the Bible teaching about each area.

1. Where we came from we call the doctrine of _____.

2. What has gone wrong with the world we call the _____.

3. What we must do to fix the world we call the doctrine of _____.

You may have answered with different words, but we normally call number 1 *the doctrine of creation*. Number 2, we call *the fall*. Number 3 may have given you more difficulty. Because we recognize that the work is not primarily ours but God's, we call what must be done *redemption*.

We have divided this study into five parts based on the concepts above. The first segment, which you are now studying, introduces the concept of worldview. The second part of our study deals with creation. The third portion deals with the fall, and the fourth deals with redemption. The final segment of our study deals with what we need to do with what we learn—how to transform culture. God has not called us to ignore the world but to be salt and light in our world. We will examine issues related to transforming culture throughout our study, but we will deal specifically with it in units 7 and 8.

The Challenge Before Us

When we understand the importance of worldviews, we see the mission of the church in new terms. Our task in this new millennium is nothing less than producing men and women who will wrest Christianity free from its fortress mentality, its sanctuary stronghold.

The church must once again establish Christianity as the great life system and cultural force that acknowledges the Creator as sovereign over all.

What evidence could you suggest that the church has developed a "fortress mentality"?

_____
_____
_____
_____
_____
_____

We must be men and women who understand that the task is more than launching spasmodic crusades to fight one battle or another over such issues as gay rights or abortion. We must be men and women who see that the struggle is one of first principles. "If the battle is to be fought with honor and with a hope of victory, then principle must be arrayed against principle." We must understand opposing views as total life systems and then "take our stand in a life system of equally comprehensive and far-reaching power."[2]

The contours of a Christian life system will become clear in the sections of our study:

- **Creation**—God spoke the universe into existence and created life;
- **Fall**—the human condition is marred by sin;
- **Redemption**—God in His grace provided a way to be reconciled to Himself;
- **Restoration**—we are called to bring these principles into every area of life and to create a new culture.

Equipped with this understanding, we can show not only that the Christian worldview gives the best answers which accord with both common sense and the most advanced science, but also that Christians can take up spiritual arms in the great cosmic struggle between conflicting worldviews.

A Place to Begin

Because we have not learned to examine worldviews, many of us have compartmentalized our Christianity. We have separated God from the "real" world. As a result we have done exactly what James warned us to avoid. James 1:8 warns that a "double-minded man" is "unstable in all he does." James was writing about a person who seeks to live combining belief and unbelief.

In the following case study circle evidences that Chris is a "double-minded" person.

CASE STUDY Chris grew up in a Christian home. At age 11 he made a profession of his faith in Christ. He believes the Bible, but he sees no connection between Scripture and the "real" world. He attends church, but makes little or no connection between Sunday and the rest of the week. He assumes that life must have evolved to its present state because there seems to be so much evidence to support the theory. He sees science as dealing with facts while religion deals with faith. Therefore, he sees no conflict between his faith and the other parts of his life.

The basis for the Christian worldview is God's revelation, yet, sadly, many believers fail to understand that Scripture is intended to be the basis for all of life. Like most people today, Chris operates on a fact/value distinction. Such people believe that science uncovers "facts," which they believe to be reliable and true, while morality and religion are based on "values," which they believe to be subjective and relative to the individual.[3]

Read the following statement carefully. Then explain what is wrong with Gould's reasoning about facts and values.

_____
_____
_____
_____
_____
_____

STATEMENT Harvard paleontologist Stephen J. Gould says that religion and science cannot conflict because they deal with different things: science is about facts, while "religion struggles with human morality."[4]

> Christianity cannot be limited to only one component of our lives, a mere religious practice or observance, or even a salvation experience. We are compelled to see Christianity as the all-encompassing truth, the root of everything else. It is ultimate reality.

Today's Prayer:
Are you willing to let God use you to help evangelize our world and transform it to reflect His wisdom? If you are, pray that God will lead you. If you are not yet ready to commit to this, ask God's guidance to start with small steps in that direction.

For the past few centuries, the secular world has driven a wedge between science and religion, between fact and value, between objective knowledge and subjective feeling. As a result, Christians often think in terms of the same false separation, allowing our belief system to be reduced to little more than private feelings and experience, completely divorced from objective facts.

Many Christians have fallen for this tactic, resulting in our often being unprepared for the intellectual battles we face in a secular culture. This is what we mean when we say a Christian must have a comprehensive worldview: a view or perspective that covers all aspects of the world. We will look more at fact/value distinctions in units 2 and 3 as we consider creation.

What examples have you seen of Christians accepting the false separation of facts and values?

_____
_____
_____
_____
_____
_____

Christianity Is a Worldview

Evangelicals have been particularly vulnerable to the false distinctions between facts and values because of our emphasis on personal commitment. We stress a personal relationship with God so highly that we may fail to see God's plan beyond our personal salvation.

Is your relationship with God only a subjective value or is it a literal, true fact? Why?

_____
_____
_____
_____
_____
_____
_____

Genuine Christianity is more than a relationship with Jesus, more than a relationship expressed in personal piety, church attendance, Bible study, and works of charity. It is more than believing a system of doctrines about God. Genuine Christianity is a way of seeing and comprehending all reality. It is a worldview.

The scriptural basis for this belief is the creation account. Everything that exists came into being at God's command and is therefore subject to Him. Thus, the truth in every area, from ethics to economics to ecology, is ultimately found in relationship to God and His revelation. God created the natural world, natural laws, our bodies and the moral laws that keep us healthy, and our minds and the laws of logic and imagination. God created us as social beings and gave us the principles for social and political institutions. God created a world of beauty and the principles of aesthetics and artistic creation. In every area of life, genuine knowledge means not only discerning the laws and ordinances by which God has structured creation, but also allowing those laws to shape how we should live.

As the church fathers used to say, all truth is God's truth.

Jesus stated His claim this way, "I am the way and the truth and the life" (John 14:6). He is the origin and end of all things, the *Alpha* and the *Omega*. Nothing has meaning apart from Him. Nothing exists apart from Him. He is the agent of creation, author of all that is and ever will be. Christ is Lord over all creation, from the human soul to the vast reaches of the cosmos (see Ps. 2; 8; 110; Phil. 2:5-11).

When we truly grasp this belief, we are compelled to see that the Christian faith cannot be reduced to John 3:16 or simple formulas. Christianity cannot be limited to one component of our lives, a mere religious practice or observance, or even a salvation experience. We are compelled to see Christianity as all-encompassing truth, the root of everything else. It is ultimate reality.

How Do You Judge a Worldview?

"For he has set a day when he will judge the world with justice by the man he has appointed. He has given proof of this to all men by raising him from the dead."—Acts 17:31

Every worldview is a proposed map of reality, a guide to navigating in the world. One effective test of any truth claim then is to ask whether we can live by it. If you follow a map but still find yourself splashing into rivers or crashing off cliffs, you can be quite sure something is wrong with the map.

Below each of the following case studies, state in your own words what you think is wrong with the person's worldview.

1. Chairman Mao believed in Marxism—that private ownership of property and the division of labor causes the evil in the world. He therefore believed that state ownership of property would bring prosperity. Mao forced his nation through more and more extreme state control, but each time the people became more desperately poor instead of more prosperous.

What was wrong with Mao's worldview?

people w/o ownership did not take responsibility

2. Dr. Benjamin Spock encouraged parents to reject the old puritan notion of children as savages, prone to evil and in need of civilizing. Instead, he urged them to understand children as evolving psyches in need of attention. For example, when a school-age child steals something, Spock suggests that parents consider whether their child might "need more … approval at home," and even a raise in his allowance![5]

What was wrong with Spock's worldview?

we are talking about 2 extremes there is the middle ground of considering the child & circumstance

Making Sense of Our World

Understanding Christianity as a total life system enables us to make sense of the world we live in and thus order our lives more rationally. It also enables us to understand forces hostile to our faith, equipping us to evangelize and defend Christian truth as God's instrument for transforming culture.

Because the world was created by an intelligent being, rather than by chance, it has an intelligible order. As Abraham Kuyper wrote, "All created life necessarily bears in itself a law for its existence, instituted by God Himself."[6]

The only way to live a rational and healthy life is to determine the nature of these divine laws and ordinances and then to use them as the basis for how we live. In the lessons to come we will see how the naturalistic worldview has led to the kinds of bumping up against reality exemplified by Chairman Mao or Dr. Spock in the previous case studies.

For Every Action

Just as certain physical actions produce predictable reactions, so moral behavior produces predictable consequences. Hollywood may portray adultery as glamorous, but it invariably produces anger, jealousy, broken relationships, even violence. Defiance of moral laws may even lead to death, whether it is the speeding drunk who kills or the drug addict who contracts and spreads AIDS. No transgression of moral law is without painful consequences.

If we want to live healthy, well-balanced lives, we had better know the laws and ordinances by which God has structured creation. Because these are the laws of our own inner nature, Kuyper notes, we will experience them not as oppressive external constraints but as "a guide through the desert," guaranteeing our safety.[7]

Interestingly, naturalists acknowledge the destruction in defying "natural law," such as the law of gravity. List a consequence of defying the following moral laws:

1. You shall not commit adultery.

broken relationships and depression leads to physical problems

2. You shall not bear false witness against your neighbor.

distruction of other lives and

Wisdom

Understanding life's laws is what Scripture calls *wisdom.* "Wisdom in Scripture is, broadly speaking, the knowledge of God's world and the knack of fitting oneself into it," said Calvin College professor Cornelius Plantinga. A wise person is one who knows the boundaries and limits, the laws, rhythms, and seasons of the created order, both in the physical and the social world. "To be wise is to know reality and then accommodate yourself to it." By contrast, nonbelievers who refuse to accommodate

opening
what is wisdom?

Proverbs 8:13 prudence

themselves to the laws of life are not only immoral but also foolish, no matter how well educated they may be. They fail to recognize the structure of creation and are constantly at odds with reality.[8]

Look up the following Scriptures that deal with wisdom and answer the questions.

1. What is the source of wisdom? (1 Kings 3:28)

God

2. What effect does obedience to God have on wisdom? (Ps. 111:10)

eternal praise

3. What will we become if we despise wisdom and discipline? (Prov. 1:7)

Fools

4. How does wisdom relate to knowing God? (Prov. 9:10)

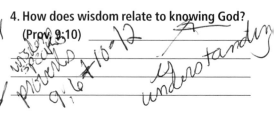

To deny God is to blind ourselves to reality. The inevitable consequence is that we will bump up against reality in painful ways, just as a blindfolded driver will crash into other drivers or run off the road.

We make the bold claim that serious Christians actually live happier, more fulfilled, more productive lives by almost every measure (and studies are beginning to bear this out). This assertion simply makes sense. Someone who accepts the contours and limits of the physical and moral order does not engage in folly—whether stepping off a cliff, committing adultery, or driving drunk.

Describe in your own words the results of wisdom in these passages:

1. Proverbs 12:8 _____

wise men are respected

_____

_____

2. Proverbs 24:14 _____

wise men have hope for the future

3. Proverbs 28:26 _____

wise men are kept safer

Making Our Mark on the World

Our calling is not only to order our own lives by divine principles but also to engage the world as Jorge Crespo did. We are to fulfill both the Great Commission and the cultural mandate—the call to create a culture under the lordship of Christ. God cares not only about redeeming souls but also about restoring His creation. Our job is to build up the church and also to build a society to the glory of God.

To engage the world, however, requires that we understand the great ideas that compete for people's minds and hearts. Philosopher Richard Weaver's book title is correct: *Ideas Have Consequences*.[10] It is the great ideas that inform the mind, fire the imagination, move the heart, and shape a culture. History is little more than the recording of the rise and fall of the great ideas—the worldviews—that form our values and move us to act.

The most fundamental weakness in modern evangelicalism is that we've been fighting cultural skirmishes on all sides without knowing what the war itself is about. We haven't identified the worldviews that lie at the root of cultural conflict—and this ignorance dooms our best efforts.

In the margin draw a tree to illustrate the content of the paragraph you just read. On your drawing write in the place of fruit or foliage some of the issues about which Christians have "skirmished" with the world. Then for the roots write in some of the underlying worldview ideas behind the differences.

The culture war is not just about abortion, homosexual rights, or the decline of public education. These are only the skirmishes. The real war is a cosmic struggle between worldviews—between the Christian worldview and the various secular and spiritual worldviews arrayed against it. This is what we must understand if we are going to be effective both in evangelizing our world and in transforming it to reflect the wisdom of the Creator.

In broadest terms the conflict of our time is theism (belief in God) versus naturalism. Is ultimate reality God or the cosmos? In tomorrow's study we will begin to trace the modern roots of this struggle.

> The real war is a cosmic struggle between worldviews—between the Christian worldview and the various secular and spiritual worldviews arrayed against it.

The Cultural Mandate

The Christian calling is, as one great scholar put it, not only to save souls but to save minds.[9] That notion might sound alien to many people, but it is surely biblical. The greatest commandment, Jesus says, is to "love the Lord your God with all your heart and with all your soul and with all your mind" (Matt. 22:37). Loving the Lord with your mind means understanding God's ordinances for all of creation, the natural world, societies, businesses, schools, the government, and for science and the arts. Sadly, many Christians have been misled into believing there is a dichotomy between faith and reason. As a result, they have actually shunned intellectual pursuits.

Today's Prayer
Praise Jesus today that He is truth on which you can build your life. Ask for God's wisdom in discerning His truth.

How We See Our World

DAY FOUR
Foundations to Build On

The wise woman builds her house, but with her own hands the foolish one tears hers down. –Proverbs 14:1

Our purpose in this study: We want you to understand the ideas that are building and destroying our world so that you can be salt and light to our generation.

René Descartes (1596-1650)

Born in a small town near Tours that now bears his name, Descartes was reared by his maternal grandmother following his mother's death.

Descartes observed that many of his preconceived childhood opinions turned out to be unreliable; so he maintained that it is necessary, "once in a lifetime" to "demolish everything and start again right from the foundations." That foundation meant to doubt everything but that he was a thinking being.

We have seen how worldviews serve like the blinders on a horse. Not only shaping what we see, a false worldview actually makes us unable to see truth. Have you noticed that some people hold beliefs that seem not only foolish but insane? For example, one communist regime after another has destroyed its own country in the name of creating a workers' paradise. Like the foolish woman in the proverb above, false beliefs can lead us to destroy the very things we value. How does such "foolishness" occur?

Think in terms of ideas as you read the words of Jesus below:
"Therefore everyone who hears these words of mine and puts them into practice is like a wise man who built his house on the rock. The rain came down, the streams rose, and the winds blew and beat against that house; yet it did not fall, because it had its foundation on the rock. But everyone who hears these words of mine and does not put them into practice is like a foolish man who built his house on sand'" (Matt. 7:24-26).

Ideas build one upon another. If we build on the firm foundation of truth, as Jesus said, we get solid results. If we build on lies, we create disasters.

Everyone feels the impact of the ideas that shape our world. Sadly, most people just play the victim role. They don't understand the ideas and worldviews. They merely feel the results.

We challenge you to be different. We challenge you to understand the great and the horrible ideas that are building and destroying our world.

Let's meet some philosophers who have shaped modern thought. We will explore them more fully later. Don't be intimidated by the term *philosophers*. These are just people who expressed ideas we can understand and examine.

Jesus compared His words (ideas) to building materials. If we examine His analogy, we can compare every person's thought-life to a building. Sadly, the modern world has been largely led to build on the sands of false ideas. Our worldview provides the foundation of our thought-life: where did we come from? what has gone wrong with the world? and what needs to be done about it?

Descartes Doubting Everything
The first thinker we want you to meet was French mathematician René Descartes. Though a lifelong Catholic, in 1610 Descartes resolved to doubt everything that could possibly be doubted. He concluded that he could doubt everything except the fact that he doubted. This conclusion led to his famous statement: "I think, therefore I am." With this, Descartes unleashed the revolutionary idea that the human mind, not God, is the source of certainty; human experience is the fixed point around which everything else revolves.

In the margin draw a house to represent your belief system. What part does God play? What foundation do you build on? Write "God" in the drawing wherever He fits in your life.

We are contrasting a biblical worldview with naturalism. Descartes did not ascribe to naturalism, but his idea opened the door for it. Once we have become the center of our universe, we begin to look for ways to dethrone and eliminate God. From the time of Descartes to the time of Darwin, the idea of evolution gained ground.

Go back to your drawing of a house. You probably labeled your foundation "God." How would Descartes's idea alter your drawing? Draw another picture replacing God with self as the basis of reality.

Rousseau and the Evil Society

Once God has been dethroned, thinkers can build some very strange dwellings. Rousseau taught that, in its natural state, human nature is good; people become evil only when they are corrupted by society.

Picture Rousseau's idea of human goodness on the first two parts of the three-part grid below.

❋ **Part 1: Creation: Man Naturally Innocent**

⬡ **Part 2: The Fall: Corruption by Society**

Rousseau believed people are naturally loving, virtuous, and selfless; it is society, with its artificial rules and conventions, that makes them envious, hypocritical, and competitive.

Rousseau rejected anything that limits freedom of the inner self, which he saw as naturally good—or, at least, unformed and undefined and capable of being made good. He opens *The Social Contract and Discourses* with the famous line, "Man is born free, and everywhere he is in chains."[11] Since individuals start out unformed, they must be free to create themselves by their own choices, free to discover their own identity. The individual's goal is to be set free from the chains of institutions, rules, customs, and traditions.

Rousseau then took his thought a step further. Since humans were basically good and corrupted by society, someone needed to step in and rescue human nature. He believed the state could fill that role.

Now we could picture Rousseau's idea with the following four steps:

1. **The individual—Naturally Good**
2. **Forces in Society—Corrupt the Naturally Good Nature**
3. **The Government—Must Step In and Remove the Corrosive Force of Society**
4. **Good Human Nature Will Then Result in a Utopian Society**

If one buys Rousseau's basic idea, the government (3) is justified to do absolutely anything necessary to destroy the forces of an evil society (2) so that natural human goodness can emerge. We'll see Rousseau's simple idea forms the basis for the most destructive systems the world has ever seen.

Remember our basic thesis? Ideas are powerful. Ideas build one upon another to develop systems of thought. Those systems of thought form the basis for everything from family living to the politics of nations.

Proverbs has much to say about building life on false ideas and behaviors. Match the following Scriptures with the appropriate applications below.

a. **"The way of a fool seems right to him" (Prov. 12:15)**

b. **"Better to meet a bear robbed of her cubs than a fool in his folly"(Prov. 17:12).**

c. **"A fool finds no pleasure in understanding but delights in airing his own opinions" (Prov. 18:2).**

_b_ **1. False ideas are extremely dangerous.**

_c_ **2. False ideas are blinding. Thus, people will build their lives on ideas even though they are extremely foolish.**

_a_ **3. Once we have adopted an idea, we tend to defend it and build on it rather than seeking truth.**

Jean-Jacques Rousseau (1712-1778)

Born in Geneva, Rousseau's mother died at his birth, and his father eventually deserted him.

Rousseau tried two apprenticeships but ran away to escape the discipline. After attending school, he served in households, and was charged with theft in one. After more wandering, he spent eight years enjoying nature and studying. Rousseau's life was marked with both dismal failures and great acclamation.

Today's Prayer
Debate can be unpleasant at times, but at least it presupposes that there are truths worth defending. Christians are increasingly being called on to stand for their beliefs. Spend time with God today, asking for His courage to stand for right.

We contend that Rousseau's concept that human nature is good is a "foolish" idea. It goes against everything in Scripture and personal experience. Yet his thought shapes our world in a thousand destructive ways. We answered the activity on page 23, 1.b; 2. a; and 3. c. We will look at a third philosopher who has shaped the modern world—Charles Darwin.

Darwin and Natural Selection

Darwin did not invent the idea of evolution. He rather proposed a mechanism called natural selection that made evolution believable. Darwin provided a "scientific" justification for evolution.

In the second drawing of the house, one student moved God from being the foundation to being the sun shining down on the house. Now Darwin made it possible to eliminate God from the picture altogether.

The Rise of Communism

Have you wondered how communists could believe what they do? How could Stalin, Mao, and Pol Pot murder millions of their own people in the name of good? Marx took the building blocks provided by previous thinkers and built the most destructive ideology yet seen on earth. His thinking fuels not only communism but dozens of other systems at work today.

Darwinism and Neo-Darwinism

Due to modern discoveries in the fields of microbiology and genetics, Darwin's original theory has been thoroughly scientifically discredited. In fact, natural selection serves to prevent evolution by screening out changes. Darwinism has been replaced by neo (new) darwinism, which considers genetic mutations as the source of evolutionary change. We have chosen to use darwinism consistently through this study to refer to the original theory, its newer form, and all evolution, though we recognize that the theory predates Darwin.

Good Human Nature

Corrupted by Something

The State as Savior

Perfect Society Results

source of corruption. We will see how these ideas lead to the ultimate irony: to build, we must destroy.

A Remarkable Phenomenon

Proverbs 9:7-8 underscores a strange fact about human nature. Once we have adopted a position, even when proved wrong, we tend to defend it rather than change our minds. In our study we will encounter this phenomenon repeatedly. Darwin's theory has been discredited, but it lives on in neo-darwinism. Marxism has been the greatest destructive failure in history but it continues in many forms.

Since he believed that human nature was good until corrupted by the family or society (Rousseau), Marx said we must destroy those forces of corruption. The state must tear down the sources of evil so the perfect society can emerge. Marx thought the private ownership of property and the division of labor was the

Why do you suppose we humans cling so tenaciously to failed and false systems? Write your thoughts for discussion in your group this week.

Pride

"Whoever corrects a mocker invites insult; whoever rebukes a wicked man incurs abuse. Do not rebuke a mocker or he will hate you; rebuke a wise man and he will love you" (Prov. 9:7-8).

DAY FIVE
The Logical Conclusion: Postmodernism

"There is a way that seems right to a man, but in the end it leads to death."—Proverbs 14:12

As we have seen, the subject of worldviews is anything but an academic issue removed from real life. Psalm 11:3 asks a haunting question: "When the foundations are being destroyed, what can the righteous do?" Never in history have the foundations been as systematically attacked as in the last century. Naturalistic philosophy has opened the door to chaos.

As we end this first week of study, we consider naturalism's impact on the heart of our political, educational, and social fabric.

Naturalism and Morality

Recently a prominent congressman connected the violence in our public schools to teaching children that they evolved from animals. Columnists scoffed at the

en·light·en·ment
\in-'li-tin-ment, en-\
n (1669) **2** *cap* : a philo-
sophic movement of the
18th century marked by a
rejection of traditional social, religious, and political
ideas and an emphasis on
rationalism —used with *the*.
(Webster's)

uto·pi·a
\yu-'to-pe-e\ *n* (1516)
2 : *often cap* : a place of
ideal perfection esp. in laws,
government, and social
conditions. **3** : an impracti-
cal scheme for social
improvement. (Webster's)

uto·pi·an \yu-'to-pe-en\
adj. often cap (1551)
1 : of, relating to, or having
the characteristics of a
utopia; *esp* : having impos-
sibly ideal conditions esp.
of social organization
(Webster's)

very idea that evolution could have anything to do with behavior. Does a connection exist between naturalism and values?
Judge for yourself.

If nature is all there is, there is no transcendent source of truth or morality. Truth
is relative, and we are left to construct
morality on our own. Every principle is reduced to a personal preference. If we are animals and have no intrinsic value, then how
is killing another human different from
killing a cow or chicken? By contrast, the
Christian believes in a God who has spoken, who has revealed an absolute and unchanging standard of right and wrong,
based ultimately on His own holy character.

Naturalism and Pragmatism

Since naturalists deny any transcendent
moral standards, they tend to take a pragmatic approach. Pragmatism says: Whatever works best is right. Actions and policies are judged on utilitarian grounds
alone. By contrast, the Christian is an idealist, judging actions not by what works but
by what ought to be, based on objective
standards.

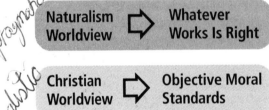

Naturalism and Utopianism

Remember Rousseau's idea that human nature is naturally good? Naturalists generally embrace the Enlightenment notion
that human nature is essentially good,
which leads to utopianism.

Utopianism says: If only we create the
right social and economic structures, we
can usher in an age of harmony and prosperity. But Christians can never give their
allegiance to utopian projects. We know
that sin is real, that it has deeply twisted
human nature, and that none of our efforts

can create heaven on earth. Heaven is a reality that can come only by divine intervention in the course of human history. In
the meantime, the human propensity to
evil and disorder must be hemmed in by
law and tradition. As we shall see in later
chapters, these truths profoundly influence
the way we organize society.

Naturalists consider only what happens
in this world, this age, this life. But
Christians see things from an eternal perspective. Everything we do now has eternal
significance, because one day there will be
a judgment, and then it will become evident that the way we have lived has consequences that last into eternity.

**How is utopianism different from our stated
objective in this course: to transform culture?**

_____

_____

_____

_____

_____

_____

_____

Naturalism's Strangest Fruit

Of all the beliefs springing from naturalism,
none are more illogical or absurd than postmodernism, the philosophy of the modern
secular campus. Postmodernist thinkers
have carried the logic of the naturalist
worldview to its logical conclusion.
Postmodernism not only rejects Christian
truth claims, it disallows *any* truth claims.
Postmodernism rejects any objective reality.
In postmodernism there can be no right or
wrong. Building a great democracy or a
Hitler's Germany are equally moral.

In 1996 I spoke at Yale Law School. A few
fearless Christian students organized a
forum asking why Yale Law School had contributed to undermining the rule of law. (It
was at Yale that Critical Legal Studies was
born, a deconstructionist move-ment to
strip the law of any objective meaning.)

I wondered if the meeting might turn into a riot—or, at the very least, some unpleasant confrontation.

I conveyed my apprehensions to Professor Stephen Carter, the brilliant Yale legal scholar and a committed Christian. "Don't worry about a riot," he chuckled. "They'll listen quietly and walk away without saying a word. When these kids come to Yale, they are taught that the law has nothing to do with morality. And they accept that. So you can have your opinions, and they'll find those interesting, but they won't even bother to argue."

As I spoke, I searched the students' eyes, hoping for some sign of engagement. Nothing. As I progressed into my material, I became more provocative, but they remained impassive.

During the question-and-answer period, no one challenged a single premise I had advanced. Carter had sized up his students well. They listened politely, took a few notes, then packed up their papers and quietly slipped out of the auditorium.

Debate can be unpleasant at times, but at least it presupposes that there are truths worth defending, ideas worth fighting for. But in our postmodernist age, your truths are yours, my truths are mine, and none are significant enough to get passionate about. And if there is no truth, then we cannot persuade one another by rational arguments. All that's left is sheer power—which opens the door to a new form of fascism.

Across the country, a generation of college graduates have marched off, degrees in hands and a postmodernist ideology in heads, to work in the nation's executive suites, political centers, and editorial rooms. The result has been the emergence of a new and influential group of professionals who control the means of public discourse; their philosophy has become dominant. The worldview framed on campuses from the 1960s on is now in the mainstream of American life.

Many people who hold a naturalistic worldview nonetheless seek to force "politically correct" positions on our society. How can people insist on enforcing a single viewpoint if all truth is relative?

_____

_____

_____

_____

Christianity in a Post-Christian Era

If we are going to make a difference in our world, we must grasp these profoundly contrary views of reality, for what people believe on this fundamental level is at the root of our cultural crisis. The dominant worldview today is naturalism which has created a culture both post-Christian and postmodernist. By post-Christian, we do not mean Americans no longer profess to be Christians or that they do not attend church. As a matter of fact, most Americans do both. Rather, by post-Christian we mean that Americans, and indeed most Western cultures, no longer rely on Judeo-Christian truths as the basis of their public philosophy or their moral consensus.

This is a significant cultural shift. At the birth of our nation, no one—not even deists and skeptics—doubted that basic biblical truths undergirded American institutions and informed the nation's values. Though the founders drew heavily from Enlightenment philosophy as well as from Christian tradition, few at the time saw any contradiction between the two. For most of our nation's history, these basic truths remained the foundation of the social consensus.

That is no longer true. To see just how rapidly the shift occurred, one need only look at Supreme Court decisions. As recently as 1952, Justice William O. Douglas wrote: "We are a religious people whose institutions presuppose a Supreme being."[12] The Court's language caused no stir; it reflected what most Americans believed.

Deconstructionism equals postmodern thinking applied to law, thus law becomes just the opinion of whoever is in power at the time.

In 1996, little more than a generation after Douglas's dictum, court watchers were scandalized when Justice Antonin Scalia announced in a speech that as a Christian he believed in miracles and in the resurrection of Jesus.[13] Cartoonist Herblock depicted the Supreme Court justices all holding law books—except Scalia, who was holding a Bible. *Washington Post* columnist Richard Cohen suggested that Scalia had disqualified himself from handling further church-state questions. (Does Cohen believe only atheists are qualified to make such decisions?) The talking heads on TV savaged Scalia for his "bias."

Similar attitudes have filtered through all levels of society. In 1997 a Boy Scout troop was denied the use of a public facility at the National Zoo, which is owned by the Smithsonian. Why? Because the Smithsonian ruled that the Boy Scout organization is "biased" when it requires that its members believe in God.[14]

The Challenge Before Us

Our challenge in post-Christian America is to confront our culture with a vibrant Christian worldview: to transform culture. The ability to articulate worldview issues is essential to that task.

Let's review the definition and three points of a worldview.
A worldview is ... _____
1. _____
2. _____
3. _____

Dare we believe that Christianity can yet prevail? We must believe it. This is a historic moment of opportunity, and when the church is faithful to its calling, it always leads to a transformation of culture. When the church is truly the church, a community living in biblical obedience and contending for faith in every area of life, it will surely transform the surrounding culture or create a new one.[15]

The hope for today's world is a renewed and vibrant spiritual order, men and women of another type arrayed for the great battle of principle against principle. A battle that begins with, "In the beginning."

[1]Friedrich Nietzsche, *The Birth of Tragedy and the Geneology of Morals,* trans. Francis Golffing (New York: Doubleday, 1956), 277-78.
[2]Abraham Kuyper, *Christianity: A Total World and Life System* (Marlborough, N.H.: Plymouth Rock Foundation, 1996), 3.
[3]C. S. Lewis, *The Abolition of Man* (New York: Touchstone, 1975).
[4]Stephen Gould, as quoted in Phillip E. Johnson, *Reason in the Balance: The Case Against Naturalism in Science, Law, and Education* (Downers Grove, Ill.: InterVarsity Press, 1995), 31. See also Stephen J. Gould, *Rocks of Ages: Science and Religion in the Fullness of Life* (New York: Ballantine, 1999).
[5]Benjamin Spock, as quoted in Dana Mack, *The Assault on Parenthood: How Our Culture Undermines the Family* (New York: Simon & Schuster, 1997), 33.
[6]Abraham Kuyper, *Christianity: A Total World and Life System,* 39-40.
[7]Ibid., 41.
[8]Cornelius Plantinga Jr., "Fashions and Folly: Sin and Character in the 90s," (presented at the January Lecture Series, Calvin Theological Seminary, Grand Rapids, Michigan, January 15, 1993), 14-15.
[9]Harry Blamires, *The Christian Mind: How Should a Christian Mind Think?* (Ann Arbor, Mich.: Servant, 1963), 80.
[10]Richard M. Weaver, *Ideas Have Consequences* (Chicago: University of Chicago Press, 1984).
[11]Jean-Jacques Rousseau, *The Social Contract* (Boston: Charles E. Tuttle, Everyman's Classic Library, 1993), 181.
[12]William Orville Douglas, *Zorach v. Clauson,* 343 US 306 (1952).
[13]Antonin Scalia, as quoted in John Pickering, "Christian Soldiers in a Secular City," *Washington Post,* 12 May 1996.
[14]Happily, this decision was overruled after being exposed in the conservative Washington journal *Human Events,* which led to congressional pressure spearheaded by Republican Senator Spencer Abraham from Michigan. See *BreakPoint* commentary, September 23, 1997.
[15]The church's primary biblical mission is not to restore or create the culture but to be faithful in serving God. As Kuyper put it, "The church exists merely for the sake of God" (*Christianity: A Total World and Life System,* 38). But in serving God, the church works toward the regeneration of the elect and testifies to the glory of God in his work among all people. So when the church is faithful, it affects all of life. It does, indeed, rejuvenate culture. See Charles Colson with Ellen Santilli Vaughn, *The Body* (Dallas: Word, 1992).

Chemicals, It's All Chemicals

Many people believe scientific facts support the theory of evolution. In this unit you will examine several scientific evidences that point to divine creation.

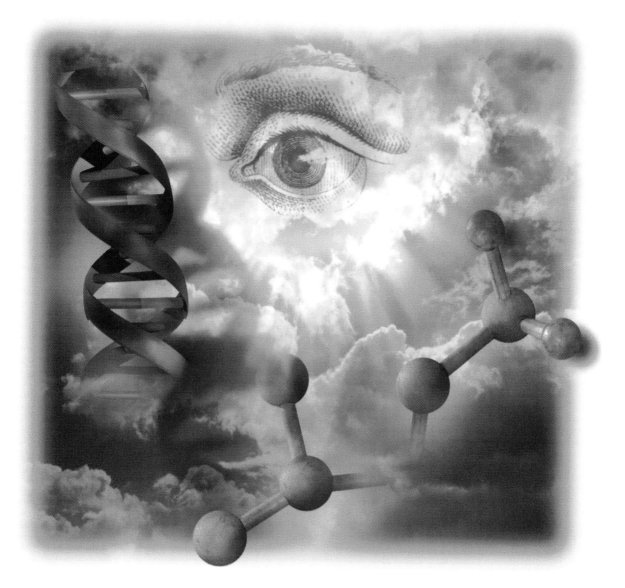

Dave and Katy's Metaphysical Adventure

Dave and his wife, Claudia, had sensed that Katy was in trouble. It wasn't only the discovery Claudia made on Sunday morning, though that in itself had sent them reeling. Worse, they felt they were losing her to a secular world smugly satisfied with itself and deeply hostile to their own. What stabbed most deeply was that Katy herself was becoming more and more antagonistic to their religious beliefs, to the point where she resisted any involvement in the church's high school group and the Sunday worship services. This from a girl who at age nine had responded to an altar call and given her life to Jesus with free-flowing tears of joy.

To get behind the emotional walls she had thrown up over the past year, Dave took Katy to Disney World for a father-daughter trip. To his dismay, Dave found Disney World to be a shrine to the belief in evolution. The repeated message that life just evolved troubled Dave, but suddenly it struck him that Katy had been hearing this message all her life. His daughter had grown up in an age when Christian children often find their faith questioned, even attacked, in the earliest grades. Katy had no reason to question the evolutionary message she was getting from her textbooks, her teachers, and even here, in the world's number one tourist attraction.

Suddenly Dave began to question, *Was Katy's rebellion against him and her mother coming from deeper doubts about God, the Bible, and Christianity?*

When he brought up the subject to Katy, she responded: "Hardly anybody believes what you and Mom believe."

"I don't think it's a question of what anyone *believes*. It's a question of what's *true*," Dave said after a painful pause.

"How does anyone know what's really true?"

"A lot of people think *they* know what's true. We just spent the day going to exhibits where a whole bunch of ideas were presented as true."

"That's science, Dad," Katy said patiently, as if teaching a child. "Science is things that are proved."

"Most of it was more like philosophy, Katy. Most of the exhibits here share one version of the truth, even when they're talking about different things. It's a story more than anything, and it goes like this: By chance the universe came into existence, by chance Earth was just right for life to exist, by chance life developed into birds and bees and butterflies, by chance human beings came along, and by chance human beings turned out to be so smart that all the world's problems will someday succumb to our technological prowess. End of story. Hallelujah, amen."

"But scientists can prove all that, Dad. No one can know for sure about God."

"Come on, how can anyone 'prove' that the universe came about by chance? Everything I know about the universe, including my incredibly beautiful daughter, indicates to me that Somebody designed it. Created it."

"My biology teacher says that's our egos talking. People want to believe they're important, so they invent religion. They invent the idea of god so they'll feel better."

"You really think life came about by chance?"

"It's chemicals. It's *all* chemicals. Scientists have done it in a test tube. I read about it in my science book."

Nothing Simple About Life

"I praise you because I am fearfully and wonderfully made; your works are wonderful, I know that full well."—Psalm 139:14

Dave put his head in his hands. So that was it. Katy had been so indoctrinated with a secular view of the world, a view backed by the prestige of "science," that Christianity no longer made sense to her. He saw it now, but what could he say to make her change her mind? She seemed to be throwing away her faith, and he had no idea how to stop her. But he made a promise to himself and to Katy: "I'll find out what's wrong with the evolution story or I'll give up my faith too."

STATEMENT When Darwin stated the theory of evolution, people thought single-celled organisms were fairly simple blobs of protoplasm. The fact that life could arise in an ancient pond containing just the right chemicals seemed reasonable, but we now know much more about the simplest possible form of life.

Question 1:
Can the first living organism have occurred by chance?

OBSERVATIONS

• We now know the simplest cell is incredibly complex.

• Many top-level secular scientists have now concluded that life cannot have begun by chance on this planet.

At least Dave now understood what had happened to his daughter. She had absorbed the idea that science is the source of truth, while religion is merely subjective opinion, something we tolerate for those weak enough to need that kind of comfort. For the first time, he realized that he had been foolishly overconfident. He had allowed his daughter to be exposed to these ideas in school, on television, and in her books without ever bothering to teach her how to respond.

If you have children, how much have you done to help them deal with the evolution story and learn to think for themselves?

NOTHING   A LOT

Now everything had changed. Dave needed to defend what he believed, if not for his own sake, then for his daughter's. "These are not just my ideas, Dad," Katy had argued that day at Disney World. "They're what I learned in school. They're what everyone believes."

"Scientists can prove evolution, Dad," Katy had said. "It's chemicals. It's all chemicals. We saw how it happened in 'The Living Seas' exhibit. Volcanoes erupting, then the ocean, then chemicals coming together. Scientists have done it in a test tube. I read about it in my science book. I even saw a photo of this thing with glass tubes and electrical sparks and then, you know, molecules came out."

Dave decided to begin with Katy's words. Had scientists really "done it in a test tube" as Katy believed?

pro·to·plasm
\'prot-e-plaz-em\ *n* (1848) a term once used for the fundamental material of which all living things were thought to be composed.

Read the following article on the Miller and Fox experiments. Then mark each of the following conclusions either true or false. The Miller and Fox experiments:

F 1. demonstrate how life began in the primitive ocean.

T 2. show that an intelligent force must operate for life to exist.

T 3. illustrate that even with scientists guiding the process, human beings can't produce anything near the simplest form of life.

At every turn, the experiments that have ignited so much excitement turn out to be artificial. As a result, even the most successful origin-of-life experiments tell us next to nothing about what could have happened under natural conditions. They tell us only what happens when a brilliant scientist manipulates the conditions, "coaxing" the materials down the chemical pathways necessary to produce the building blocks of life.

The Stanley Miller Experiment

In 1953, newspapers across the country carried photos of Stanley Miller, of the University of Chicago, reporting on his sensational claim that he had accomplished the first step toward creating life in a test tube.

Miller mixed simple chemicals and gases in a glass tube, then zapped them with an electrical charge to induce chemical reactions. To everyone's surprise, what emerged at the other end of the laboratory apparatus were amino acids, the building blocks of protein. Miller's success seemed to provide dramatic evidence for a naturalistic account of life's origin.[1]

The problem is that no one is asking critical questions about what the experiments really prove. The conventional wisdom is that they support the theory that life evolved spontaneously from simple chemicals in a primeval pond about four billion years ago. But do they?[2]

First, amino acids are to the simplest living cell like a single brick is to the Empire State Building. The cell is enormously more complex. The amino acid is just one of the simplest building blocks. What is more, the amino acids formed by such experiments are useless for life anyway. Amino acids come in two forms, left-handed and right-handed. Living things use only the left-handed form. But Miller got both kinds—an even fifty-fifty mix. In fact, this is what happens every time anyone mixes the chemicals randomly in the laboratory. No natural process produces only left-handed amino acids, the kind required by living things.

And that's only the first problem. The next step to "creating life" is to get amino acids to link up and form proteins. In 1958 Sidney Fox, a chemist at the University of Miami, started with already existing amino acids and boiled them in water to induce them to react with one another. The result was proteinlike chains of amino acids, and, like Miller, Fox was promptly inducted into the Modern Hall of Scientific Heroes.

Once again, life is much more selective than anything we get from a test tube. The proteins in living things are comprised of amino acids hooked together in a very particular chemical bond called a peptide bond. But amino acids are like Tinkertoys: They're capable of hooking together in all sorts of different ways, forming several different chemical bonds. And in the test tube, that's exactly what they do. They hook up in a variety of ways, never producing a genuine protein capable of functioning in a living cell.

So what do these experiments really prove? That *life can be created only by an intelligent agent directing, controlling, and manipulating the process.* The latest scientific findings do not discredit biblical faith; rather, they provide positive evidence that the origin of life requires an intelligent agent, a creator.

If you answered 1. false; 2. true; and 3 true, you are correct. Experiments support the impossibility of undirected evolution and point to a creator. Even the non-living cell parts we can synthesize require human intervention. With all our technology we can no more build the simplest living cell than a three-year old can build a supercomputer with items from a toy box.

The Simplest Form of Life

How could Dave get Katy to see that life could not have come from non-life? He prayed and asked God what he should do. Then he had a wonderful idea. He realized that Katy had uncritically accepted the propaganda she had seen about evolution. Instead of challenging what Katy believed, he would help Katy learn to think for herself.

In his search, Dave found a Web site on genetics. Because the Web site was run by secular scientists, Katy agreed to study it with her dad. Together they explored the workings of the cell. They found that even the simplest cell is an incredibly complex factory with many layers of interacting parts, none of which can operate independently or exist alone.

Dave and Katy found and summarized the following information from a Web site called "the Gene School." Each step in their summary moves to a vastly smaller level.

- Cells are the smallest unit of life other than viruses (viruses technically aren't alive).
- Most cells' genetic information is organized into chromosomes.

The Complexity of a Cell

April 12, 1999: A computer model of a cell requires a minimum of 127 genes.
A group led by biologist and computer scientist Masaru Tomita at Keio University in Fujisawa, Japan, has built a computer model of a cell. The "bare-bones" model, called "E-CELL," requires 127 genes, the minimum needed to model a cell, they find.[3]

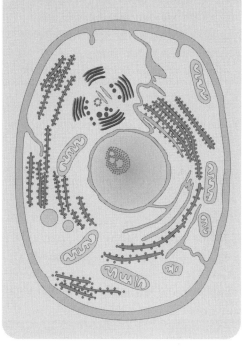

- Each chromosome contains from hundreds to thousands of smaller pieces of information called genes.
- Each gene is a chemical blueprint for a specific type of protein.
- Proteins are made of smaller units called amino acids.
- There are 20 types of amino acids. The DNA tells the cell how to manufacture these amino acids.
- The DNA molecule ultimately guides the production of all the above. One DNA molecule contains more information than a stack of phone books.[4]
- The RNA operates like a tiny chemical copy machine. RNA "translates" the instructions from the DNA molecule to create amino acids and proteins.

Katy became fascinated by the information about living cells. She found that cells are tremendously complex and more complicated than any machine ever built. Even the smallest bacterial cell has 100 proteins, DNA, RNA, and contains one hundred billion atoms.

Dave hoped that Katy was beginning to think for herself instead of just buying the evolution story. If you were Katy's parent, what would you like Katy to begin asking herself about evolution and the origin of life?

_____
_____
_____
_____
_____
_____
_____

Dave hoped Katy would ask how a cell with hundreds of thousands of essential parts could possibly assemble itself, but, wisely, Dave held his tongue. He knew starting an argument would only drive Katy to defend her belief in evolution. Since he began to understand the issues of creation and evolution, he no longer needed to convince his daughter. He realized that he needed to help Katy question the evolution story for herself and to pray that God would open her eyes to the truth.

Which requires more faith?
❑ belief in God
❑ belief that something as complex as a living cell occurred by accident

Dave and Katy discovered something else amazing. They found a long list of prominent scientists who, on purely scientific grounds, have rejected the possibility that life came from non-life. Because these scientists reject belief in God, they have concluded that life must have come from outer space. Their theory is called "panspermia" or "cosmic ancestry."

Katy looked up cosmic ancestry on a web site *(http://www.panspermia.org)* and found the following questions and answers. Remember these statements come from secular scientists:[5]

Q. Why is Cosmic Ancestry necessary? Isn't the theory that life on Earth arose here spontaneously a perfectly adequate theory?

A. No. The theory that life can arise spontaneously from nonliving chemicals is speculative and "will remain so until living creatures have been synthesized in the biochemical laboratory. We are a long way from that goal." J.B.S. Haldane wrote those words in "The Origin of Life," in 1928. Seventy years later, the goal looks farther away now than it did then.

Q. Isn't life as likely to have started here on Earth as anywhere else?

A. Yes. But that likelihood is still effectively zero.

We began today's study with a question, *Can the first living organism have occurred by chance?*

Katy began to see for herself that the answer must be no! The likelihood that life came from non-life is "still effectively zero." Katy had seen for herself a major contradiction in the evolution story. Many secular scientists have rejected the possibility that life began as previously supposed, yet she had been taught that "scientists" were all in agreement about evolution. Slowly, Katy was beginning to think for herself and to question the rest of the evolution story.

Today's Prayer
Thank You, God, for the precious gift of life. I have been lovingly crafted by Your creative power. Give me the wisdom to understand who I am and what is the meaning of my life.

From Goo to You

"God created the great creatures of the sea and every living and moving thing with which the water teems, according to their kinds, and every winged bird according to its kind. And God saw that it was good."—Genesis 1:21

Dave began to feel that he was making some progress. After studying the incredible complexity of all living cells, Katy admitted that God may have started the process of life on earth. "But everyone knows that once life was here, it evolved just as Darwin said it did." She said, "I saw it in my textbook at school." Katy rustled through her backpack and pulled out a heavy biology textbook, opening it to a full spread of colorful, eye-catching photos showing several breeds of dogs and horses as well as a vast variety of orchids and roses. Here, the caption proclaimed, "is evolution in action." Evolution happening before our very eyes.

Even if we could believe that a single-celled bacteria somehow came to exist, evolution has another impossible hurdle to jump. Can life progress? Can one kind of life form change into another? Harold Hill, Mary Elizabeth Rogers, and Irene Burk Harrell wrote a book with a wonderful title that sums up the idea of evolution from single-celled to complex life. They called it *From Goo to You by Way of the Zoo*. Katy considered the hurdle posed to evolution by the origin of life. Now she began to consider whether life could evolve from there.

Question 2:
Does change of species occur? Does one form of plant or animal life change, either gradually or suddenly, into another form?

OBSERVATIONS

- Variation within a species has nothing to do with evolutionary change from one species to another.
- Typical examples used to support evolution actually provide evidence for creation and against evolution.

Change Does Not Equal Evolution
Dave took the book from her hands and felt his stomach tighten. He hadn't covered these issues yet, and those colorful photos certainly were impressive.

Katy gazed at him triumphantly. "It's right in the book, Dad."

Dave didn't answer. His eyes had moved down to the text to find out exactly what his daughter was learning. Katy waited a few moments, then walked out of the room, leaving him sitting with the textbook still open on his lap. Dave clenched his hands. *God,* he prayed, *no wonder she keeps fighting me—fighting you. Everything she gets at school is saying that nature can do it on its own, that you are irrelevant.*

What about Katy's argument? Does the variety of sizes and shapes among dogs, horses, orchids, and roses support the concept of evolution? Why or why not?

_____

_____

_____

_____

Natural selection is the idea that nature permits positive changes while eliminating negative changes. You can picture natural selection like a screen that allows only helpful changes to continue.

mu·ta·tion
\myü-ta-shen\ *n* (14c)
1 : a significant and basic alteration : CHANGE
3 a : a relatively permanent change in hereditary material involving either a physical change in chromosome relations or a biochemical change in the codons that make up genes.

The Phony Arguments

One of the most maddening parts of seeking the truth about origins comes when people use facts that clearly contradict evolution to support the theory. We must challenge such faulty reasoning.

Organisms Stay True to Type

The best argument against Darwinism has been known for centuries by farmers and breeders, and it can be stated in a simple principle: natural change in living things is limited. Or stated positively: organisms stay true to type.

Take the pictures in Katy's textbook. They tout the variation in dogs and horses and roses as "evolution in action." The Darwinist seems to overlook the obvious fact that the dogs are all still dogs, the horses are still horses, the roses are still roses. None of the changes have created a novel kind of organism. Dog breeding has given rise to varieties ranging from the lumbering Great Dane to the tiny Chihuahua, but no variety shows any tendency to leave the canine family. None of the examples cited in biology textbooks show evolution that rises to a new level of complexity; they all simply illustrate variation around a mean.

What the textbooks cite as evidence of evolution actually shows the wonder of creation. God created every variety of plants and animals with the ability to adapt to a range of changing conditions. Breeding is nothing more than choosing from among the thousands of genes in the originally created type.

Sugar Beet

Consider one historical example. In 1800 plant breeders started trying to increase the sugar content of the sugar beet, with excellent success. Over seventy-five years of selective breeding, they increased the sugar content of beets from 6 percent to 17 percent. But then they could go no further. Although the same intensive breeding was continued for another half century, the sugar content never rose above 17 percent. At some point, biological variation always levels off and stops.

Why does progress halt? Because once all the genes for a particular trait have been selected, breeding can go no further. Breeding shuffles and selects among existing genes in the gene pool, combining and recombining them, much as you might shuffle and deal cards from a deck. Breeding does not create new genes, any more than shuffling cards creates new cards. A bird cannot be bred to grow fur. A mouse cannot be bred to grow feathers. A pig cannot grow wings. Moreover, when an organism is no longer subject to selective pressure, it tends to revert to original type.

How would you use the example of the sugar beet as an argument supporting the idea that one species cannot become another?

_____

_____

_____

Darwin was simply mistaken in his conclusion. Whether in the breeding pen or in nature, the minor change produced by shuffling genes is not an engine for unlimited change. The natural tendency in living things is not to continue changing indefinitely but to stay close to the original type.

Mutations and Natural Selection

Since breeding only shuffles existing genes, the only way to drive evolution to new levels of complexity is to introduce new genetic material. The only natural source of new genetic material in nature is mutations. In our neo-Darwinism, the central mechanism for evolution is random mutation and natural selection.

The concept of mutations was popularized for the younger set a few years ago by the Teenage Mutant Ninja Turtles, and today virtually every sci-fi movie features mutants. But what exactly is a mutation?

Since a gene is like a coded set of instructions, a mutation is akin to a typing error—a changed letter here, an altered punctuation mark there, a phrase dropped, or a word misspelled. These typing errors are the only source of novelty in the genetic code.

Already there is an obvious problem. Typing errors seldom improve reports. An error is more likely to make nonsense than better sense. The same is true of errors in the genetic code. Most mutations are harmful or lethal to the organism. If mutations were to accumulate, the result would more likely be *de*volution than evolution—more degeneration than growth.

Neo-Darwinists, to make this theory work, must hope that some mutations, somewhere, somehow, will be beneficial. And since the evolution of a single new organ or structure may require many thousands of mutations, neo-Darwinists must hope that vast numbers of these rare beneficial mutations will occur in a single organism. The improbabilities are staggering.

If we take neo-Darwinism into the laboratory and test it experimentally, the difficulties only multiply. The handiest way to study mutations in the laboratory is with the help of the ordinary fruit fly—the kind you see hovering around overripe bananas in the kitchen. Since this tiny fly reaches sexual maturity in only five days, the effects of mutations can be observed over several generations. Using chemicals or radiation to induce mutations, scientists have produced flies with purple or white eyes; flies with oversized wings or shriveled wings or even no wings; fly larvae with patchy bristles on their backs or larvae with so many bristles that they resemble hedgehogs.[6]

All this experimentation has not advanced evolutionary theory in the slightest. For nothing has ever emerged except odd forms of fruit flies. The experiments have never produced a new species of insect. Mutations alter the details in *existing* structures—like eye color or wing size—but

they do not lead to the creation of *new* structures. The fruit flies have remained fruit flies. Like breeding, genetic mutations produce only minor, limited change.

Further, the minor changes observed do not accumulate to create major changes—the principle at the heart of Darwinism. Hence, mutations are not the source of the endless, limitless change required by evolutionary theory. Whether we look at breeding experiments or laboratory experiments, the outcome is the same: Change in living things remains strictly limited to variations on the theme. We do not see new and more complex structures emerging..

Think for a moment about Darwin's idea of natural selection—the survival of the fittest. Does natural selection contribute to change or does it screen out the tiny changes produced by mutation? Explain.

_____

_____

_____

_____

The same pattern holds throughout the past, as we see in the fossil record. The overwhelming pattern is that organisms appear fully formed, with variations clustered around a mean, and without transitional stages leading up to them. Indeed, the fossil record as a whole gives persuasive evidence against Darwinism.[7]

Mastering these basic facts gives us the tools to think critically about the examples typically used to support evolution. Take Darwin's famous finches, whose variation in beak size helped inspire his initial theory. A recent study designed to support Darwinism found that the finches' beaks actually grow larger in dry seasons, when the seeds they eat are tough and hard, but grow smaller again after a rainy season, when tiny seeds become available once more. This is evolution happening "before [our] very eyes," the author of the study concluded, but in fact, it is precisely the opposite. The change in finch beaks is a cyclical fluctuation that allows the finches to adapt and survive, points out Phillip Johnson in *Reason in the Balance*. In other words, it's a minor adjustment that allows finches to … stay finches. It does not demonstrate that finches are evolving into a new kind of organism or that they originally evolved from another kind of organism.[8]

The same holds for all the frequently cited "confirmations" of evolution, such as organisms that develop a resistance to antibiotics and insects that develop resistance to insecticide. Even more disturbing, some of the most famous examples have been exposed as hoaxes—most recently, England's black-and-white peppered moths.

The Infamous Peppered Moth

Standard textbooks assert that during the Industrial Revolution, when the tree trunks were darkened by soot, a light-colored variety of the moth became easier for birds to see and were eaten up, while a darker moth flourished.

Think for a moment. If the moth story were true, would it support evolution or creation? Why? _____

_____

_____

_____

The textbooks touted this as a classic illustration of natural selection, the theory that nature preserves those forms that function better than their rivals in the struggle for existence. But recently it was discovered that photographs showing the light moths against the darkened tree trunks were faked. Peppered moths fly about in the upper branches of trees and don't perch on the trunks at all. Even more recently, biologist Theodore Sargent of the University of Massachusetts admitted that he glued dead samples of the moths onto the tree trunks for a *NOVA* documentary.

The respected journal *Nature* says the moth example, once the "prize horse in our stable" to illustrate evolution by natural selection, must now be thrown out.[9]

Why do you suppose so many naturalists have faked their results to support evolution? _____

_____

_____

_____

That researchers have faked evidence to support evolution indicates what we will explore further in the next unit. Evolution is not primarily a scientific theory but, rather, a religious belief system. Therefore, adherents to the worldview of naturalism seek to support their belief system, often in direct contradiction of the facts.

No scientific finding has contradicted the basic principle that change in living things is limited. Luther Burbank, regarded as the greatest breeder of all time, said the tendency for organisms to stay true to type is so constant that it can be considered a natural law—what he called the law of the Reversion to the Average. It's a law, he said, that "keeps all living things within some more or less fixed limitations."[10]

Despite what the textbooks say, Darwin did not prove that nature is capable of crossing those "fixed limitations." He suggested only that it was theoretically possible—that minor changes might have accumulated over thousands of years until a fish became an amphibian, an amphibian became a reptile, and a reptile became a mammal. But after more than 150 years, it has become clear that Darwin's speculation flies in the face of all the results of breeding and laboratory experimentation, as well as the pattern in the fossil record.

The simple words from Genesis 1 still stand firm: And God made every living thing to reproduce "after their kind" (see Gen. 1:11-12,21,24-25, NASB).

We began today's study with a question, *Does change of species occur?* Every scientific fact we know indicates that the answer is *no*. Belief in evolution remains a statement of belief—belief in a system that has broken down. Belief that requires vast amounts of faith when you learn the facts.

DAY THREE
Irreducible Complexity

"Do you know the laws of the heavens? Can you set up God's dominion over the earth?"—Job 38:33

The great Christian evangelist Francis Schaeffer used to offer an argument against evolution that was simple, easy to grasp, and devastating: Suppose a fish evolves lungs. What happens then? Does it move up to the next evolutionary stage? Of course not. It drowns.

Living things cannot simply change piecemeal—a new organ here, a new limb there. An organism is an integrated system, and any isolated change in the system is more likely to be harmful than helpful. If a fish's gills were to begin mutating into a set of lungs, it would be a disaster, not an advantage. The only way to turn a fish into a land-dwelling animal is to transform it all at once, with a host of interrelated changes happening at the same time—not only lungs but also coadapted changes in the skeleton, the circulatory system, and so on.

Question 3:
How can complex organisms survive long enough to evolve?

OBSERVATIONS

• Evolution cannot explain the development of the eye, feathers, bat wings, skeletal changes, or hundreds of other features.
• Natural selection demonstrates that a partially-developed organ means the death of the organism.

The term to describe this kind of interdependent system is *irreducible complexity*. The fact that organisms are irreducibly complex is yet another argument that they could not have evolved piecemeal, one step at a time, as Darwin proposed. Darwinian theory states that all living structures evolved in small, gradual steps from simpler structures—feathers from scales, wings from forelegs, blossoms from leaves, and so on. But anything that is irreducibly complex cannot evolve in gradual steps, and thus its very existence refutes Darwin's theory.

ir·re·duc·ible
\ˈir-i-d(y)ü-se-bel\ *adj*
(1633): impossible to transform into or restore to a desired or simpler condition. (Webster's)

cant change onething at a time

The concept of irreducible complexity was developed by Michael Behe, a Lehigh University professor of biochemistry, in his 1993 book *Darwin's Black Box.* Behe's homey example of irreducible complexity is the mousetrap. A mousetrap cannot be assembled gradually, he points out. You cannot start with a wooden platform and catch a few mice, add a spring and catch a few more mice, add a hammer, and so on, each addition making the mousetrap function better. No, to even *start* catching mice, all the parts of the trap must be assembled from the outset. The mousetrap doesn't work until all its parts are present and working together.[11]

Many living structures are like the mousetrap. They involve an entire system of interacting parts all working together. If one part were to evolve in isolation, the entire system of interacting parts would stop functioning; and since, according to Darwinism, natural selection preserves the forms that function better than their rivals, the nonfunctioning system would be eliminated by natural selection—like the fish with lungs. Therefore, there is no possible Darwinian explanation of how irreducibly complex structures and systems came into existence.

Nature is full of examples of complex organs that could not possibly have been formed by numerous, slight modifications—that is, they are irreducibly complex.

Take the example of the bat. Evolutionists propose that the bat evolved from a small, mouselike creature whose forelimbs (the "front toes") developed into wings by gradual steps. But picture the steps: As the "front toes" grow longer and the skin begins to grow between them, the animal can no longer run without stumbling over them; and yet the forelimbs are not long enough to function as wings. And so, during most of its hypothetical transitional stages, the poor creature would have limbs too long for running and too short for flying. It would flop along helplessly and soon become extinct. There is no conceivable pathway for bat wings to be formed in gradual stages.

No such system could arise in a blind, step-by-step Darwinian process. The most rational explanation of irreducibly complex structures in nature is that they are products of the creative mind of an intelligent being.

As Dave and Katy examined the scientific facts, they discovered a mountain of evidence that evolution could not have taken place as Katy had been taught. Katy began to see that science is not casting up new challenges to Christian faith, as she had been told. Instead, it is uncovering increasingly powerful evidence that the Christian worldview is true on all levels, including the natural world.

Now that Katy was thinking and studying for herself, she thought, *I see the evidence that evolution did not create our world; is there evidence that God did?* Next we'll see what she found.

The Amazing DNA Molecule

On all fronts, scientists are being forced to face up to the implications of an intelligent cause. The discovery of the information content in DNA is also forcing biologists to recognize an intelligent cause for the origin of life.

Question 4:
Can information arise by natural forces alone? Or does it require an intelligent agent?

OBSERVATIONS Scientists committed to naturalism must try to construct an explanation of life based solely on physical-chemical laws. They must explain the information in DNA as a product of natural processes at work in the chemicals that comprise living things. Recall Katy's words to her father at Epcot: "It's chemicals. It's all chemicals."

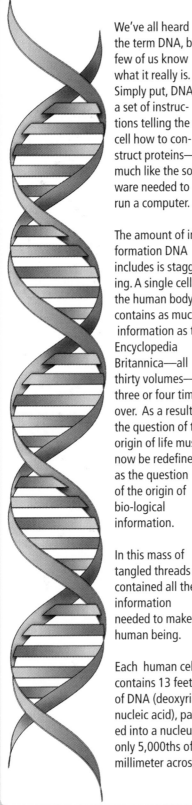

DNA: The Thread of Life

We've all heard the term DNA, but few of us know what it really is. Simply put, DNA is a set of instructions telling the cell how to construct proteins—much like the software needed to run a computer.

The amount of information DNA includes is staggering. A single cell of the human body contains as much information as the Encyclopedia Britannica—all thirty volumes—three or four times over. As a result, the question of the origin of life must now be redefined as the question of the origin of bio-logical information.

In this mass of tangled threads is contained all the information needed to make a human being.

Each human cell contains 13 feet of DNA (deoxyribonucleic acid), packed into a nucleus only 5,000ths of a millimeter across.

The Language of Life

You probably know that computers operate on a binary code. No matter how complex the message in a computer document—a novel, symphony, or a scientific program—at the machine level it's all zeros and ones. You may be surprised to know that DNA coding works almost exactly the same way.

What makes DNA function as a message is not the chemicals themselves but rather their *sequence,* their pattern. The chemicals in DNA are divided into molecules (called *nucleotides)* that act like letters in a message, and they must be in a particular order if the message is going to be intelligible. Scientists picture the DNA molecule as the famous double-helix. Picture a ladder twisted into a spiral-staircase shape. Each rung of the ladder contains a pattern of only 4 nucleotides—like the computer program of 1234,2143,1243, and so on. God designed the incredibly wonderful living cell to read the DNA code like a computer program. The message in the DNA tells every other part of the cell how to do its work. The crucial question becomes whether the sequence of chemical "letters" arose by natural causes, or does it require an intelligent source? Is it the product of law or design?

Accident or Intelligent Agent?

More than 200 years ago, the English clergyman William Paley framed the classic argument for design by comparing a living organism to a watch. Upon finding a watch lying on the beach, no one would say, "Oh, look what the wind and the waves have produced." Instead, we instantly recognize that a watch has a structure that can be produced only by an intelligent agent. Likewise, Paley argued, living things have a type of structure that can be produced only by an intelligent agent.[12]

In everyday life, we weigh natural versus intelligent causes all the time without thinking much about it. If we see ripples on a sandy beach, we assume they were formed by natural processes. But if we see words written in the sand—"John loves Mary"—immediately we recognize a different kind of order, and we know that a couple of lovers recently lingered there.

How would you explain that a message scribbled in the sand on a beach was the work of an intelligent agent?

_____

_____

In the same way, when scientists probed the nucleus of the cell, they came across something analogous to "John loves Mary"—the only difference being that DNA contains vastly more information. What this means is that we can now revive the design argument using a much closer analogy than Paley's analogy between living things and watches. The new analogy is between DNA and written messages. Are there natural forces capable of writing a book, programming a computer disk, or writing a symphony? Clearly not. The discovery of DNA provides powerful new evidence that life is the product of intelligent design. It's an argument that is simple, easy to explain, and based solidly on experience.

No known physical laws are capable of creating a structure like DNA with high information content. Based on both the latest scientific knowledge and on ordinary experience, we know only one cause that is up to the task: an intelligent agent.

When it comes to the origin of life, science is squarely on the side of creation by an intelligent agent. We have nothing to fear from the progress of science. Parents like Dave have solid answers to give their questioning teens.

How would you defend belief in creation from the information content of DNA?

_____

_____

_____

_____

Information Theory

Since DNA contains information, the case can be stated even more strongly in terms of information theory, a field of research that investigates the ways information is transmitted. As we said earlier, the naturalistic scientist has only two possible ways to explain the origin of life—either chance or natural law. But information theory gives us a powerful tool for discounting both these explanations, for both chance and law lead to structures with low information content, whereas DNA has a very high information content.[13]

A structure or message is said to have high or low information content depending on the minimum number of instructions needed to tell you how to construct it. To illustrate, a random sequence of letters has low information content because it requires only two instructions: (1) select a letter of the English alphabet and write it down, and (2) do it again (select another letter and write it down). By the same token, a regular, repetitive pattern of letters has low information content as well. Using your computer to create Christmas wrapping paper requires only a few instructions: (1) type in "M-e-r-r-y C-h-r-i-s-t-m-a-s," and (2) do it again. By contrast, if you want your computer to print out the poem "The Night before Christmas," you must specify every letter, one by one. Because the process of writing down the poem requires a large number of instructions, it is said to have high information content.

Similarly, in nature, both random patterns and regular patterns (like ripples on a beach) have low information content. By contrast, DNA has a very high information content. It would be impossible to produce a simple set of instructions telling a chemist how to synthesize the DNA of even the simplest bacterium. You would have to specify every chemical "letter," one by one—and there are literally millions. Thus DNA has a completely different structure from the products of either chance or natural law, and information theory gives us the conceptual tools to debunk any such attempts to explain the origin of life.

Science cannot tell us everything we might wish to know about this intelligent cause, of course. Biology cannot reveal who the Creator is, and it cannot explain God's plan of salvation. These are tasks for theology. But a study of the design and purpose in nature does clearly reveal God's existence—so clearly that, as the apostle Paul wrote in the New Testament, we stand before Him without excuse.

"For since the creation of the world God's invisible qualities—his eternal power and divine nature—have been clearly seen, being understood from what has been made, so that men are without excuse" (Rom. 1:20).

Today's Prayer
Father God, we marvel that You have created all things. The intricate construction of a cell is far beyond our understanding. Thank You that You not only created us but communicate with us. All the praise is Yours, O God, for You have dominion over all the earth.

DAY FOUR
The Big Bang, God's Thumbprint

"Where were you when I laid the earth's foundation?"—Job 38:4
"God said, 'Let there be light,' and there was light."—Genesis 1:3

Throughout the modern debate over origins, creationists have faced a virtual brick wall in an accepted scientific belief. Until recent discoveries, scientists were convinced that the universe was eternal and that matter had always existed.

Dave was about to discover one of the most exciting breakthroughs in recent scientific research. After maintaining for centuries that the physical universe is eternal and therefore needs no creator, science today has uncovered dramatic new evidence that the universe did have an ultimate origin, that it began at a finite time in the past—just as the Bible teaches.

Question 4:
What evidence of divine creation does the big bang theory provide?

OBSERVATIONS

- The big bang confirms the biblical truth that the universe had a beginning.
- The implications of the big bang have shaken scientists to the core, destroying many of the assumptions on which evolution was built.

Imagine a court case on the order of the Scopes "monkey trial" in the year 1900. You are seeking to prove that creation should be taught in public schools. One authority after another testifies that the universe has always existed. What argument could you present for a creationist viewpoint?

_____
_____
_____
_____

To grasp just how revolutionary this beginning-time viewpoint is, we must under-

Christians hold opinions that vary about the age of the earth. Some believe the earth is only a few thousand years old. Others understand the Bible to allow room for much greater age, but those discussions do not alter this issue. The point at hand is simple: the evolution story was built on the belief that matter had always existed. Now scientific findings have demonstrated the falsehood of such a "steady state" universe.

stand that most ancient cultures believed that the universe is eternal—or, more precisely, that it was formed from some kind of primordial material that is eternal. Ancient Greeks argued that the idea of an ultimate beginning was rationally inconceivable.

The Greek argument was revived during the late Middle Ages and Renaissance, when classical literature was rediscovered. Then, in the eighteenth century, scientists formulated the law of conservation of matter (that matter can be neither created nor destroyed), and it became a weapon in the hands of materialists, who argued that science itself now ruled out any ultimate creation. "Today the indestructibility or permanence of matter is a scientific fact," wrote a nineteenth-century proponent of materialism. "Those who talk about an independent or supernatural creative force" that created the universe from nothing "are in antagonism with the first and simplest axiom of a philosophical view of nature."[14]

There things stood. The idea that the universe had a beginning was reduced to a bare article of religious faith, standing in lonely opposition to firmly established science. To the activity on page 43, you could only present your faith in opposition to "scientific fact."

A Revolution in Science

Then, in the early twentieth century, several lines of evidence began a curious convergence. Each demonstrated that the prevailing belief was in error.

1. Einstein's general relativity theory suggested that the universe is expanding.
2. Scientists discovered that the stars exhibit a "red shift," implying that they are moving away from each other.
3. Scientists realized that the laws of thermodynamics actually make it imperative to believe in a beginning to the universe.

The second law of thermodynamics, the law of decay, implies that the universe is in a process of gradual disintegration—im-placably moving toward final darkness and decay. In other words, the universe is running down, like a wound-up clock. And if it is running down, then there must have been a time when it was wound up. In the eloquent words of Lincoln Barnett in *The Universe and Dr. Einstein*, "the inescapable inference is that everything had a *beginning*: somehow and sometime the cosmic processes were started, the stellar fires ignited, and the whole vast pageant of the universe brought into being."[15]

Think back to the previous activity with the court case. Suppose you are a judge in the court of appeals reviewing the case. Now all the most prominent physicists and astronomers of the twentieth century testify, beginning with Albert Einstein. Each agrees. Their colleagues in the original trial were wrong. The universe did have a specific moment in which it began. What will be your ruling now?

❏ **I would rule that the original trial verdict was correct, that science proves evolution.**
❏ **I would rule that the original trial verdict was in error, that science supports the belief that the universe began at a specific moment.**
❏ **I would rule that the new information made no difference in the verdict of the original trial.**

The Big Bang Theory

Does the courtroom scenario sound far-fetched? In fact, the various lines of scientific evidence joined forces in the 1960s and led to the formulation of the big bang theory, which asserts that the universe began billions of years ago with a cosmic explosion. The new theory hit the scientific world like a thunderclap. It meant that the idea of an ultimate beginning was no longer merely religious dogma. Science itself now indicated that the universe burst into existence at a particular time in the past.

What's more, the first law of thermodynamics (the conservation of matter) implies

Explosive Evidence of Creation

Understanding the "Big Bang" has been one of the most exciting scientific developments of our century. Evidence from several areas of physics shows that the universe came into existence at a specific time in the past. Science now proves what the Bible has said all along—the Universe had a beginning point. "In the beginning, God created…" (Gen. 1:1).

that matter cannot just pop into existence or create itself. And therefore, if the universe had a beginning, then something *external* to the universe must have caused it to come into existence—something, or Someone, transcendent to the natural world. As a result, the idea of creation is no longer merely a matter of religious faith; it is a conclusion based on the most straightforward reading of the scientific evidence.

The big bang theory delivers a near-fatal blow to naturalistic philosophy, for the naturalist regards reality as an unbroken sequence of cause and effect that can be traced back endlessly. But the big bang represents a sudden discontinuity in the chain of cause and effect. It means science can trace events back in time only to a certain point; at the moment of the big bang explosion, science reaches an abrupt break,

an absolute barrier. In fact, when the theory was first proposed, a large number of scientists resisted it for that reason. The great physicist Arthur Eddington summed up the feelings of many of his colleagues when he stated that the idea of a beginning is philosophically "repugnant."[16] Albert Einstein fiddled with his equations in the vain hope of avoiding the conclusion that the universe had a beginning. Astronomer Robert Jastrow, an agnostic who nevertheless delights in tweaking the noses of his naturalistically minded colleagues, maintains that science has reached its limit, that it will never be able to discover whether the agent of creation was "the personal God of the Old Testament or one of the familiar forces of physics."[17]

Yet many secularists still squirm to avoid the clear implications of the theory. Some argue that the big bang actually advances naturalistic philosophy—that it has extended naturalistic explanations back to the moment of the origin of the universe itself. That means that if God exists, He has been pushed back to a shadowy first cause who merely started things off, with no role to play after that. But this is sheer bluster. Far from supporting naturalism, the big bang theory shows the *limits* of all naturalistic accounts of reality by revealing that nature itself—time, space, and matter—came into existence a finite period of time ago.

Perhaps the most common strategy among scientists and educators today is simply to ignore the startling implications of the big bang, labeling them "philosophy" or "religion" and shunting them aside. We deal only with science, they say. Discussion of the ultimate cause *behind* the big bang is dismissed as philosophy and is given no place in the science classroom. As a result, schoolchildren never dream what fascinating vistas are veiled from their sight, what interesting questions they are essentially forbidden to ask. This is the approach Dave Mulholland witnessed at Disney World, when Bill-Nye-the-Science-Guy, with theatrical flourish, directed the audience's attention to an artistic rendering of the big bang. A thundering wave of light swept over the screen, but not a word was uttered about what came before the primeval explosion or what caused it.

Still other scientists try to get around the big bang by tweaking the theory in ways that allow them to insist that matter is eternal after all. For example, Carl Sagan proposed that the explosion that started our universe was only one of a series—that the universe is expanding today, but at some point the process will reverse itself and begin to contract, until it is once again a tiny point, which will then explode once again, starting the entire process over. This oscillation will go on forever in endless repetition, like an accordion opening and closing.[18] But Sagan's speculation runs up against the basic laws of physics: Even an oscillating universe would use up the available energy in each cycle, and it would eventually run down. The second law of thermodynamics, the law of decay, shoots down any notion of an eternal universe.

Other scientists face the facts of an ultimate beginning, but in an effort to avoid the idea of a creator, they craft strange ideas. Some speak of the self-generation of the universe, overlooking the obvious logical contradiction in such a notion (if the universe doesn't exist yet, there is no "self" to do the generating.) Others, like Stephen Hawking of Cambridge University, probably the best-known theoretical physicist today, propose that the early universe existed in "imaginary time," an idea that is for all purposes little more than fantasy. Still others have proposed that the universe simply popped into existence—completely uncaused—out of nothing. For example, philosophy professor Quentin Smith proposes that the universe "came from nothing, by nothing, for nothing."[19] But this is to leave the domain of science for sheer magic. One of the most established laws of experience is that something cannot come out of nothing.

Naturalists simply have no way to avoid the challenge posed by the big bang theory without twisting themselves into impossible logical contortions. The facts clearly indicate that the universe is not eternal, that it cannot originate itself. The implication is that the universe began at a definite moment in time, in a flash of light and energy. Science has begun to sound eerily like Genesis 1:3, "God said, 'Let there be light.'"

We can make these arguments when we encounter people hostile to Christian faith.

Review the contents of this unit. Briefly explain why each of the following areas provides potent evidence against evolution.

1. The origin of life from non-life: _____
_____
_____
_____

2. The development from simple to complex life forms:_____
_____
_____
_____

3. Irreducible complexity: _____
_____
_____
_____

4. The information content of DNA: _____
_____
_____
_____

5. The big bang theory: _____
_____
_____
_____
_____
_____

We ought to raise questions such as, What came before the big bang? What caused it? If the big bang was the origin of the universe itself, then its cause must be something *outside* the universe. The truth is that the big bang theory gives dramatic support to the biblical teaching that the universe had an ultimate beginning—that space, matter, and time itself are finite. Far from being a challenge to Christian faith, the theory actually gives startling evidence *for* the faith.

And the case for creation is even stronger if we look at the *nature* of our universe. It is a universe that speaks at every turn of design and purpose.

Today's Prayer

God, our universe speaks at every turn of Your design and purpose. The very water, dirt, and sunlight are Your miracles. You indeed are worthy of glory, honor, and praise for Your being Creator of the earth and all that is in it.

DAY FIVE
Designed with Us in Mind

"God's voice thunders in marvelous ways;
he does great things beyond our understanding."—Job 37:5

As Dave and Katy both learned more about the science supporting creation, they talked about the message from "The Living Seas." They began to see the irony of the evolutionist message. A small sphere, the planet Earth, "just happened" to be the right size and "just happened" to be the right distance from the sun so that life "just happened" to arise. And through a process of random mutations and natural selection, we humans "just happened" to appear on the scene.

STATEMENT

Many coincidences make life on Earth possible. These matters of physics and chemistry may seem theoretical or trivial, but they are causing great consternation with naturalistic scientists. These unexplained and precise values provide evidence of a divine hand in creation. As Einstein said, "God does not play dice with the cosmos."

Question 6:
Do the many precise coincidences that make life possible give evidence of God's design in the structure of the universe?

OBSERVATIONS

- The earth's orbit, the existence and characteristics of water, and several features of the atom, all combine to make life on this planet possible.
- These "coincidences" demonstrate God's care in the very structure of the universe.

Are all these coincidences really just coincidences? Or did Someone design the universe this way? What Dave discovered, to his surprise, is another dramatic shift in the latest scientific thought.

In the following paragraph, look for the meaning of the term *anthropic principle.*

Not only are scientists acknowledging an ultimate beginning, but they are also recognizing that the physical structure of the universe gives striking evidence of purpose and design. They have proposed what is known as the *anthropic principle,* which states that the physical structure of the universe is exactly what it must be in order to support life.

The term *anthropic principle* comes from the Greek word *anthropos,* which means human being, and it begins to appear that the laws of physics were exquisitely calibrated from the outset for the creation of human life. Of course, many scientists shy away from this conclusion because it presupposes a creator, and they have been trained to believe that such a concept has no place in science.

How would you explain to a friend the anthropic principle? _____
_____

As we learn more about our universe, it has become clearer than ever that Earth is unique. It boasts a wealth of characteristics that make it capable of supporting life—a nearly endless list of preconditions that have been exquisitely met only, as far as we know, on our planet.

How does Earth happen to be so special? Is it just coincidence? Luck? Or was it designed by a loving Creator who had us in mind from the outset?

Earth's Orbit

Consider, for example, Earth's orbit. If Earth were even slightly closer to the sun, all its water would boil away, and life would be impossible. If it were only slightly farther away from the sun, all its water would freeze and the terrestrial landscape would be nothing but barren deserts.

And it's not only the landscape that is affected by the position of our planet. The processes inside our bodies also rely on these hospitable conditions. The chemical reactions necessary for life to function occur within a narrow temperature range, and Earth is exactly the right distance from the sun to fall within that range. What's more, for all this to happen, Earth must remain about the same distance from the sun in its orbit; that is, its orbit must be nearly circular—which it is, in contrast to the elliptical orbits of most other planets in our solar system. Are these finely calibrated distances a product of mere happenstance? Or were they *designed* to support life?

Water

Consider the existence of water, that common substance we take for granted. Water has a host of unique properties absolutely indispensable for life. For example, it is the only known substance whose solid phase (ice) is less dense than its liquid phase. This allows ice to form on the top of oceans and lakes instead of on the bottom, allowing fish and other marine life to survive the winter. On the microscopic level, water molecules exhibit something called the hydrophilic effect, which gives water the unique ability to shape proteins and nucleic acids in DNA. From a molecular standpoint, "the various properties of water are nothing short of miraculous," writes Michael Corey; "no other compound even comes close to duplicating its many life-supporting properties."[20]

Cosmic Coincidences

Evidence of the anthropic principle aren't confined to this planet. Earth would not support life unless the cosmos itself had the right physical properties. The anthropic principle draws together a staggering number of "cosmic coincidences" that make life possible. For example, the big bang had to have exploded with just the right degree of vigor for our present universe to have formed. If it had occurred with too little velocity, the universe would have collapsed back in on itself shortly after the big bang because of gravitational forces; if it had occurred with too much velocity, the matter would have streaked away so fast that it would have been impossible for galaxies and solar systems to subsequently form. This same "lucky coincidence" could be stated in another way: The force of gravity must be fine-tuned to allow the universe to expand at precisely the right rate (accurate to within 1 part in 1060). The fact that the force of gravity just happens to be the right number with "such stunning accuracy," writes physicist Paul Davies, "is surely one of the great mysteries of cosmology."[21]

The Structure of the Atom

Everything in the universe is made of atoms, from the stars in the farthest heavens to the cells in your body—and the atom itself is a bundle of fortuitous "coinci-dences." Within the atom, the neutron is just slightly more massive than the proton, which means that free neutrons (those not trapped within an atom) can decay and turn into protons. If things were reversed—if it were the proton that was larger and had a tendency to decay—the very structure of the universe would be impossible.

If free protons had a tendency to decay, then everything made of hydrogen would decay. The sun, which is made of hydrogen, would melt away. Water, a liquid oxide of hydrogen (H_2O) would be impossible. In fact, the universe itself would decay, since about 74 percent of the observed universe consists of hydrogen.

And why is the neutron larger than the proton? No one knows. There is no physical cause to explain why the neutron is larger. It is simply a fact. So apparently the only "reason" for the difference in size is that it allows the universe to exist and to support life.

Not only do atomic particles have a size, but they also have an electrical charge. Electrons have a negative charge, and protons have a positive charge. The charge of the proton exactly balances that of the electron, and it's a good thing it does. If the electron carried more charge than the proton, all atoms would be negatively charged. In that case—since identical charges repel—all the atoms composing all the objects in the universe would fly apart in a catastrophic explosion. On the other hand, if the proton carried more charge than the electron, all atoms would be positively charged—with the same disastrous consequences.

There is no known physical reason, no natural explanation, for the precise balance in the electrical charges of the proton and the electron—especially when you consider that the two particles differ from one another in all other respects: in size, weight, magnetic properties, and so on. And since there is no natural explanation, no natural law to account for this extraordinarily

The Atom

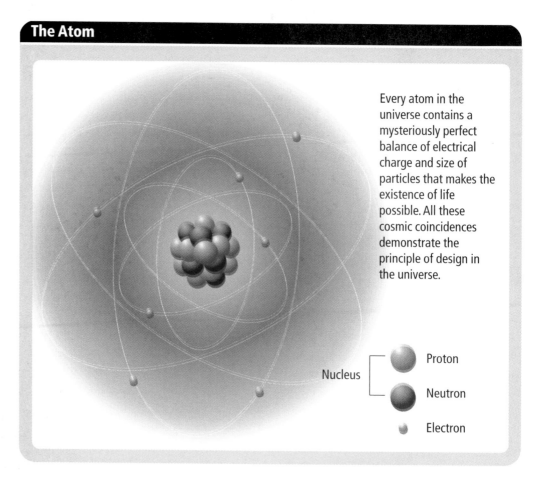

Every atom in the universe contains a mysteriously perfect balance of electrical charge and size of particles that makes the existence of life possible. All these cosmic coincidences demonstrate the principle of design in the universe.

Nucleus — Proton

Neutron

Electron

precise adjustment, is it not reasonable to conclude that this intricate arrangement is the product of a choice, a plan, a design?

The list of "coincidences" goes on and on. It turns out that the slightest tinkering with the values of the fundamental forces of physics would have resulted in a universe where life is utterly impossible. The anthropic principle states that in our own universe, all of these seemingly arbitrary and unrelated values in physics have one strange thing in common: they are precisely the values needed to get a universe capable of supporting life.

Why should we care about these coincidences? These technical issues and values in physics may seem trivial to the non-scientist, but non-Christian scientists scramble to cope with their implications. They add up to a message that says: "The heavens declare the glory of God; the skies proclaim the work of his hands" (Ps. 19:1).

Proposed Solutions to the Anthropic Principle

Since many secular scientists rule out God as a solution, they must look elsewhere for answers. One of the widely held versions of the anthropic principle is the "many worlds" hypothesis. According to this theory, an infinite number of universes exist, all with different laws and different values for fundamental numbers. Most of these universes are dark, lifeless places. But by sheer probability, some will have just the right structure to support life. The "fit" universes survive, while the "unfit" are weeded out. Our own, of course, happens to be a universe "fit" for life.

How do we know whether these numberless universes really exist? The answer is, we *cannot* know. The idea is purely a product of scientific imagination. Even if alternative universes did exist, they'd be inherently impossible to detect.

Why do you suppose secular thinkers are going to such lengths to explain the anthropic principle? _____

_____

_____

_____

_____

_____

_____

_____

Candid scientists admit that the whole idea is motivated by a desire to avoid the theological implications of the anthropic principle. Physicist Heinz Pagels says that if the universe appears to be tailor-made for life, the most straightforward conclusion is that it *was* tailor-made, created by God; it is only because many scientists find that conclusion "unattractive" that they adopt the theory of multiple universes, Pagels explains. And he adds wryly, "It is the closest that some atheists can get to God." In other words, atheists are squirming every which way to avoid the obvious.[22]

A Universe That Wants to Be Known

Another version is the *participatory anthropic principle*. Drawing a wild conclusion from quantum mechanics, this version says that the universe did not fully exist until human beings emerged to observe it. And so, in order to become fully real, the universe decided to evolve human consciousness. In the words of Nobel prize-winning biologist George Wald, "The universe wants to be known."[23]

This is indeed a strange picture of the universe—as if it had a heart, longing to be known, and a mind, deciding to evolve human beings. Yet it seems to be a picture shared by physicist Freeman Dyson, who says, "I find that the universe in some sense must have known that we were coming."[24] And astronomer George Greenstein echoes a similar refrain: "If this is the best way to make a universe, how did the universe find that out?"[25]

Here we have a concept of the universe as a quasi-intelligent being that can know and be known, that can plot and plan. It is astonishing that scientists will dismiss the idea of a Creator as unscientific, yet turn around and embrace the bizarre, almost mystical concept of a conscious universe.

Scientists are not being forced to these speculative forms of the anthropic principle by the facts; instead, they are driven by a religious motive—or rather, by an *anti*religious motive. So strong is their desire to avoid the conclusion of divine creation that they will resort to irrational notions, such as the existence of millions of unknowable universes or a pantheistic universe that "knew" we were coming. As Patrick Glynn writes, the fact that so many scientists are willing to accept "wild speculations about unseen universes for which not a shred of observational evidence exists suggests something about both the power of the modern atheistic ideology and the cultural agenda of many in the scientific profession." Then Glynn delivers this searing indictment: "The mainstream scientific community has in effect shown its attachment to the atheistic ideology of the random universe to be in some respects more powerful than its commitment to the scientific method itself."[26] Precisely.

We intuitively recognize the products of design versus the products of natural forces. According to the anthropic principle, evidence for design is found throughout the physical universe. If the universe exhibits design, it is logical to conclude that there is a designer. The most obvious inference is that the universe *appears* to be designed because it *is* designed—powerful evidence for the biblical worldview that a loving God created the world.

In our next unit we will explore why those who believe the evolution story work so hard to ignore the facts against evolution and the evidence for creation.

Today's Prayer

Father, I thank You that Your truth endures, even when human wisdom does not accept it. You are the Designer and Creator of all things. Thank You for caring enough for Your creations to design us down to the tiniest parts of atoms.

[1] The following discussion draws heavily from Charles B. Thaxton, Walter L. Bradley, and Roger L. Olsen, *The Mystery of Life's Origin: Reassessing Current Theories* (Dallas: Lewis & Stanley, 1992). See also Stephen C. Meyer, "Explanatory Power of Design," in *Mere Creation: Science, Faith, and Intelligent Design,* ed. William A. Dembski (Downers Grove, Ill.: InterVarsity Press, 1998), 113.

[2] Stanley L. Miller, *From the Primitive Atmosphere to the Prebiotic Soup to the Pre-RNA World* (Washington, D.C.: National Aeronautics and Space Administration, 1996).

[3] *(http://www.panspermia.org/whatis2.htm).*

[4] *(http://library.advanced.org/19037/ebasics.html).*

[5] *(http://www.panspermia.org).*

[6] Rick Weiss, "Mutant Moniker: A Tale of Freaky Flies and Gonzo Genetics," *Science News* 139, no. 2 (January 12, 1991): 30; and Dan L. Lindsley and Georgianna Zimm, "The Hard Life of a Mutant Fruit Fly," *Harper's Magazine* 284, no. 1703 (April 1992): 24.

[7] Given the simplicity of Darwin's theory of evolution, it was reasonable for paleontologists to believe that they should be able to demonstrate with the hard evidence provided by fossils both the thread of life and the gradual transformation of one species into another. Although paleontologists have, and continue to claim to have, discovered sequences of fossils that do indeed present a picture of gradual change over time, the truth of the matter is that we are still in the dark about the origin of most major groups of organisms. They appear in the fossil records as Athena did from the head of Zeus—full blown and raring to go—in contradiction to Darwin's depiction of evolution as resulting from the gradual accumulation of countless infinitesimally minute variations, which, in turn, demands that the fossil record preserve an unbroken chain of transitional forms. See Jeffrey H. Schwartz, *Sudden Origins: Fossils, Genes, and the Emergence of Species* (New York: Wiley & Sons, 1999), 3.

[8] Phillip E. Johnson, *Reason in the Balance: The Case against Naturalism in Science, Law, and Education* (Downers Grove, Ill.: InterVarsity Press, 1995). See also Nancy R. Pearcey, "Naturalism on Trial," *First Things,* no. 60 (February 1996): 64.

[9] Jerry A. Coyne, "Not Black and White," *Nature* 396 (November 5, 1998): 35-36; Jonathan Wells, "Second Thoughts about Peppered Moths," *http://www.trueorigin.org/pepmoth1.htm.*

[10] Luther Burbank, as quoted in Norman Macbeth, *Darwin Retried* (New York: Delta, 1971), 36.

[11] Michael J. Behe, *Darwin's Black Box: The Biochemical Challenge to Evolution* (New York: Touchstone, 1996), 40-48. The functional integration of parts is a classic argument against Darwinism; it was first developed in the nineteenth century by George Cuirer. See Michael Denton, *Evolution: A Theory in Crisis* (Bethesda, Md.: Adler and Adler, 1985).

[12] See Michael J. Behe, *Darwin's Black Box: The Biochemical Challenge to Evolution* (New York: Free Press, 1996), 210-16.

[13] See Thaxton, *The Mystery of Life's Origin; Pearcey and Thaxton, The Soul of Science;* and Stephen C. Meyer, "The Origin of Life and the Death of Materialism," *Intercollegiate Review* 31, no. 2 (spring 1996).

[14] Ludwig Büchner, as quoted in Gordon H. Clark, *The Philosophy of Science and Belief in God* (Nutley, N.J.: Craig Press, 1964), 50.

[15] Lincoln Kinnear Barnett, *The Universe and Dr. Einstein* (New York: William Morrow, 1968), 114 (emphasis in the original).

[16] Arthur Eddington, as quoted in Hugh Ross, "Astronomical Evidences for a Personal, Transcendent God," in *The Creation Hypothesis,* ed. J. P Moreland (Downers Grove, Ill.: InterVarsity Press, 1994), 145-46.

[17] Robert Jastrow, *Until the Sun Dies* (New York: Norton, 1977), 51.

[18] Carl Sagan, *Cosmos* (New York: Random, 1980), 259.

[19] William Lane Craig and Quentin Smith, *Theism, Atheism, and Big Bang Cosmology* (new York: Oxford University Press, 1993), 135.

[20] M.A. Corey, *God and the New Cosmology: The Anthropic Design Argument* (Lanham, Md.: Rowman & Littlefield, 1993), 105.

[21] Paul C. Davies, *The Accidental Universe* (Cambridge: Cambridge University Press, 1982), 90.

[22] Heinz Pagels, "A Cozy Cosmology," *The Sciences* (March/April 1985): 38.

[23] George Wald, as quoted in Dietrick E. Thomsen, "A Knowing Universe Seeking to Be Known," *Science News* (February 19, 1983): 124.

[24] Freeman Dyson, as quoted in Martin Gardner, "Intelligent Design and Phillip Johnson," *Skeptical Inquirer* (November 21, 1997): 17.

[25] George Greenstein, *The Symbiotic Universe: Life and Mind in the Cosmos* (New York: William Morrow, 1988), 197.

[26] Patrick Glynn, "The Atheistic Assumptions of Modern Society Are Being Challenged by the New Science," *National Review* 48, no. 8 (May 6, 1996): 32. See also Patrick Glynn, *The Evidence: The Reconciliation of Faith and Reason in a Postsecular World* (Rocklin, Calif.: Prima, 1997).

Science or Religion?

Evolution continues to be presented as a scientific fact, but this idea is deceptive. In this unit you will examine the evidence that evolution is a religious belief system.

A Struggle Between Two Worldviews

Naturalistic scientists try to give the impression that they are fair-minded and objective, implying that religious people are subjective and biased in favor of their personal beliefs. But this is a ruse, for naturalism is as much a philosophy, a worldview, a personal belief system as any religion is. The core of the controversy is not science; it is a titanic struggle between opposing worldviews—between naturalism and theism. Is the universe governed by blind material forces or by a loving personal Being? Only when Christians understand this, only when we clear away the smoke screens and get to the core issue, will we stop losing debates. Only then will we be able to help our kids, like Katy, face the continual challenges to their faith.

In this unit we will look at five questions. These five questions clarify the nature of the struggle.

- Is the theory of evolution genuine science or is it at heart part of a religious belief system?
- How did the theory of evolution develop? From where did it come?
- How did the theory of evolution become accepted? How did it become the mainstream belief system of modern society?
- What is at stake? Does the naturalist vs. creationist debate really matter?
- What has resulted from the theory of evolution? What practical difference has it made in our world?

DAY ONE
Is the Theory Science or Religion?

"there is a God in heaven who reveals mysteries."–Daniel 2:28

Is the theory of evolution genuine science or is it at heart part of a religious belief system?

The dominant view in our culture today is radically one-dimensional: that this life is all there is, and nature is all we need to explain everything that exists. At heart, the philosophy of naturalism permeates the classroom curriculum and is expressed widely in popular culture from Disney World to television nature shows to children's books.

Every worldview has to begin with a theory of how the universe began. Naturalism begins with the fundamental assumption that the forces of nature alone are adequate to explain everything that exists. Whereas the Bible says, "In the beginning God created the heavens and the earth" (Gen. 1:1), naturalists say that in the beginning were the particles, along with blind, purposeless natural laws.

Naturalists say that nature is our creator. That nature created the universe out of nothing, by random processes. That nature formed our planet, with its unique ability to support life. That nature drew together the chemicals that formed the first living cell. And naturalism says that nature acted to evolve complex life-forms and, finally, human beings, with the marvels of consciousness and intelligence.

Naturalists portray Christians as biased, unthinking simpletons who want to ban books and eliminate the teaching of evolution. Why do you think evolutionists are so opposed to Christianity?
❑ **Christians are closed-minded, book-burning enemies of learning.**
❑ **Naturalism is a religion hiding behind the false veil of science.**
❑ **Christians have sometimes unwisely provided naturalists with ammunition because believers have opposed evolution instead of championing truth.**

What should our approach be to the teaching of evolution in schools?
❑ **We need to ban the teaching of evolution and substitute the teaching of a biblical view of creation.**
❑ **We need all the scientific evidence taught about origins—including that which supports and that which contradicts evolution.**

Christians don't want less taught in the classroom, we want *more* taught. Students should know the basics of evolutionary theory and all the evidence cited in its favor. But they should also learn the evidence *against* evolution.

Naturalism begins with premises that cannot be tested. One such premise is that nature is "all that is or ever was or ever will be," to use a line from the late Carl Sagan's popular science program *Cosmos.* This is not a scientific statement, for there is no conceivable way it could be tested. Naturalism is an assumption, a philosophy,

a religious belief. It is the philosophy that supports the entire evolutionary enterprise, from its assertions about the beginning of the universe to the beginning of life to the appearance of complex life-forms.

The Nature Religion of Carl Sagan

As much as anyone else, Sagan popularized the naturalistic worldview and entrenched it firmly in the mind of the average American. Week after week, through his program *Cosmos,* he brought stunning images of exploding stars and sprawling nebulae to the nation's homes and classrooms.

Pictures are not all Sagan brought. With his engaging manner, he was a televangelist for naturalism, the philosophy he held with all the fervor of a religion. He was being consistent, for whatever you take as the starting point of your worldview does function, in effect, as your religion.[1]

In the following three paragraphs, circle the evidences you find that Sagan's naturalism was a religious belief system.

Sagan's trademark phrase from his book and TV series was "The Cosmos is all that is or ever was or ever will be."[2] Anyone from a liturgical church recognizes Sagan was using a liturgical form. Since the early church, Christians have sung the Gloria Patri: "Glory be to the Father, and to the Son, and to the Holy Ghost; As it was in the beginning, is now, and ever shall be, world without end." Sagan is clearly offering a substitute liturgy, a cadence to the cosmos. The sheer fact that he capitalizes the word *Cosmos,* just as religious believers capitalize the word God, is a dead giveaway that he was gripped by religious fervor.

On point after point, Sagan offers a naturalistic substitute for traditional religion. While Christianity teaches that we are children of God, Sagan says that "we are, in the most profound sense, children of the Cosmos," for it is the cosmos that gave us birth and daily sustains us.[3]

Carl Sagan (1934-1996)

Born Nov. 9, 1934, in Brooklyn, N.Y. , Carl Sagan is famous for his research on the origins of life and his belief that life exists elsewhere in the universe.
Sagan became a leading figure in the search for extraterrestrial intelligence with his involvement in the Mariner, Viking, and Voyager spacecraft expeditions to Venus and the outer planets.
Sagan passed away on December 20, 1996.

"It is said that men may not be the dreams of the Gods, but rather that the Gods are the dreams of men." –Carl Sagan

In a passage that is almost certainly autobiographical, Sagan hints that the astronomer's urge to explore the cosmos is motivated by a mystical recognition that the chemicals in our bodies were originally forged in space—that outer space is our origin and our true home: "Some part of our being knows this is from where we came. We long to return."[4] And the astronomer's "awe" is nothing less than religious worship. "Our ancestors worshiped the Sun, and they were far from foolish." For if we must worship something, "does it not make sense to revere the Sun and the stars?"[5]

[handwritten margin note: this is a moral duty]

Summarize the evidences you found in the previous three paragraphs to suggest Sagan's naturalism was a religious belief.

[handwritten: Cosmos being God + Our being its children]

In Sagan's television program and books, he makes it clear that he has no use for the transcendent Creator revealed in the Bible. The cosmos is his deity. In one of his many best-selling books, Sagan mockingly described the Christian God as "an outsized, light-skinned male with a long white beard, sitting on a throne somewhere up there in the sky, busily tallying the fall of every sparrow."[6] In place of the biblical God, Sagan regarded the cosmos as the only self-existing, eternal being: "A universe that is infinitely old requires no Creator."[7] Did you note that Sagan worshiped the cosmos using liturgical forms, capitalized the word as a reference to deity, and described the cosmos as the creator?

Compare the quote from Sagan about the infinitely old universe with what you have learned about the "Big Bang" theory. Mark each of the following statements either T (true) or F (false).

[handwritten: F] ___ 1. Sagan's statement is true. Scientific studies indicate that the universe is infinitely old.
[handwritten: T] ___ 2. Sagan's statement is false. Both scientific and biblical evidence agree that the universe is not infinitely old.
___ 3. As a scientist, Sagan knew that the world is not infinitely old.
[handwritten: F] ___ 4. Sagan made a statement of scientific fact.
[handwritten: T] ___ 5. Sagan made a statement of religious belief veiled as scientific fact.

Like any religion, Sagan's worship of the cosmos prescribes certain moral duties for its adherents. He believed the cosmos created human life in its own image—"Our matter, our form, and much of our character is determined by the deep connection between life and the Cosmos"—and in return, we have a moral duty to the cosmos.[8] According to Sagan, what is that duty? It is an "obligation to survive," an obligation we owe "to that Cosmos, ancient and vast, from which we spring."[9]

The evidence is clear. Carl Sagan used the mantle of "science" to influence millions of people, but he was in fact a salesman for his naturalist worldview—his religion. His statements were religious faith pretending to be scientific and often specifically contradicting scientific fact. In the learning activity above, statements 1 and 4 are false. Statements 2, 3, and 5 are true.

We hear much about the "separation of church and state." How would recognizing naturalism as a religion change the debate over what is allowable in public schools?

_____
_____
_____

Cosmic Salvation

Sagan's worship of the cosmos even tells us how to be saved. He believed that threats to human survival—pollution, war, food shortages—have nothing to do with moral failings. Instead, Sagan wrote that they result from technological incompetence, which is hardly surprising since he believed that humanity is still in its evolutionary childhood.[10]

Which answer to human misery do you think more nearly fits reality?

- ☑ human selfishness and greed (sin)?
- ☐ technical incompetence because we haven't evolved sufficiently?

How would you explain your answer to a person who did not believe in sin?

These same problems existed before technology

Since Sagan believed our problems came from incomplete evolution, he thought the solutions may well come from more advanced civilizations somewhere out there, descending to Earth to save us. For this reason Sagan was an avid supporter of efforts to scan the far reaches of space for radio messages.[11] "The receipt of a single message from space would show that it is possible to live through such technological adolescence," he writes breathlessly, for it would prove that an advanced extraterrestrial race has survived the same stage and gone on to maturity.[12]

If this isn't a vision of salvation, what is? The cosmos will speak to us. It is there, and it is not silent.

In every human being is a deep, ongoing search for meaning and transcendence—part of the image of God in our very nature.

Even if we flee God, the religious imprint remains. Everyone worships some kind of god. Everyone believes in some kind of deity—even if that deity is an impersonal substance such as matter, energy, or nature. That's why the Bible preaches against idolatry, not atheism. Naturalism may parade as science, marshalling facts and figures, but it is a religion.

Brainwashing for Toddlers

This religion is being taught everywhere in the public square today—even in the books your child reads in school or checks out of the public library. Not long ago, Nancy picked up a Berenstain Bears book for her son. In the book, part of a popular picture-book series for children, the Bear family invites the young reader to join them for a nature walk. We start out on a sunny morning, and after running into a few spider webs, we read in capital letters sprawled across a sunrise, glazed with light rays, those familiar words: Nature is "all that IS, or WAS, or EVER WILL BE!"[13]

Sound familiar? Of course. It is Sagan's famous opening line, now framed in cute images of little bears and bugs and birds—the philosophy of naturalism peddled for toddlers. And to drive the point home, the authors have drawn a bear pointing directly at the reader—your impressionable young child—and saying, "Nature is you! Nature is me!"[14] Human beings, too, are nothing more than parts of nature.

Think for a moment. Why would a writer of a children's book include such a statement?

If you noted that the reason to include such a statement is because the writers sought to spread their religious conviction, you were on the right track. Is there any more poignant example of why Christians

Today's Prayer
Father God, I praise you for being the Creator of all the universe. I confess that I am too easily influenced by the theories and philosophies of our culture. Lead me in making firm my worldview and in educating myself to be able to present facts about creation in a way that will bring honor and glory to You. Do not let me be a stumbling block to anyone who disagrees with me, but let Your light shine through me to show Your truth.

need to learn how to argue persuasively against naturalism? It is pressed on our children's imagination long before they can think rationally and critically. It is presented everywhere as the only worldview supported by science. It is a religion held with all the fervor and conviction of any other religion. And it is the exact opposite of Christianity.

We began today with a question: "Is the theory of evolution genuine science or is it at heart part of a religious belief system?"

Can there be any real doubt concerning the answer?

DAY TWO

How Did the Theory Arise?

"The fear of the Lord is the beginning of wisdom; all who follow his precepts have good understanding."–Psalm 111:10

"The fear of the Lord is the beginning of wisdom, and knowledge of the Holy One is understanding."–Proverbs 9:10

How did the theory of evolution arise, or from where did it come?

Evolution promises to tell us where we came from, but have you ever asked where it came from? How did the theory of evolution come to be? Most people probably assume something like this: Scientist Charles Darwin set sail on the ship called the Beagle. During his travels in the South Pacific he studied various forms of wildlife. From what he saw, he began to realize that they had evolved into their present state. From those observations, he developed the theory that all life had evolved.

Did the evidence lead to the theory? No, the theory led Darwin to find supportive facts. Even before he formulated his theory, Darwin had already turned against the idea of creation and had developed a settled conviction that, as he put it, "Everything in nature is the result of fixed laws."[15] In other words, the deck was already stacked. Darwin set out to frame a naturalistic account of life before he actually uncovered any evidence.

How does knowing that Darwin had already decided to reject creation affect what you think of his theory?

❑ **no effect**
❑ **believe he was neutral and objective**
❑ **makes me suspicious**

Describe how you would feel about walking into a courtroom with a judge who had already decided against you.

_____
_____
_____
_____

It should come as no surprise to us that Charles Darwin had the same attitude that Carl Sagan displayed. Nature became a substitute religion for the father of evolution. His son William wrote, "As regards his respect for the laws of Nature, it might be called reverence if not a religious feeling. No man could feel more intensely the vastness and the inviolability of the laws of nature."[16] With an attitude akin to religious worship, it is not surprising that Charles Darwin eventually attributed godlike creative powers to natural selection.

Separate Genuine Science from Philosophy

The Christian must be ready to separate genuine science from underlying religious beliefs. Evolution, as it is typically presented in textbooks and museums, confuses the two; what most secular scientists label as "science" is actually their personal philosophy or religion. Science has come to be defined as naturalistic philosophy; the "scientific" answer is always the theory that appeals to natural forces alone. *Science based on a natural theory*

But why should we let secularists make the definitions? Let's be clear on the distinction between empirical science and philosophy, and then let's answer science with science and philosophy with philosophy.

In a cartoon reacting to the battle over evolution, two students are talking. One is carrying a jar. He says the jar contains his brain, that he had it pickled and put in a jar. When the other character asks why, he explains: "My creation science project." Mark the following true or false.

____ 1. The cartoonist thinks the battle over evolution pits science versus religion.
____ 2. The cartoon reflects an attitude that Christians oppose science.
____ 3. The cartoonist seems to understand that evolution is a belief system requiring faith just as does creationism.
____ 4. Christians need to oppose bad science with better science.

Being clear becomes all the more imperative when we realize what we're up against. The moment a Christian questions evolution, he or she is labeled a backwoods Bible-thumper, an ignorant reactionary who is trying to halt the progress of sci-

ence. Like Katy, most schoolchildren today have seen the movie *Inherit the Wind* or have witnessed its counterpart on television, and their imaginations are peopled with blustery, ignorant Christians going toe-to-toe with intelligent, educated, urbane defenders of Darwin. When we question evolution in public, we are viewed through the grid portrayed in these media pieces. In the activity above, all but the third response is true.

One day my wife, Patty, came home from a Bible study and told me how outraged the entire group was over an episode at the local school. One of the women in the group had a thirteen-year-old son who had received a low grade for giving a wrong answer on his weekly quiz for his earth science class. To the question, "Where did Earth come from?" Tim had written, "God created it." His test came back with a big red check and twenty points marked off his grade. The "correct" answer, according to the teacher, was that Earth is the product of the big bang. *Tim*

The women in Patty's Bible study urged Tim's mother to march into the classroom and show the teacher what the Bible says. "It's right there in Genesis 1," they said. "God created the heaven and the earth." *Do you*

How would you approach the teacher in a similar situation?

_____
_____
_____
_____

As soon as Patty told me the story, I reached for the phone to call Tim's mother. "Don't go to the teacher with Bible in hand," I said.

She was taken aback. "But the Bible shows that the teacher was wrong."

"As believers, we know that Scripture is inspired and authoritative," I explained, "but Tim's teacher will dismiss it out of hand. She'll say, 'That's religion. I teach science.'"

What we need to avoid in such situations is giving the mistaken idea that Christianity is opposed to science. If we are too quick to quote the Bible, we will never break out of the stereotype spread by *Inherit the Wind*. We should not oppose science with religion; we should oppose *bad* science with *better* science.

Our first task, then, before we can even expect to be heard, is to shatter that grid, to break that stereotype. We must convince people that the debate is not about the Bible versus science. The debate is about pursuing an unbiased examination of the scientific facts and following those facts wherever they may lead. We must challenge the assumption that science by definition means naturalistic philosophy.

The real battle is worldview against worldview, religion against religion. As you continue this week's study, look for evidence that can help Tim and his mother support his test answer.

If we continue to use the Bible against those who don't believe in it, they will continue to see us a ignorant + arogant Bible thumpers.

DAY THREE

How Did the Theory Become Accepted?

"He has made everything beautiful in its time. He has also set eternity in the hearts of men; yet they cannot fathom what God has done from beginning to end."—Ecclesiastes 3:11

How did the theory of evolution become accepted? How did it become the mainstream belief system of modern society?

How could most of humanity come to believe the idea of evolution? To answer that question we need to clearly recognize two biblical truths about humans. First, we are made to worship. As Ecclesiastes says, God has set eternity in our hearts. We do not have the option of being non religious. We only have the choice of what we will worship. Second, we are rebellious against God. We want to be the boss. We want to dethrone God and take His place. The theory of evolution has tremendous appeal because it gives human beings the excuse to eliminate God from their thinking.

Katy's teacher said that belief in God is just wishful thinking, something we make up to feel better. How could belief in evolution be wishful thinking?

_____

_____

_____

Modern Darwinists insist that evolution is so obviously supported by the facts that anyone who dissents must be ignorant or dishonest. Darwin was more candid. He knew quite well he had not proved his theory of natural selection. He described it as an inference, grounded chiefly on analogy.

Darwin said it can be judged only by how useful it is, how well "it groups and explains phenomena."[17]

Likewise, many of Darwin's earliest and most ardent supporters were quick to spot the weaknesses in his theory. Yet they, too, chose to champion it because they saw it as a useful means of promoting naturalistic philosophy.

Read the following paragraph about Herbert Spencer. Then answer the question: Why did Spencer choose evolution?

_____
_____
_____
_____
_____
_____

Herbert Spencer, the first person to extend evolution into every discipline, from ethics to psychology, explains frankly that he felt an enormous internal pressure to find a naturalistic alternative to the idea of creation. "The Special Creation belief had dropped out of my mind many years before," he wrote, "and I could not remain in a suspended state: acceptance of the only conceivable alternative was peremptory." Moreover, Spencer admitted, once you accept the philosophy of naturalism, some form of naturalistic evolution is an "inevitable corollary."[18] The strength of the scientific evidence is a secondary matter.

Check the response that most nearly expresses Spencer's motivation for supporting evolution.

❏ He carefully studied the scientific evidence and came to a conclusion based on the facts.

❏ He first disbelieved in creation; then he needed a justification for his disbelief.

Thomas Huxley christened himself "Darwin's bulldog" and fought fiercely for the cause, and yet by his own admission, he never thought Darwin's theory amounted to much scientifically. He, too, rallied to the cause for philosophical reasons. Long before his encounter with Darwin, Huxley had rejected the biblical teaching of creation and was actively looking for an alternative. Darwin, he recalls, "did the immense service of freeing us forever from the dilemma—Refuse to accept the creation hypothesis, and what have you to propose that can be accepted by any cautious reasoner?"[19] Apparently Huxley was willing to champion any naturalistic theory, even one he found scientifically flawed, as long as it provided an alternative to creation.

Why did Thomas Huxley fight for Darwin's theory? _____
_____
_____
_____
_____
_____
_____

It is becoming clear that the contest over evolution in the nineteenth century was philosophically "rigged." Darwinism won not because his theory fit the evidence, but because it provided a scientific rationale for naturalism. If the world is governed by uniformly operating laws, as Huxley said, then the successive populations of beings "must have proceeded from one another in the way of progressive modification."[20] The operative word here is "must." Once you accept philosophical naturalism, then something very much like Darwinism _must_ be true—regardless of the facts.

Philosophy not Science

Darwinism is the official creed in our public schools, not because of what we see through the microscope or the telescope; it's what we hold in our hearts and minds.

Darwinism functions as the cornerstone propping up a naturalistic worldview, and therefore the scientists who are committed to naturalism before even walking into the laboratory are primed to accept even the flimsiest evidence supporting the theory. They accept the most trivial change in living things as confirmation of the most far-flung claims of evolution, so they tout minor variation in finch beaks or insecticide resistance as evidence that finches and flies both evolved ultimately from the slime by blind, unguided natural processes.

In Darwin's day so little was known about biology that belief in evolution made some degree of sense. Even in our grandparents' day Christians had relatively little scientific evidence to argue against Darwinism. List several of the reasons Christians today have enormously more evidence to support creation now than then. If necessary, review unit 2. _____

_____

_____

_____

_____

_____

_____

_____

_____

The Anatomy of a Lie

Are we saying that everyone who believes the theory of evolution is dishonest and rebelling against God? Absolutely not. Lies are much more subtle than that. Most people have accepted the lie as fact because they have failed to think for themselves. Those who have been indoctrinated with the lie now continue to propagate the theory without realizing how it developed or that it is a religious belief rather than a scientific fact. They don't know how much scientific evidence has been misinterpreted or kept from them because it contradicts the evolution story. They don't realize that

evolution developed through the following steps:

1. In our rebellious human nature, we want to replace God and be our own boss. We either surrender to Him or continue to rebel.
2. Those who choose rebellion must eliminate God from their thinking, but they still have a problem: "The heavens declare the glory of God; the skies proclaim the work of his hands." (Ps. 19:1).
3. Therefore, they must resolve the conflict by getting rid of the necessity for a creator.
4. They observe natural change within species (varieties of finch beaks, pigeons, dogs).
5. They make the quantum leap of logic that just as creatures change within a species (micro-evolution) they can change from one species to another (macro-evolution) and that life itself can originate from non-life.
6. They begin to teach the theory.
7. The theory becomes accepted scientific dogma. Millions of people believe the theory because "science says so."

Order the following steps in the development and propagation of the concept of evolution by placing a 1 by the first step, 2 by the second, and so on.

6 a. We accept the theory of evolution without thinking for ourselves.

2 b. We come to believe that God does not exist.

1 c. In our rebellion, we humans want to be free of God's control and interference in our lives.

5 d. We formulate the theory of evolution.

4 e. We need an alternate explanation of origins.

3 f. We want to believe that God does not exist.

Some believe in evolution like Huxley. They want a way to eliminate God. Millions of others accept evolution because they assume it must be supported by the facts.

The modern fragmentation of science also contributes to the lie. Science is broken into biology, chemistry, physics, and dozens of more specialized fields such as microbiology or particle physics. Scientists in each area could easily see the holes in evolution, but due to the specialization, each discipline tends to think, "this doesn't make sense to me, but the scientists over in the (biology, chemistry, or physics) department understand." I answer-ed the activity on page 62: a. 6; b. 2; c. 1; d. 5; e. 4; f. 3.

The Method Fits the Conclusion

One of the most explicit recent statements of the philosophical motivation behind Darwinism comes, surprisingly enough, from Harvard geneticist Richard Lewontin, who explains why scientists have such disdain for religion—which he groups with things such as UFOs and channeling. Admittedly, science has its own problems, Lewontin says. It has created many of our social problems (like ecological disasters), and many scientific theories are no more than "unsubstantiated just-so stories." Nevertheless, "in the struggle between science and the supernatural," we "take the side of science." Why? "Because we have a prior commitment to materialism."[21]

Note carefully those last few words. The hostility to religion that is fashionable in the scientific establishment is not driven by the facts but by materialistic philosophy.

And there is more, for Lewontin says even the methods of science are driven by materialistic philosophy. The rules that define what qualifies as science in the first place have been crafted by materialists in such a way as to ensure they get only materialistic theories. Or, as Lewontin puts it, "we are forced by our *a priori* (a decision reached before examining the facts) adherence to material causes to create an apparatus of investigation and a set of concepts that produce material explanations."[22]

This is a stunning admission. The authority of science rests primarily on its public image—on the impression that its theories rest firmly on a foundation of empirical facts. But Lewontin has pulled back the curtains in Oz to reveal the wizard's strings and levers.

On what does the authority of science rest today?
_____
_____
_____
_____
_____
_____
_____

How has Richard Lewontin helped to expose this false wizard?
_____
_____
_____
_____
_____
_____
_____

In the face of so much contradictory evidence, why do naturalistic scientists continue to hold on to evolution?
because of a commitment to materialism
_____
_____
_____
_____

The truth is that much of Darwinism is not science but, rather, naturalistic philosophy masquerading as science. So an honest debate between Darwinism and Christianity is not fact versus faith but philosophy versus philosophy, worldview versus worldview.

a pri•or•i
\.ä-pre-'o(e)r-e\ *adj* (1652):
1 a : DEDUCTIVE **2 a :** being without examination or analysis : PRESUMPTIVE **b :** formed or conceived beforehand (Webster's)

Today's Prayer
Father, God,
I frequently try to be my own boss. My life is so much better when I surrender my will to Yours instead of rebelling against it. I humbly ask You now to guide me and change me to be like You.

What Is at Stake?

What is at stake? Does the naturalist vs. creationist debate really matter?

"Simon, Simon, Satan has asked to sift you as wheat. But I have prayed for you, Simon, that your faith may not fail. And when you have turned back, strengthen your brothers."
—Luke 22:31-32

We began this study with a look at the power of ideas. We must be clear what is at stake in the battle for the mind. As long as Darwinism reigns in our schools and elite culture, the Christian worldview will be considered the madwoman in the attic—irrational and unbelievable. That's why we can no longer allow naturalists to treat science as a sanctuary where their personal philosophy reigns free from challenge.

This debate has tremendous importance for the nature and fate of society. Evolution is not a benign scientific theory that does not matter. It is a devastatingly destructive idea that continues to take a toll on our societies, families, and our children. Consider some of the results of evolution in our society.

Implications of Evolution: Ethics

If a transcendent God created us for a purpose, then the most rational approach is to ask, What is that purpose and how must we live in order to fulfill it? The answer is found in divine revelation; its moral commands tell us how we can become the people God created us to be. Hence, Christian morality is not subjective, based on our personal feelings; it is objective, based on the way God created human nature. Skeptics often dismiss Christianity as "irrational," but if we were indeed created, then the truly irrational course is to ignore the Creator's moral rules.

Compare for yourself the two models. With each of the following issues describe all the results you can think of that will naturally follow the "created" model of recognized rules and the "evolved" model of no moral rules.

SEXUALITY
Created _____
_____
_____
_____

Evolved _____
_____
_____
_____

VALUE OF HUMAN LIFE
Created _____
_____
_____
_____

Evolved _____
_____
_____
_____

BUSINESS ETHICS
Created _____
_____
_____
_____

Evolved _____
_____
_____
_____

Naturalism claims that God did not create us; rather, it is we who created the idea of God. He "exists" only in the minds of those who believe in him. If this claim is true, then the most rational course is to dismiss religion as wishful thinking and to base morality squarely on what is real—on scientific knowledge. If humans are products of evolutionary forces, then morality is nothing more than an idea that appears in our minds when we have evolved to a certain level. Consequently, there is no ultimate objective basis for morality; humans create their own standards. The only objective reality that exists is the natural world, and it is in constant evolutionary flux. Hence, our ideas about right and wrong are constantly changing as well. The result is radical relativism, not only in ethics but also in law and education, and every other aspect of culture.

In the activity above you can quickly see how unworkable and destructive the lack of morality becomes. You may have noted that "restrictive" biblical ethics encourage such things as:
- stable marriages and children with parents who care for them;
- a high respect for human life that results in efforts to eliminate poverty, disease, war, and all forms of abuse;
- a business ethic of honesty, hard work, and personal responsibility.

On the other hand, you probably noted that the absence of a biblical foundation results in promiscuity, selfishness, and disregard for anything but our own gratification.

The Bible presents the options of life in Galatians 5:19-23. Which set of behaviors are the natural outgrowth of naturalism?

_____

_____

We need to help people face the stark choice: either a worldview that leads to moral anarchy and that opens the door to tyranny, or a worldview that makes possible an ordered and morally responsible society. The price for the biblical worldview is acknowledging a transcendent standard and our accountability for sin before a holy God.

The opponents of Christianity have portrayed Christians as the greatest threat to liberty. They think Christians want to take away our freedoms. How would you respond to those charges? _____

_____

_____

_____

_____

_____

When Jewish theologian Dennis Prager gives speeches, he often asks audiences to imagine that they are walking down a dark city alley at night and they suddenly see a group of young men coming toward them. Prager then asks: "Would you be frightened or relieved that they are carrying Bibles and that they've just come from a Bible study?" Audiences invariably laugh and admit that they would be relieved.[23]

Relativism in Law

A nation's laws were traditionally understood to be based on a transcendent moral order (ultimately on divine law). The belief was that "men do not make laws. They do but discover them. Laws … must rest on the eternal foundation of righteousness."[24] These words may sound like they came from the pen of a sixteenth-century divine, but they were written in the early twentieth century by our thirtieth president, Calvin Coolidge.

But if Darwinism is true, there is no divine law or transcendent moral order, and hence, there is no final, authoritative basis for law. The influential legal theorist Oliver Wendell Holmes, an avowed Darwinian, taught that laws are merely a codification of political policies judged to be socially and economically advantageous. Law is re-

John Dewey
(1859-1952)

John Dewey was an American philosopher and educator whose writings and teachings have had profound influences on education in the United States. Dewey's philosophy of education, instrumentalism (also called pragmatism), focused on learning-by-doing rather than rote learning and dogmatic instruction, the practice of his day.

duced to a managerial skill used in the service of social engineering, the dominant view in the legal profession today.

Evolution's Effect on Education

Darwinism has molded not only the content but also the methodology of teaching. The key figure is John Dewey, who sought to work out what Darwinism means for the learning process. If human beings are part of nature and nothing more, he reasoned, then the mind is simply an organ that has evolved from lower forms in the struggle for existence—just as wings or claws have evolved—and its value depends on whether it works, whether it enables the organism to survive.

Dewey rejected the traditional belief that an idea is an insight into an objective reality, to be judged by whether it is true or false. Instead, he argued that ideas are merely hypotheses about what will get the results we want, and their validity depends on whether they work. Dewey's pragmatic philosophy is the source of much of the relativism that has gutted both academic and moral education today.

If you were a teacher, in what practical ways would Dewey's ideas change the way you would teach children?

_____

_____

_____

Darwin and Postmodernism

Darwinism is even a key source of postmodernism, which dismisses the idea of universal truth. Because Darwinism eliminates the transcendent, postmodernism draws the inevitable conclusion that there is no transcendent truth. Each of us is locked in the limited perspective of our race, gender, and ethnic group. The "search for truth" that supposedly motivates education is a sham; there is only the black perspective, the feminist perspective, the Hispanic perspective, and so on. Any claim

to universal truth is considered an attempt to impose the perspective of one group on all the others.

Does postmodernism have the one absolute truth? ❏ yes ❏ no
What do you think it is? _____

_____

_____

_____

Despite its flamboyant skepticism toward objective truth, ironically, postmodernism rests on an assumption that something is objectively true—namely, Darwinism.

If tying Darwinism to postmodernism seems a bit of a stretch, listen to the personal odyssey of the influential postmodernist guru Richard Rorty. In an autobiographical essay, Rorty reveals that he was once attracted to Christianity. But finding himself "incapable" of "the humility that Christianity demanded," he turned away from God—only to discover that a world without God is a world without any basis for universal truth or justice.[25] Rorty then determined to work out a philosophy consistent with Darwinism. Like Dewey, he accepted the Darwinist notion that ideas are problem-solving tools that evolve as means of adapting to the environment. Human beings are not oriented "toward Truth," Rorty writes, but only "toward its own increased prosperity."[26] Truth claims are just tools that "help us get what we want."[27] (Which means, of course, that Rorty's own ideas are just tools for getting what he wants—including the idea of postmodernism. Thus, postmodernism refutes itself.)

Darwinism forms the linchpin to the debate between Christianity and naturalism. Since modern culture has given science authority to define the way the world "really is," Darwinism provides the scientific justification for a naturalistic approach in every field. As British biologist Richard Dawkins puts it, Darwin "made it possible to be an intellectually fulfilled atheist."[28]

Many Christians shrink from drawing such a stark contrast between theism and Darwinism. They hope to combine Darwin's biological theory with belief in God—suggesting that God used evolution as his method of creating. Yet Darwin himself insisted that the two are mutually exclusive.[29] If God were guiding evolution, he argued, we wouldn't need natural selection to act as a sieve, sifting out harmful variations in living things and preserving helpful variations; God would ensure that each variation was beneficial from the start. Natural selection would be, in his own words, "superfluous."[30] The whole point of Darwin's theory was to identify a natural process that would mimic design, thus making design unnecessary.

What is at stake? Does the naturalist vs. creationist debate really matter? Why?

_____
_____
_____
_____
_____
_____
_____
_____

DAY FIVE
What Has the Theory Done?

"Elijah went before the people and said, 'How long will you waver between two opinions? If the Lord is God, follow him; but if Baal is God, follow him.' But the people said nothing."
—1 Kings 18:21

Do evolution and religion really conflict? For public relations purposes many Darwinists veil their antagonism toward religion. While Darwinism is a scientific theory and must be answered with scientific evidence, it is more fundamentally a worldview—or, more precisely, a crucial plank in the worldview of naturalism.. Unless we engage it on that level, we will remain ineffective in answering its challenges.

Perhaps nowhere in Scripture is the clash of worldviews more powerfully observed than in the story of the temptation of Christ in

Matthew 4:1-11. Read these verses carefully. Who are the opponents and what is at stake in the outcome?

The opponents: _____
_____
_____
_____

At stake in the outcome: _____
_____
_____
_____
_____

What has the theory of evolution done? What practical difference has it made in our world?

prag·ma·tism
\'prag-'ma,-ti-zem\
_n_ (ca. 1864) **2** : an American movement in philosophy founded by C.S. Peirce and William James and marked by the doctrines that the meaning of conceptions is to be sought in their practical bearings, that the function of thought is to guide action, and that truth is preeminently to be tested by the practical consequences of belief. (Websters)

rel·a·tiv·ism \ rel-et-iv-iz-em\ *n* (1865) **1 a:** a theory that knowledge is relative to the limited nature of the mind and the conditions of knowing **b:** a view that ethical truths depend on the individuals and groups holding them

In what ways do Satan's temptations appeal to pragmatism? To relativism?

_____
_____
_____

How did Christ correct Satan's false thinking and assert a biblical worldview?

_____
_____
_____

One evolutionist who is boldly up-front about the underlying worldview of naturalism is biologist William Provine of Cornell University. He declares forthrightly that Darwinism is not just about mutations and fossils; it is a comprehensive philosophy stating that all life can be explained by natural causes acting randomly—which implies that there is no need for the Creator. And if God did not create the world, he notes, then the entire body of Christian belief collapses.

Provine preaches his message on college campuses across the country, often flashing the following list on an overhead projector to hammer home what consistent Darwinism means: "No life after death; no ultimate foundation for ethics; no ultimate meaning for life ; no free will."[31] The only reason anyone still believes in such things as ethics and free will, Provine says, is that people have not yet grasped the full implications of Darwinism.

His ideas may sound radical, but Provine is being brutally honest. He recognizes that the biblical teaching of creation is not just a theological doctrine; it is the very foundation of everything Christians believe.

Why is Darwinism such a dangerous idea? What "non-scientific" areas of life does it threaten to subvert?

_____
_____
_____
_____

Cosmos or Creation?

In William Steig's *Yellow & Pink,* a delightfully whimsical picture book for children, two wooden figures wake up to find themselves lying on an old newspaper in the hot sun. One is painted yellow, the other pink.

Suddenly, Yellow sits up and asks, "Do you know what we're doing here?"

"No," replies Pink. "I don't even remember getting here."

So begins a debate between the two marionettes over the origin of their existence.

Pink carefully surveys their well-formed features and concludes, "Someone must have made us."

Yellow disagrees. "I say we're an accident," and he outlines a hypothetical scenario of how it might have happened. A branch might have broken off a tree and fallen on a sharp rock, splitting one end of the branch into two legs. Then the wind might have sent it tumbling down a hill until it was chipped and shaped. Perhaps a flash of lightning struck in such a way as to splinter the wood into arms and fingers. Eyes might have been formed by woodpeckers boring in the wood.

"With enough time, a thousand, a million, maybe two and a half million years, lots of unusual things could happen," says Yellow. "Why not us?"

The two figures argue back and forth.

In the end, the discussion is cut off by the appearance of a man coming out of a nearby house. He strolls over to the marionettes, picks them up, and checks their paint. "Nice and dry," he comments, and tucking them under his arm, he heads back toward the house.

Peering out from under the man's arm, Yellow quietly whispers in Pink's ear: "Who is this guy?"[32]

"Who is this guy?" is precisely the question each one of us must answer, and it's no storybook fantasy. It is deadly serious. Beyond the public debates and rhetoric, beyond the placard-waving and politicizing, at the heart of every worldview are the intensely personal questions: Who made me, and why am I here?

Every worldview has to begin somewhere—God or matter, take your choice. Everything else flows from that initial choice. This is why the question of creation has become such a fierce battleground today. It is the foundation of the entire Christian worldview. For if God created all of finite reality, then every aspect of that reality must be subject to him and his truth.

Everything finds its meaning and interpretation in relation to God. No part of life can be autonomous or neutral, no part can be sliced off and made independent from Christian truth.

Because creation includes the whole scope of finite reality, the Christian worldview must be equally comprehensive. It must include every aspect of our lives, our thinking, and our choices. Both friends and foes of Christianity realize that everything stands or falls on the doctrine of creation.

A Starting Place for Evangelism

Christians often seek to evangelize others by starting with the message of salvation—John 3:16 and the gospel message. And for an earlier generation, that approach worked. Most people had some kind of church experience in their background, even if they did not have strong personal beliefs. But in today's post-Christian world, many people no longer even understand the meaning of crucial biblical terms. For example, the basic term sin makes no sense to people if they have no concept of a holy God who created us and who therefore has a right to require certain things of us. And if people don't understand sin, they certainly don't comprehend the need for salvation.

Consequently, in today's world, beginning evangelism with the message of salvation is like starting a book at the middle—you don't know the characters, and you can't make sense of the plot. Instead, we must begin with Genesis, where the main character, God, establishes himself as the Creator, and the "plot" of human history unfolds its first crucial episodes.

I saw a dramatic example of this principle when I met with Bulgaria's minister of justice, an uncompromising communist. I had spoken at a prison on the theme that crime is ultimately a moral problem and that the solution, therefore, is moral reformation. The minister of justice asked if I would come by his office. So the next morning, I went to see him. He seated himself at the head of a long conference table and immediately started firing questions in a brisk, businesslike voice, speaking flawless English. "Mr. Colson, yesterday you said crime is a moral problem. What do you mean by that?"

I said, "Crime is a matter of people choosing to do wrong. It is the individual's moral failure. People are genuine moral agents, and they make real moral choices."

The minister of justice replied, "It seems to me that crime is caused by social and economic forces, that people respond to environmental conditions."

As our conversation continued, the outlines of the minister's own worldview became clear, and I could see why he was having trouble understanding me. Educated in a communist school system, he had been steeped in Marxist philosophy. Because of this, the minister couldn't even grasp what I meant by individuals making moral choices. "What I don't understand," he said, "is why some people know the law of the land but blatantly disregard it."

The minister set his cigarette pack on the table, using it to symbolize the barrier that the law sets up against certain behavior; then his hand jumped over the pack to illustrate a criminal ignoring the law. "It seems that only fear will stop people from committing crimes."

"No, sir," I responded. "Fear does not stop people. If it did, no one would smoke." The official juggled his cigarette pack nervously, and we both smiled. "Only love changes human behavior," I said. "If I love

apol·o·get·ics
\e-pä-le-'je-'tiks\ *n pl but sing or pl in constr*
(ca. 1733) **1** : systematic argumentative discourse in defense (as of a doctrine) **2** : a branch of theology devoted to the defense of the divine origin and authority of Christianity

another person, I want to please him or her; if I love God, I want to please him and do what he wants. Only love can overcome our sinful self-centeredness."

I soon realized, however, that before I could even begin to explain these biblical concepts to this man, I would have to engage in what the late Francis Schaeffer called "pre-evangelism." In other words, I would have to address the huge gap between his worldview and mine, the gap that kept him from grasping concepts such as sin and guilt, responsibility and forgiveness. For the next hour, I challenged this man's basic presuppositions.

"At the core," I said, "people are spiritual beings, not pawns of economic forces." He arched his eyebrows at me as I challenged his most basic belief.

Then I explained the reality of the Fall and sin, so tragically evident in the horrors of the twentieth century, which, in naked evil, surpasses all previous centuries. Sin begins in the heart, I said, where it battles for control of our very being. And when the darker side of our nature prevails, we do wrong things. This is the source of crime.

At each point, trying to remain sensitive to his feelings, I gently rebutted the basic Marxist assumptions, showing how they fail to conform to the reality of human experience. I saw understanding slowly dawning in his eyes. It was as if a new world gradually opened to him, a new way to see human nature.

Finally he asked about my own life, and I shared the gospel, telling the story of how I met Jesus Christ in the darkest days of Watergate. Then I saw his face light up, as if a dark cloud had lifted, and for the first time he could see clearly. We even prayed together at the end of the meeting.[33]

What is apologetics? _____
_____
_____
_____

What is pre-evangelism? _____
_____
_____
_____

The best way of combating the religion of naturalism is by defeating it on its own turf, then bringing the gospel and the Word of God into the void that has been created. This is a biblical strategy, used by the apostle Paul in Acts 17:16-34.

According to verses 32-34, what three reactions did listeners have to Paul's message in Athens? _____
_____
_____
_____

What does Paul do in verses 16-18? What verbs describe his manner of speech among the Athenians?_____
_____
_____
_____

On Mars Hill, did Paul begin with the Bible or something else? (vv. 22-23)_____
_____
_____
_____

What does he purpose to do for the Athenians? (See the last part of v. 23.)
_____
_____
_____
_____

What kinds of results can you expect if you take seriously the challenge of witnessing to those who believe in naturalism? What can you expect if you don't?
_____
_____
_____
_____

How Now Shall We Live?

We began this week's study with a plan to answer five questions:

- Is the theory of evolution genuine science or is it at heart part of a religious belief system?
- How did the theory of evolution arise, or from where did it come?
- How did the theory of evolution become accepted? How did it become the mainstream belief system of modern society?
- What is at stake? Does the naturalist vs. creationist debate really matter?
- What has the theory of evolution done? What practical difference has it made in our world?

We hope that your study has made the answers clear. We must not allow the worldview issues of our day to be seen as science against Christianity. We must help people see that the struggle pits worldview against worldview and that Christians are committed to follow truth wherever it leads. In next week's study we will discover the key to that process. Only the biblical worldview accurately describes what has gone wrong with the world.

[1]The following discussion owes much to Norman Geisler's book *Cosmos: Carl Sagan's Religion for the Scientific Mind* (Dallas: Quest, 1983).
[2]Carl Sagan, *Cosmos* (New York: Random, 1980), 4.
[3]Ibid., 242.
[4]Ibid., 5.
[5]Ibid., 243.
[6]Carl Sagan, *Broca's Brain* (New York: Random, 1979), 282.
[7]Ibid., 287.
[8]Sagan, *Cosmos,* 243.
[9]Ibid.
[10]Sagan, *Broca's Brain,* 271-75.
[11]Carl Sagan was one of the scientists who formed the SETI Institute (Search for Extra-Terrestrial Intelligence). Sagan wrote the novel *Contact,* on which the movie *Contact* was based.
[12]Sagan, *Broca's Brain,* 275.
[13]Stan and Jan Berenstain, *The Berenstain Bears' Nature Guide* (New York: Random, 1984), 11.
[14]Ibid., 10.
[15]Nora Barlow, ed., *The Autobiography of Charles Darwin 1809-1882 with Original Omissions Restored* (New York: Norton, 1958), 87.
[16]William Darwin, as quoted in John Durant, "Darwinism and Divinity: A Century of Debate," in *Darwinism and Divinity: Essays on Evolution and Religious Belief,* ed. John Durant (New York: Basil Blackwell, 1985), 18.
[17]Francis Darwin, ed., *Life and Letters of Charles Darwin,* vol. 2 (New York: D. Appleton, 1899), 155.
[18]David Duncan, *Life and Letters of Herbert Spencer,* vol. 2 (New York: D. Appleton, 1908), 319.
[19]Leonard Huxley, *Life and Letters of Thomas Henry Huxley,* vol. 1 (New York: Macmillan, 1903), 246.
[20]Thomas Henry Huxley, "Science and Religion," *The Builder* 17 (1859): 35.
[21]Richard Lewontin, "Billions and Billions of Demons," *New York Review of Books* (January 9, 1997): 31.
[22]Ibid.
[23]Dennis Prager, as quoted in "Religious Right Takes Heat for Salting and Lighting Cultural Debate," *Orlando Sentinel,* 26 August 1995.
[24]Calvin Coolidge, as quoted in *The Journal,* (a Summit Ministries newsletter), 7.
[25]Richard Rorty, "Trotsky and the Wild Orchids," *Wild Orchids and Trotsky: Message from American Universities,* ed. Mark Edmundson (New York: Viking, 1993), 38.
[26]Richard Rorty, "Untruth and Consequences," *New Republic* (July 31, 1995): 27.
[27]Richard Rorty, as quoted in Roger Lundin, *The Culture of Interpretation: Christian Faith and the Postmodern World* (Grand Rapids: Eerdmans, 1993), 15.
[28]Richard Dawkins, *The Blind Watchmaker: Why the Evidence of Evolution Reveals a Universe without Design* (New York: Norton, 1987), 6.
[29]Barlow, *The Autobiography of Charles Darwin 1809-1882 with Original Omissions Restored,* 87.
[30]The following discussion of Darwin and his contemporaries is based on Nancy R. Pearcey, "You Guys Lost," in *Mere Creation: Science, Faith, and Intelligent Design,* ed. William A. Dembksi (Downers Grove, Ill.: InterVarsity Press, 1998): 73.
[31]William B. Provine and Phillip E. Johnson, "Darwinism: Science or Naturalist Philosophy?" (videotape of debate held at Stanford University, April 30, 1994). Available from Access Research Network, P.O. Box 38069, Colorado Springs, CO 80937-8069, phone (888) 259-7102.
[32]William Steig, *Yellow & Pink* (New York: Farrar, Strauss & Giroux, 1984).
[33]Shortly thereafter, in the political upheaval of 1997, the minister of justice was removed from office. Father Nikolai and other Christians have continued to minister to him. The story is not finished yet.

Today's Prayer
God, thank You for desiring personal relationships with Your children. How thankful I am that we don't have to look up and say, Who is this guy?, but we can know without a shadow of a doubt that we are Yours.

The Fall

Any worldview must answer the question of evil. The biblical model accounts for the universal human experience better than any other belief system.

The Problem of Evil

Turmoil filled Katy's mind and heart as she climbed the steps to her school. After examining the evidence for herself, Katy realized she had believed the lie of evolution. She had started attending church services again, and for the first time she really listened. In Sunday's sermon the pastor spoke of something he called "the mystery of human evil." He said that all human beings are naturally depraved.

Katy didn't know exactly what *depraved* meant, but she did know it wouldn't fit with what she had been learning about human nature. Her psychology teacher said that human beings are naturally good unless they are corrupted by things like poverty or a dysfunctional family.

I think I have some more digging to do, Katy thought to herself as she entered the building.

de·praved \di-'pravd\ *adj* (14c) : marked by corruption or evil; *esp* : PERVERTED (Webster's)

DAY ONE
Two Views of Evil

" 'You will not surely die,' the serpent said to the woman. 'For God knows that when you eat of it your eyes will be opened, and you will be like God, knowing good and evil.'

When the woman saw that the fruit of the tree was good for food and pleasing to the eye, and also desirable for gaining wisdom, she took some and ate it. She also gave some to her husband, who was with her, and he ate it."–Genesis 3:4-6

The Biblical View of Evil

The first and most fundamental element of any worldview is the way it answers the question of origins—where the universe came from and how human life began. The second element raises the issue of evil: what has gone wrong with us and with the world? The biblical worldview has an answer for the question of evil, and it accounts for the universal human experience better than any other belief system. Scripture teaches that God created us in His image—to be holy, to live by His commands. Yet God loved us so much that He imparted to us the unique dignity of being free moral

Persons in developing countries readily admit they are sinnners and are willing to repent, but many persons in Western cultures do not believe they are sinners.

agents—creatures with the ability to make choices, to choose either good or evil. To provide an arena in which to exercise that freedom, God placed one moral restriction on our first ancestors: He forbade them to eat of the tree of the knowledge of good and evil.

The Fall

The original humans, Adam and Eve, exercised their free choice and chose to do what God had commanded them not to do, thus rejecting His way of life and goodness, opening the world to death and evil. The theological term for this catastrophe is *the Fall.*

Sin has wrought havoc throughout God's creation. We are all tempted and tainted by sin. None of us escapes its powerful effects, but what is sin?

❏ missing the mark
❏ disobedience
❏ pride
❏ all of the above

In short, the Bible places responsibility for sin, which opened the floodgates to evil, squarely on the human race—starting with Adam and Eve, but continuing on in our own moral choices. The Bible doesn't give a simple answer to the mystery of human sin. Rather it describes sin with such words as *disobedience, pride,* and *rebellion.* We could say sin at its root is our attempt to dethrone God and become our own master.

In that original choice to disobey God, human nature became morally distorted and bent so that from then on humanity has had a natural inclination to do wrong. This is what theologians call *original sin,* and it haunts humanity to this day. Since humans were granted dominion over nature, the Fall also had cosmic consequences as nature began to bring forth "thorns and thistles," becoming a source of toil, hardship, and suffering. In the words

of theologian Edward Oakes, we are "born into a world where rebellion against God has already taken place and the drift of it sweeps us along."[1]

Check the explanation of original sin that best fits the description in the paragraph above.

❏ We are blamed and condemned for Adam and Eve's action.
❏ We are damaged by the fall so that our character is naturally bent.
❏ Original sin refers only to Adam and Eve; we are condemned only by our own sin.

Mark each of the following statements true (T) or false (F).

___The Bible places responsibility for sin squarely on the human race.
___Since the fall, every human being has had a natural inclination to do wrong.
___The fall only affected human beings.

The problem with the Bible's answer is not that it isn't clear, but that it is unpalatable to many people because it implicates each one of us in the twisted and broken state of creation. The second explanation above best fits the facts of the fall. The first two statements are true; the third is false.

Read Romans 5:12-21 in your Bible. Describe in your own words the connection between the fall and the cross, between Adam and Christ. _____
_____
_____
_____
_____
_____
_____

These are complex concepts. You could have written a book or two on the issue of Adam and Christ. I hope you indicated that just as sin entered the world through one man, eventually implicating all humanity, so redemption has come to all through one man. Righteousness is available to all through belief in Christ's atoning sacrifice.

The Enlightenment View of Evil

The Christian view of sin may seem harsh, even degrading, to human dignity. That's why in modern times, many influential thinkers have dismissed the idea of sin as repressive and unenlightened. They have proposed instead a *utopian* view that asserts that humans are intrinsically good and that under the right social conditions, their good nature will emerge.

How do people who hold a naturalistic worldview try to account for evil?

_____
_____
_____
_____
_____
_____
_____
_____

Utopia was an imaginary ideal country in a book by Sir Thomas Moore. The word has come to mean *a perfect society*. The utopian view has roots in the Enlightenment, when Western intellectuals rejected the biblical teaching of creation and replaced it with the theory that nature is our creator—that the human race arose out of the primordial slime and lifted itself to the apex of evolution.

Under the utopian view people would no longer live under the shadow of guilt and moral judgment; no longer would they be oppressed and hemmed in by moral rules imposed by an arbitrary and tyrannical deity. The biblical doctrine of sin was cast aside—a holdover from what the Enlightenment philosophers disdainfully called the Dark Ages, from which their own age had so triumphantly emerged.

If the problem is not sin, then what is the source of disorder and suffering? Enlightenment thinkers concluded that these must be the product of an environment that contained ignorance, poverty, or other undesirable social conditions. They decided that all it takes to create an ideal society is to create a better environment: improve education, enhance economic conditions, and reengineer social structures. Given the right conditions, human perfectibility has no limits. Thus was born the modern utopian impulse.

Original Innocence

Corrupting Influence

Solution: to eliminate the corrupting influence...

You see the utopian concept portrayed above. If you consider poverty to be the corrupting influence, the idea seems benign enough—eliminate poverty and utopia results. However, utopian thinkers have substituted every imaginable cause as the source of corruption.

Imagine that you are seen as the corrupting influence … the solution becomes to eliminate you. How do you feel about this benign plan now? _____
_____
_____
_____
_____
_____
_____
_____
_____

Does the idea seem farfetched? Ask the Jews who suffered at Auschwitz or the university professors who suffered under Chairman Mao. We will see that the utopian impulse has born bitter fruit in our modern world in many different ways. One of the great ironies of human existence surfaces when we adopt utopian attitudes; disregarding human sin makes life and society not better but infinitely worse.

What prayer requests come to mind as a result of studying today's material?

_____
_____
_____
_____
_____
_____
_____

DAY TWO
The Test of Reality

"It is dangerous and it will turn out badly for you to keep kicking against the goad [to offer vain and perilous resistance]."
—Acts 9:5, Amplified

Saul of Tarsus did not believe Jesus to be the Messiah. Saul carried out his belief by persecuting followers of Jesus. In Acts 9 the Sovereign Lord confronted Saul. First, Jesus directly confronted Saul's false belief: "I am Jesus, whom you are persecuting." Then the Amplified version tells us Jesus added the pointy comment above. The "goad" refers to an oxgoad, a sharp stick. Today we would say a cattle prod.

Sometimes we play the part of Saul. We hold false beliefs and as a result we find ourselves kicking against the sharp and unyielding points of what is. Each of us must determine which of these worldviews, the biblical or the modern utopian, meets the test of reality. Which fits the world and human nature as we actually experience it?

One can hardly say that the biblical view of sin is unrealistic, with its frank acknowledgment of the human disposition to make wrong moral choices and inflict harm and suffering on others. Not when we view the long sweep of history. Thirty-five centuries of human experience have verified original sin.

Look carefully at Romans 3:10-18. According to Paul, how does sin affect each of the following?

Our moral life: _____
_____
_____
_____
_____
_____

Our understanding of things: _____
_____
_____
_____
_____
_____
_____

Our speech and conversation: _____

_____

_____

_____

_____

_____

Our relationships with other people: _____

_____

_____

_____

_____

_____

According to Romans 3:19-20 and 7:7, how does God's law help us to understand sin?

❑ It tells us how to identify the sins of others.
❑ It makes us conscious of the fact that we are sinners.
❑ It gives us detailed definitions of what sin is and what sin is not.

Where must we begin in the battle to roll back sin? (Rom. 6:23)

_____

_____

_____

_____

_____

_____

_____

The Bible does not give us a philosophical discussion of sin. Rather, the Holy Spirit uses the law to make us conscious of the fact that we are sinners so that we will turn to God for restoration. By contrast, the "enlightened" worldview has proven to be utterly irrational and unlivable.

Denying our sinful nature breeds the utopian myth and leads not to beneficial social experiments but to tyranny. The confidence that humans are perfectible provides a justification for trying to make them perfect … *no matter what it takes.* And with God out of the picture, those in power are not accountable to any higher authority. They can use any means necessary, no matter how brutal or coercive, to remold people to fit their notion of the perfect society.

The triumph of the Enlightenment worldview, with its fundamental change in presuppositions about human nature, was in many ways the defining event of the twentieth century, which explains why the history of this era is so tragically written in blood. As William Buckley trenchantly observes: Utopianism "inevitably … brings on the death of liberty."[2]

In your own words, describe how utopianism leads to oppression and loss of liberty.

_____

_____

_____

_____

_____

_____

_____

_____

_____

Edward T. Oakes stated the facts of the matter clearly: "If the experience of human history from Rousseau to Stalin means anything, it must be that we are stuck, like it or not, with a doctrine— nay the reality—of original sin." As political philosopher Glenn Tinder writes, if one acknowledges "no great, unconquerable evils in human nature," then it seems possible to create a heaven right here on earth.[3]

How does the human attempt to bring about "heaven on earth" really work out? The philosophy doesn't match reality. When moral convictions and personal commitments are torn away or destroyed, the result is not a great release of human goodness. Instead, the individual becomes malleable, controllable by anything or anyone

to·tal·i·tar·ian
\(')to-tal-e-ter-e-en\ *adj*
[total + -itarian (as in
authoritarian)]
1 a : of or relating to cen-
tralized control by an auto-
cratic leader or hierarchy
b : of or relating to a political regime based on subor-
dination of the individual
to the state and strict control of all aspects of the life
and productive capacity of
the nation esp. by coercive
measures (as censorship
and terrorism)

Today's Prayer
God, I know that only
the gospel can deliver
us from sin's power.
I ask You to give me
the opportunity and
courage to share this
good news with others.

who steps in to take the place of family,
church, and village. Utopians start with the
promise to liberate the individual from
such things as economic oppression, crime-
ridden streets, or ancient superstitions. And
the bargain is always the same: Give me
power, and I'll use it to liberate human
goodness and create an ideal society.

Can we say, then, that the modern utopian worldview produces a rational, sus-
tainable life system? Most emphatically
not. It tells us we are good, but it un-
leashes the worst evil. It promises enlightenment, but it thrusts us into darkness. As
Reinhold Niebuhr put it, "The utopian illusions and sentimental aberrations of the
modern liberal culture are really all derived from the basic error of negating the
fact of original sin."[4]

**List several ways society's rejection of God's
law affects our culture.**

_____
_____
_____
_____

**According to Romans 6:11-19, what does the
Christian worldview prescribe as the proper
attitude toward sin? (Check all that apply).**

❏ **Do not offer the parts of your body to sin.**
❏ **Fear the power of sin to disrupt your life.**
❏ **Offer your body in slavery to righteousness
leading to holiness.**
❏ **Count yourselves dead to sin but alive to
God in Christ Jesus.**
❏ **Humans are incapable of independence—
either we will serve Christ or we will be
slaves to sin.**

The Christian worldview avoids both the
utopianism that fails to take sin seriously
and the fatalistic view that sees victory
over sin as an impossibility. Romans 6
paints a realistic view of human sinfulness.
We checked all but the second response.

**Revelation 12 gives us additional insights
into the origins of evil and suffering on earth.
According to verses 7-9 and 13, how did evil
come to be on the earth?**

_____
_____
_____
_____
_____
_____
_____

**Since only the gospel can deliver people
from the power of sin, how can we effectively bring the Gospel message to those
around us?**

_____
_____
_____
_____
_____
_____

Will the Western nations see through
their delusion and change course before it
is too late? That is a pressing question
raised in the following chapters, where we
will probe the consequences of the false
worldview of human goodness, in both the
totalitarian systems of the East and the welfare state of the West. We will trace this
worldview's effects in politics, psychology,
crime, welfare, and education, and we will
reveal its fatal weaknesses. Against the
utopian worldview, we will pose the
Christian worldview, which we submit is
demonstrably the only philosophy that fits
universal human experience.

But first we must look at how the myth
of utopianism was born and why it has
such a grip on the modern mind. We cannot begin to counter the myth until we understand how the utopian vision came to
replace what had been for sixteen centuries the settled understanding of human
nature and society. Whatever became of
the biblical notion of sin?

How Now Shall We Live?

Whatever Became of Sin?

"Sin is crouching at your door; it desires to have you, but you must master it."—Genesis 4:7

In 1973 psychiatrist Karl Menninger posed a provocative question in his best-selling book titled *Whatever Became of Sin?* He sounded like an Old Testament prophet thundering against the moral relativism of our age.[5] Let's not talk about what's progressive or unprogressive, what's appropriate or inappropriate, he said, cutting through the fog of fashionable cover-up words like a brisk breeze. Let's talk about good and evil, right and wrong.

What did become of sin? Good question. To solve the mystery, we must travel back to the mid-eighteenth century and to the influential writings of a young Swiss-born philosopher named Jean-Jacques Rousseau. Persuasive ideas are typically launched in the writings of one person who gives expression to what becomes a powerful trend. Such was the case when Rousseau burst upon the European intellectual scene, winning instant notoriety with an essay arguing a surprising thesis: that the progress of civilization had been harmful for human beings, not beneficial. In its natural state, human nature is good, he contended; people became evil only when corrupted by society.

From the time of Aristotle, most philosophers had taught that humans are naturally social—that they fulfill their true nature by participating in the civilizing institutions of family, church, state, and society. Rousseau insisted that human nature is at its best prior to and apart from social institutions. He said people are naturally loving, virtuous, and selfless, and it is society, with its artificial rules and conventions, that makes people envious, hypocritical, and competitive.

Stop for a moment and think. Why in the world do you think people would embrace the notion that humans are naturally good, in the face of the obvious evidence to the contrary? (check any that apply and add your own thoughts.)

❑ The idea makes us personally responsible for our actions.
❑ The idea makes us feel good about ourselves.
❑ The idea gives us a scapegoat to blame for our own failures.
❑ Your Response: _____
_____
_____

If human nature is essentially good, then Rousseau was correct. If evil and corruption are created by a false and hypocritical society, you are wise to throw off the restraints of civilization and explore your natural, spontaneous self—the true self that underlies social forms.

Pretend for a moment that you are on a debate team. The statement put before you is that human nature is good until it is corrupted by society. What arguments would you put forward in favor of the statement?
_____
_____
_____
_____
_____

What arguments would you put forward against the statement?

_____

_____

_____

_____

Rousseau's notion that civilization is artificial is perhaps less surprising when you realize that the society he lived in was just that. Picture the French aristocracy of the 1700s. Women concealed themselves beneath powdered wigs, pasty white makeup, and ornate dresses dripping with jewels and ribbons. Men pranced about in long, curly, powdered wigs; silk waistcoats and frilly cuffs; satin britches; clocked hose; and high-heeled, buckled shoes.

"Better a poor man whose walk is blameless than a fool whose lips are perverse" (Prov. 19:1).

Read the article below about the lifestyle of Rousseau. How does Proverbs 19:1 apply to his lifestyle? _____

_____

_____

_____

What irony that Rousseau's philosophy of radical and unbounded freedom spawned the most oppressive regimes of the modern world, inspiring revolutionaries like Robespierre, Marx, Lenin, Hitler, and Mao. Even Pol Pot and his cadre of Paris-educated terrorists were known to have studied Rousseau while their henchmen were slaughtering a quarter of the Cambodian population. How did this happen?

The key is that Rousseau did not define freedom as the assertion of rights against the *state;* freedom meant liberation from the forms and institutions of *society*—family, church, class, and local community—while the state was the liberator.

What did Jesus say would set us free (John 8:32)? _____

Who is the Truth (John 14:6)? _____

What danger do you immediately identify in Rousseau's idea that the state can set us free? _____

_____

Check each of the following that was a part of Rousseau's philosophy.

❏ We are naturally good if we discover our inner, spontaneous self.
❏ The state is made up of sinful individuals, so the power of the state must be restrained.
❏ The state is naturally good and must use its power to free us from the corrupting effects of society.
❏ We are sinners and require the civilizing influence of home, church, and society.

The Rousseau Lifestyle

Rousseau fled the powdered and polished society of his day, denouncing it as false to the core and retreated to small country houses where he could be close to nature. Rousseau painted the state as the great liberator. Historian Paul Johnson offers an intriguing explanation.[6] Rousseau abandoned his five children to an orphanage, even though most of the babies placed in this institution died; the few who survived became beggars. In several of his books and letters, Rousseau made vigorous attempts to justify his actions. He insisted he was merely following the teachings of Plato, who had declared the state was better equipped than parents to raise good citizens.

When Rousseau turned to writing political theory, his personal excuses seem to be sublimated into general maxims. His ideal state turns out to be one that liberates its citizens from troubling personal obligations. In particular, he urged that responsibility for educating children should be taken away from parents and given to the state. Was there a connection between Rousseau the man, fleeing from the obligations of fatherhood, and Rousseau the political theorist?

Rousseau's idea gave birth to what one historian calls "the politics of redemption," the idea that politics can be the means not only of creating a better world but of actually transforming human nature, creating "the New Man."[7] For Rousseau, the state "is the agency of emancipation that permits the individual to develop the latent germs of goodness heretofore frustrated by a hostile society."[8]

In the following paragraph identify what is distinct about the concept of revolution built on Rousseau's thought.

STATEMENT This explains why Rousseau's philosophy gave birth to the modern concept of revolution, which involves not just political rebellion to overthrow a particular ruler but also the wholesale destruction of an existing society in order to build a new, ideal society from scratch. Whereas traditional social theory justified any given action by an appeal to the past—to the normative human nature created by God— modern revolutionaries justify their actions by an appeal to the future—to the ideal society they will create. The bloodiest atrocities can be justified by invoking the perfect society that the revolutionaries promise to build on the ashes of the old.[9]

Why didn't anyone in Rousseau's legions of disciples foresee these disastrous consequences? Why didn't anyone consider that absolute power is sure to corrupt?

Stop. Before you read further, explain why you think Rousseau's disciples continue to fail to see the danger of their ideas.

_____
_____
_____
_____
_____
_____

Utopianism creates a peculiar blindness. Believing the individual to be naturally good, Rousseau was confident that the all-powerful state would likewise be good, since the state was simply a merging of individual wills into a "General Will." In his view Rousseau actually believed that the state would always be right, always tending toward the public good—"always constant, unalterable, and pure."[10] And if some recalcitrant individuals failed to agree with the General Will? That merely proved that they had been corrupted and that they must be coerced into seeing that their true liberty lay in conforming to the General Will. As Rousseau put it, the individual must "be forced to be free."[11]

Marx and the Perfect Society

You can see this same basic pattern in the philosophy of Karl Marx, whose vision of a perfect society has fueled one failed utopian experiment after another in nations around the globe. The fatal flaw in Marxism's utopian view of the state is once again the denial of the basic Christian teaching of the Fall. If one is to believe there is such a thing as sin, one must believe there is a God who is the basis of a transcendent and universal standard of goodness. Marx denied all of this. For him, religion and morality were nothing but ideologies used to rationalize the economic interests of one class over another.

The desire to be free of God's law is very old. Look at Psalm 2:1-3. In what ways does this picture capture the liberationist hopes of Marxism? _____
_____
_____
_____
_____
_____
_____
_____
_____

If one is to believe there is such a thing as sin, one must believe there is a God who is the basis of a transcendent and universal standard of goodness.

Small wonder that the totalitarian states created by Marxism acknowledged no universal moral principles, no transcendent justice, and no moral limits on their murderous brutality. The party, like Rousseau's General Will, was considered always right. We will consider more about Marx and his philosophy in the section on redemption.

It is paradoxical indeed that such horrors flowed from the idealistic-sounding philosophy of innate human goodness. As Anatole France once observed, never have so many been murdered in the name of a doctrine as in the name of the principle that human beings are naturally good.[12]

Explain in your own words how the idea of human goodness actually led to murderous actions. _____
_____
_____
_____
_____

How might Romans 1:21-22 apply to what you have studied today? _____
_____
_____
_____
_____
_____

DAY FOUR
We're All Utopians Now

"Therefore, dear friends, since you already know this, be on your guard so that you may not be carried away by the error of lawless men and fall from your secure position."—2 Peter 3:17

The famous theologian Reinhold Niebuhr said that "the utopian illusions and sentimental aberrations of modern liberal culture are really all derived from the basic error of negating the fact of original sin."[13]

When the Berlin Wall came tumbling down, the rejoicing on this side of the Atlantic had an almost smug ring to it. The Western model of democracy had triumphed, once and for all, over the great tyrannies that had dominated so much of the twentieth century. Indeed, the collapse of the communist behemoth was a profoundly significant political event, but what happened to the ideas that created communism? Have these changed?

Not at all. In fact, many Americans and other Western people continue to cherish the same utopian myth that produced such bitter fruit in the totalitarian nations: the same assumption that human nature is basically good, the same rejection of transcendent morality as confining and oppressive, and the same grandiose dreams of social engineering.

Unless we change these basic presuppositions, we are headed down our own path to tyranny in a form the great French statesman Alexis de Tocqueville called "soft despotism," an over solicitous nanny state that debilitates its citizens just as thoroughly, but by coddling them, instead of coercing them.[14]

Time for a reality check. Have you also absorbed the ideas of the utopian myth? Check each of the following ideas with which you agree.

❏ Crime is caused by things such as poverty and dysfunctional families.
❏ Children are naturally innocent. They would not lie or make up stories about such things as abuse.
❏ Proper education can cure the ills of poverty, racism, and crime that plague our societies.

Each of the responses above indicate utopian thinking. Certainly poverty and the quality of family life have an effect on crime, but the cause of crime is our own moral choices. Think about the second response. Abuse of a child is a terrible thing, but psychologists and law enforcement officials in the 1980s believed anything a child said was true, with the result that parents and day-care workers went to jail for abuse. In many cases we later learned that the abuse never happened.

Think for a moment. Why did officials believe that whatever a child said was true?

_____
_____
_____
_____

If you responded that the officials were influenced by the ideas of Rousseau and the naturalist worldview, you were right on target. Remember, the great danger of our worldview is that we often don't think. Our worldview does our thinking for us. It controls the media and shapes what we see and hear.

Utopianism with an American Twist

American utopianism traces its ancestry to Rousseau's notion of human goodness, but it also exhibits a unique technological, pragmatic cast that is rooted in the scientific rev-olution and that appeals to the Yankee, can-do mind-set. Isaac Newton's dramatic discovery that a single law—the law of gravity—explained a variety of phenomena, both in the heavens and on the earth, led to an image of the universe as a vast machine, running by natural laws. Many people extended this machine image into every area of life, including society itself.[15]

In the eighteenth and nineteenth centuries, social thinkers fervently believed that science would not only explain the physical world but also show us how to order our lives together harmoniously. They searched for some principle that would explain society in the same way Newton's law of gravity explained motion. They sought an experimental physics of the soul that would enable them to craft a science of government and politics to conquer the age-old plagues of ignorance, oppression, poverty, and war.

Which of the following represents the view of human beings reflected by the social thinkers in the paragraph above?

❏ They held a high view of the person's worth and dignity, treating people as unique individuals.
❏ They held a low view of the person, treating people as cogs in a machine.
❏ They gave dignity to the individual by considering people as responsible moral agents.

What do you think results when we treat people as objects to be controlled and manipulated? _____
_____
_____
_____
_____

Of course, nowhere has this vision of scientific utopianism become a reality. And the reason it continually fails is lodged in

the logic of the scientific method itself. If we turn human beings into objects for scientific study, we implicitly assume that they are objects to be manipulated and controlled, like scientific variables. That means we have to deny things like the soul, conscience, moral reasoning, and moral responsibility. When we apply these assumptions to real social problems, we inevitably dehumanize and demoralize people, placing them at the mercy of social scientists in the employ of the technocratic state. In short, by denying moral responsibility, we end up not with utopia but with another form of despotism.

Utopianism in Psychology

Beginning in the nineteenth century, Sigmund Freud did more than anyone else to destroy the very notion of moral responsibility. Freud reduced humans to complex animals, rejecting explanations of behavior couched in "old-fashioned" theological terms—such as *sin, soul,* and *conscience*—and substituting scientific terms borrowed from biology, such as *instincts* and *drives.* In Freud's theory, people are not so much rational agents as pawns in the grip of unconscious forces they do not understand and cannot control. A committed Darwinist, Freud proposed an evolutionary scheme in which our primitive impulses (the id) belong to the oldest, most animal part of the human brain, while the rational mind (the ego) is a later development from the more highly evolved cerebral cortex. Thus, the things that society labels "bad" are not really evil; they simply reflect the more ancient, animal part of the brain.[16]

Psychologists who followed Freud carried this process of reduction even further by seeing humans not as animals but as machines. The first book ever published about experimental psychology was titled *Elements of Psychophysics*, as if psychology were a branch of physics. Its author, Gustav Fechner, another radical Darwinist, argued

that humans are complicated stimulus-response mechanisms, shaped by forces in their environment. [17]

In the 1960s, B. F. Skinner's *Walden Two* introduced millions of college students to behaviorism, a school of psychology that flatly denies the reality of consciousness or mental states. Because these things cannot be observed, Skinner argued, they cannot be described scientifically; therefore, they are not real. Only observable, external behavior is real.[18]

By denying the reality of the mind, Skinner and the behaviorists believed they were "purifying" psychology of all philosophical prejudices and rendering it purely scientific and objective. In reality, of course, they were simply injecting their own philosophical prejudices. They were also creating a new brand of "scientific" utopianism, which said that the flaws in human nature are a result not of moral corruption but of learned responses—responses that can be *un*learned so that people can then be reprogrammed to be happy and adjusted, living in harmony in a utopian society.

Do you think that people can be successfully programmed to be happy and adjusted? Why or why not? _____
_____
_____
_____
_____
_____

Will people you know be receptive to the idea that sin lies at the root of the human dilemma? Why or why not? _____
_____
_____
_____
_____
_____
_____
_____

Utopianism in Education

One of results of this utopian thinking was a shift in education. Classical education had always aimed at the pursuit of truth and the training of moral character. But if human nature was nothing more than a reactive mechanism, then it could be manipulated and shaped by the laws that science discovered. Thus, education became a means of conditioning, with the child being treated as essentially passive rather than as an active moral agent.

Of course, this dehumanizing philosophy is always presented in the language of utopian promise. In the words of J. B. Watson, the founder of behaviorism, "Give me the baby and ... the possibility of shaping in any direction is almost endless."[19] Forget trying to reform behavior through religion and morality; these are merely forms of oppression. Through education the world can be "unshackled from leg- endary folklore ... free of foolish customs and conventions ... which hem the individual in like taut steel bands." Watson promised to bring up children with "better ways of living," who "in turn will bring up their children in a still more scientific way, until the world finally becomes a place fit for human habitation."[20]

Which of the following options best describes Watson's idea that he could shape a baby in any direction he chose?
❑ a statement of scientific fact
❑ a statement of pure faith in his worldview

From what you know of our society, what have been the results of the "scientific" method of rearing ever more perfect children? _____
_____
_____
_____

DAY FIVE
The Bitter Fruits of Utopianism

"Discipline your son, for in that there is hope; do not be a willing party to his death."—Proverbs 19:18

The utopian myth has even taken hold in the home, where the same ideas are served up through magazines, parenting seminars, maternity classes, and books on child development. In the most influential book ever written for parents, Dr. Benjamin Spock encouraged parents to reject the old puritan notion of children as savages, prone to evil and in need of civilizing. Instead, he urged them to understand children as evolving psyches in need of attention. For example, when a school-age child steals, Spock suggests that parents consider whether their child might "need more ... approval at home," and even a raise in his allowance![21]

Thus, even in the home, the heart and hearth of society, a sense of duty has been replaced by a sense of entitlement, a sense that we have a right to what we want, even if it means violating standards of proper behavior. Adults who once gave firm and unequivocal moral direction—parents, teachers, even pastors—have been indoctri-

> Even Christians are prone to use the vocabulary of therapy instead of the sterner language of morality.

nated with the idea that the way to ensure healthy children is not to tell them what's right and wrong, but to let them discover their own values. As a result, most Americans have lost even the vocabulary of moral accountability. Sin and moral responsibility have become alien concepts.[22]

To what degree would you say your own attitudes toward parenting have been affected by the utopian myth?

NOT AFFECTED AT ALL   AFFECTED GREATLY

Just how deeply this has affected us was evident in an MTV network special news report on "The Seven Deadly Sins," which aired in August 1993. The program's description looked promising enough—interviews with celebrities and ordinary teens talking about the seven deadly sins: lust, pride, anger, envy, sloth, greed, and gluttony, but the main message that came across was the participants' shocking moral ignorance.

Rap star Ice-T glared into the camera and growled, "Lust isn't a sin ... These are all dumb."

One young man seemed to think sloth was a work break. "Sloth ... Sometimes it's good to sit back and give yourself personal time."

Pride was the sin the MTV generation found the hardest to grasp. "Pride isn't a sin—you're supposed to feel good about yourself," one teen said. Actress Kirstie Alley agreed. "I don't think pride is a sin, and I think some idiot made that up," she snapped.

Amazingly, the program offered not one word about guilt, repentance, or moral responsibility. Instead, it was littered with psychotherapeutic jargon, as if sin were a sickness or addiction. Even the program narrator joined the chorus: "The seven deadly sins are not evil acts, but rather universal human compulsions."[23]

Put yourself in the place of those who gave such answers. How would the respondents feel about Christianity's stance against the seven deadly sins?

❑ They would see the church as the real source of evil because it teaches restrictive rules.
❑ They would believe that the church is right to teach moral values.
❑ They would see the importance of teaching clear standards of right and wrong.

The utopian mind-set has become so pervasive that most people in Western culture have no intellectual resources to identify or to deal with genuine wrongdoing. For example, when a respected historian wrote a book about mass murderers such as Hitler and Stalin, all he could say was that they were subject to "mental disorders."[24] Every one of us is affected by this degeneration of moral discourse, to the point where even Christians are prone to use the vocabulary of therapy instead of the sterner language of morality. Is it any wonder that the church is often portrayed as the real villain, preventing happiness by spreading guilt?

Results in Law

The same ideas were applied to law. Traditionally in the West, positive law (man-made law) was based on a transcendent standard of justice derived from God's law. But in the late nineteenth century, legal thinkers such as Oliver Wendell Holmes, influenced by Darwin and the rise of social science, began to shift these foundations, as we will see later, reducing the law to summaries of the social and economic policies that could be determined scientifically to work best. The law was redefined as a tool for identifying and manipulating the right factors to create social harmony and progress.

How much social harmony and progress has resulted from the shift in the basis for law?

- ❑ much _____
- ❑ some _____
- ❑ little_____
- ❑ none _____

Results in the Welfare State

The same scientific utopianism explains the rise of the welfare state. The idea that both law and government policy should be transformed into social engineering took root in the New Deal of the 1930s and blossomed in the Great Society programs of the 1960s. Many American politicians became enthusiastic converts, sincerely believing that all it would take to solve the problems of poverty and crime would be some well-designed, well-funded government programs. They were confident that they could win President Lyndon Johnson's "war on poverty."

Well, the war is over, and poverty won. The welfare state has backfired, creating both a near-permanent underclass of dependency and a host of attendant social pathologies, from broken families and teen pregnancy to drug abuse and crime. What went wrong?

Novelist Dean Koontz discovered the answer through hard experience. In the 1960s, young, idealistic, and eager to change the world, Koontz signed up as a counselor in Title III of the Appalachian Poverty Program. He intended to work with problem students, giving them one-on-one tutoring and counseling that would help them break out of the area's depressed economic situation. But when Koontz showed up for work, he discovered that many of the students had criminal records. In fact, the man who preceded him on the job had been beaten up by the kids he was there to help, and the man had ended up in the hospital. Koontz soon realized these kids needed a lot more than education. They needed moral guidance and disci-

pline, which they were not getting at home or at school. By the end of his first year in the program, a discouraged Koontz realized that the notion of reforming society through government programs was itself misguided. The failed Great Society programs, he writes, are an illustration of "humanity's hopeless pursuit of utopia through government beneficence."[25]

Write your own moral to the story of Dean Koontz and the poverty program.

_____
_____
_____
_____
_____
_____
_____
_____
_____
_____
_____

Koontz puts his finger squarely on the problem: the "hopeless pursuit of utopia." The Great Society offered no real answer to the dilemma of moral breakdown, to crime and social disorder, because it redefined moral maladies as technical problems that could be solved by bureaucrats. Instead of treating human beings as moral agents who must be addressed in the language of duty and responsibility, the Great Society treated them as objects to be shaped and manipulated. As a result, its programs tended to undercut the moral dignity of their recipients, leaving millions dependent and demoralized.

Again we see the irony: When we deny the Christian worldview and reject its teachings on sin and moral responsibility in favor of a more "enlightened" and "scientific" view of human nature, we actually end up stripping people of their dignity and treating them as less than human.

When we deny the Christian worldview and reject its teachings on sin and moral responsibility in favor of a more "enlightened" and "scientific" view of human nature, we actually end up stripping people of their dignity and treating them as less than human.

> Liberalism regards crime as the outcome of impersonal forces in society, and it also locates responsibility for crime outside the criminal.

Results in Criminal Justice

Welfare is not the only area of public policy that illustrates the pernicious effects of the utopian myth. When it comes to crime, America's criminal justice policy swings back and forth between liberal and conservative approaches: from an emphasis on rehabilitation and social engineering to calls for tougher laws and harsher sentences. Yet both approaches exemplify, in different ways, the same utopian worldview.

Traditional liberalism fixes responsibility for crime on poverty and other social ills. Crime is not a matter of the soul, says the liberal; it is a technical problem that can be solved by engineering the right social conditions: devising the right public policies, distributing money to the right places, and arranging the right physical environment. This view was expressed at the dawn of the Great Society by then Attorney General Ramsey Clark. He first blamed crime on social conditions such as "the dehumanizing effect on the individual of slums, racism, ignorance and violence, of corruption and impotence to fulfill rights, of poverty and unemployment and idleness, of generations of malnutrition, of congenital brain damage and prenatal neglect, of sickness and disease, of pollution, of decrepit, dirty, ugly, unsafe, overcrowded housing, of alcoholism and narcotics addiction, of avarice, anxiety, fear, hatred, hopelessness, and injustice."

Astonishingly, after reciting this horrendous litany, Clark concluded optimistically: "They can be controlled." Never mind how universal, how endemic, how intractable these problems are; they are all merely technical malfunctions that can be fixed by applying the right technical solution.[26]

Since liberalism regards crime as the outcome of impersonal forces in society, it also locates responsibility for crime outside the criminal. Already at the turn of the century, Clarence Darrow, the lawyer who achieved notoriety defending Darwinism in the Scopes trial, was portraying criminals as helpless victims of their circumstances. He declared that "there is no such thing as a crime as the word is generally understood ... I do not believe that people are in jail because they deserve to be. They are in jail simply because they cannot avoid it on account of circumstances which are entirely beyond their control and for which they are in no way responsible."[27]

Today, Darrow's heirs fill courtrooms across the country, wringing pity from juries by presenting wrongdoers as victims of forces beyond their control. This loss of moral responsibility has spread across the entire spectrum of our culture, ushering in "The Golden Age of Exoneration."[28] When people are consistently told that they are victims of outside forces, they begin to believe it. When things go wrong, someone else must be to blame.

Conservative calls for stiffer sentencing also demonstrate utopian thinking. Such views treat people like stimulus-response machines. Put in the right stimulus, harsher punishment, and people will respond by avoiding crime. Like their liberal cousins, utopian conservatives have missed the point of moral responsibility.

How do liberal policies toward crime demonstrate a utopian mind-set?_____

_____

_____

_____

_____

_____

_____

How do conservative policies toward crime often also demonstrate a utopian mind-set?

_____

_____

_____

_____

_____

_____

_____

Of course, acknowledging responsibility means attributing real praise and blame—and blame, in turn, implies the legitimacy of punishment. That's what makes moral accountability so bittersweet. Yet punishment actually expresses a high view of the human being. If a person who breaks the law is merely a dysfunctional victim of circumstances, then the remedy is not justice but therapy; and the lawbreaker is not a person with rights but a patient to be cured. The problem, said C. S. Lewis, is that "to be 'cured' against one's will ... is to be put on a level with those who have not yet reached the age of reason or those who never will; to be classed with infants, imbeciles, and domestic animals. But to be punished, however severely, because we have deserved it, because we 'ought to have known better,' is to be treated as a human person made in God's image."[29]

Denial of sin may appear to be a benign and comforting doctrine, but in the end, it is demeaning and destructive, for it denies the significance of our choices and actions. It reduces us to pawns in the grip of larger forces: either unconscious forces in the human psyche or economic and social forces in the environment. Social planners and controllers then feel perfectly justified in trying to control those forces, to remake human nature and rebuild society according to their own blueprints—and to apply any force required toward that end.

"Of all tyrannies a tyranny sincerely exercised for the good of its victims may be the most oppressive," wrote Lewis. "Those who torment us for our own good will torment us without end for they do so with the approval of their own conscience."[30]

The Great Irony

Utopianism depends on a kind of willful blindness to the reality of human sin and moral responsibility. But in denying the reality of sin, we lose the capacity to deal with it, and thus, in the end, we actually compound its effects. Therein lies the greatest paradox of all attempts to deny the Fall: In denying sin and evil, we actually unleash its worst powers.

The fatal flaw in the myth of human goodness is that it simply fails to correspond with what we know about the world from our own ordinary experience.

In any society, only two forces hold the sinful nature in check: the restraint of conscience or the restraint of the sword. The less citizens have of the former, the more the state must employ the latter. A society that fails to keep order by an appeal to civic duty and moral responsibility must resort to coercion—either open coercion, as practiced by totalitarian states, or covert coercion, where citizens are wooed into voluntarily giving up their freedom. It's not much of a stretch to imagine Americans eventually being so frightened of their own children that they will welcome protection by ever-greater government control. That's why utopianism always leads to the loss of liberty.

The only alternative to increased state control is to be honest about the human condition. The only solution for the pathologies that plague our society is to expose the modern myth of human goodness and to return to biblical realism. Sociologists are constantly searching for the root causes of crime and other dysfunctions in society. But the root cause has not changed since the temptation in the Garden. It is sin.

Having studied the second worldview question—what has gone wrong with the world?_____

_____

_____

What difference does it make to you that we live in a fallen world marked by sin?

_____

_____

_____

_____

_____

Denial of sin is demeaning and destructive, for it denies the significance of our choices and actions.

Today's Prayer
Father, I live in a world marked by sin. I cannot be perfect, but I strive with Your help to follow Jesus' perfect example. You are greater than anything that is in the world. Help me to focus on You instead of the world.

[1] Edward T. Oakes, "Original Sin: A Disputation," *First Things* (November 1998): 21.

[2] William F. Buckley Jr., *Nearer My God: An Autobiography of Faith* (New York: Doubleday, 1997), 232.

[3] Glenn Tinder, *Political Thinking: The Perennial Questions* (New York: HarperCollins, 1995), 199.

[4] Reinhold Niebuhr, as quoted in Edward T. Oakes, "Original Sin: A Disputation," *First Things* (November 1998): 21.

[5] Karl Menninger, *Whatever Became of Sin?* (New York: Hawthorn Books, 1973).

[6] Paul Johnson, *Intellectuals* (New York: Harper & Row, 1988), 22-23.

[7] Robert Nisbet, *The Quest for Community: A Study in the Ethics of Order and Freedom* (San Francisco, ICS Press, 1990), 127.

[8] Tinder, *Political Thinking*, 200.

[9] Historian Glenn Tinder puts it well: "Political leaders claim that power that the Old Testament attributes to God alone—that of erasing and avenging all in justice and of guiding humanity to its destined fulfillment." (Ibid., 201)

[10] Rousseau, *The Social Contract,* 275.

[11] Ibid., 195.

[12] Oakes, Original Sin, 16.

[13] Reinhold Niebuhr, as quoted in Edward T. Oakes, "Original Sin: A Disputation," *First Things* (November 1998): 21.

[14] Alexis de Tocqueville, *Democracy in America,* trans. George Lawrence, *Great Books of the Western World,* ed. Mortimer Adler (Chicago: Encyclopedia Britannica, 1991), 374-77.

[15] Nancy R. Pearcey and Charles B. Thaxton, *The Soul of Science: Christian Faith and Natural Philosophy* (Wheaton, Ill.: Crossway, 1994), 71-73.

[16] The following discussion about Freud, Fechner, and Pavlov is based on "Evolution and the Humanities," a presentation made by Willem J. Ouweneel at the National Creation Conference, August 1985.

[17] Gustav T. Fechner, *Elements of Psychophysics* (New York: Holt, Rinehart & Winston, 1966).

[18] B.F. Skinner, *Walden Two* (New York: Macmillan, 1976).

[19] J.B. Watson, *The Way of Behaviorism* (New York: Harper, 1928), 35ff.

[20] John B. Watson, *Behaviorism* (New York: The People's Institute, 1924), 248. American philosopher and educator John Dewey used even stronger utopian language, heralding the teacher as "the prophet of the true God and the usherer in of the true kingdom of God" (John Dewey, *My Pedagogic Creed* [Washington, D.C.: The Progressive Education Association, 1929], 17).

[21] Benjamin Spock, as quoted in Dana Mack, *The Assault on Parenthood: How Our Culture Undermines the Family* (New York: Simon & Schuster, 1997), 33.

[22] For Spock "the 'good' parent was no longer the parent who got his children to behave, but rather the parent who understood why his children might not behave" (Mack, *The Assault on Parenthood,* 33).

[23] "Seven Deadly Sins," MTV (August 1993).

[24] Alan Bullock, as quoted in Charles Maier, *A review of Hitler and Stalin: Parallel Lives,* by Alan Bullock, New Republic (June 15, 1992):42.

[25] Dean Koontz, as quoted in Nick Gillespie and Lisa Snell, "Contemplating Evil: Novelist Dean Koontz on Freud, Fraud, and the Great Society," *Reason 28,* no. 6 (November 1996): 44.

[26] Ramsey Clark, *Crime in America: Observations on Its Nature, Causes, Prevention, and Control* (New York: Simon & Schuster, 1970), 17-18.

[27] Clarence Darrow, *Attorney for the Damned,* ed. Arthur Weinberg (New York: Simon & Schuster, 1957), 3-4.

[28] John Leo, "The It's-Not-My-Fault Syndrome," *U. S. News & World Report* 108, no. 24 (June 18, 1990): 16.

[29] C. S. Lewis, "The Humanitarian Theory of Punishment," *God in the Dock* (Grand Rapids: Eerdmans, 1970), 292.

[30] Ibid.

Redemption and the Myth of Progress

*All people are religious. Some make God the object
of their religious affections. Others create their own gods.
In this unit you will explore some novel forms of redemption
that are being pursued in modern culture.*

The Redemption of Bernie Nathanson

One day in late autumn 1996, my secretary informed me of a surprising phone call. Dr. Bernard Nathanson was inviting my wife and me to his baptism at St. Patrick's Cathedral. Cardinal John O'Connor would be presiding. I was stunned. "Are you sure you've got the right name?" I asked. "Bernard Nathanson?" "That's it," she said with a smile. In the early 1970s, Dr. Nathanson ran the largest abortion clinic in the United States. Since that time he had undergone an interesting journey. With the advent of ultrasound, Dr. Nathanson came face to face with the realization that abortion took the life not of a fetus but of a baby.

Bernard Nathanson soon became convinced that human life existed within the womb from the onset of pregnancy. In an article he wrote for *The New England Journal of Medicine*, he confessed that he had presided over "60,000 deaths." In abortion "we are taking life," he wrote, "and the deliberate taking of life, even of a special order and under special circumstances, is an inexpressibly serious matter." While he did not conclude that abortion was wrong, he did say that physicians "must work together to create a moral climate rich enough to provide for abortion, but sensitive enough to life to accommodate a profound sense of loss."[1]

Nathanson's article caused a tremendous controversy, and the public attention forced him to think even more closely about the morality of abortion. He had always believed that a society's morality must be judged by its treatment of the weak and defenseless, and his own early work for abortion reform had been inspired by a concern for the poor. But ultrasound technology had revealed to him an even more vulnerable class: the unborn. For purely scientific reasons Nathanson became active in the pro-life movement.

As Nathanson's ideas changed, he also began a profound examination of his conscience. The guilt he felt drove him to consider suicide. He turned to a serious study of spiritual issues.

I had known that Nathanson was interested in Christianity; in fact, the two of us had been trying to meet for some time, but we had been unable to coordinate our schedules. I confess my initial disappointment that I hadn't introduced him to Christ and my Baptist tradition. Though I disagree with Catholic doctrine on specific issues concerning their view of salvation, the news that the man who was once the nation's leading abortionist had turned to Christ made this an invitation I couldn't refuse.

A few weeks later, on a cold December morning, Patty and I stepped along briskly as we walked the few blocks from our Manhattan hotel to St. Patrick's for the 7:30 service. We had been told to go to the back entrance of the massive cathedral, where we were greeted by a smiling young man who led us to a small basement chapel, chilly and damp, where about fifty people were seated on folding chairs. No pomp or ceremony, just a group of believers surrounding a small altar. We could have been the first-century church, gathered in the catacombs, about to witness the baptism of a new believer in the name of the resurrected Christ.

Nathanson was escorted forward by a young woman whom I immediately recognized as Joan Andrews (now Joan Andrews Bell). How God delights in ironies, I thought. Joan Andrews was a former nun who had spent five years in a Florida prison for nonviolent resistance at abortion clinics. In the prison, thieves and murderers came and went, while Joan—her parole consistently denied by a stubborn judge—sat silently in her cell praying. Eventually, most people forgot who Joan Andrews was. She might have wondered if her years of prison were worth the cost; but God uses every act of faithful obedience, and there she was, with one of the world's leading abortionists now professing his faith in Christ.

It was a striking moment of spiritual victory. Most of the time, Christians fight in the trenches, seeing only the bloody warfare around us. But every so often God permits us a glimpse of the real victory. This was one of those rare, illuminating moments, as we watched Bernie Nathanson—a Jew by birth, a man who had been an atheist by conviction, a brilliant but amoral doctor by profession—kneeling before the cross of Christ.

DAY ONE

Hegel and the Escalator Fallacy

"Then they said, 'Come, let us build ourselves a city, with a tower that reaches to the heavens, so that we may make a name for ourselves and not be scattered over the face of the whole earth.'"
—Genesis 11:4

Not all of us, of course, are driven to the depths of despair that Bernie Nathanson was. Yet all human beings yearn, deep in their hearts, for deliverance from sin and guilt. Many try to suppress the longing, to rationalize it away, to mute it with lesser answers. But ultimately, it is impossible to evade. This is the great human predicament: Sooner or later, even the most decent among us know that there is a rottenness at our core. We all long to find freedom from our guilt and failures, to find some greater meaning and purpose in life, to know that there is hope.

What is the "great human predicament" and how does Bernard Nathanson's experience illustrate it?

_____

_____

_____

This need for salvation has been imprinted on the human soul since the first couple went astray in the Garden. The desire is universal, and every religion and worldview offers some form of redemption. For the Buddhist, it is nirvana; for the Jew, it is the atonement of good works; for the

George Friedrich Hegel (1770-1831)

G. W. F. Hegel was born in Stuttgart, Germany, studied and taught theology and philosophy. He was an idealist philosopher who has influenced many areas of modern philosophy; his strongest influence was on Karl Marx. According to Hegel, reality is Absolute Mind, Reason, or Spirit, which manifests itself in history.

Muslim, it may be heaven after the perilous walk across the sword of judgment.

But religions and philosophies are not the only ones offering redemption. Any belief system in the marketplace of ideas, any movement that attracts followers, anything that has the power to grab people's hearts and win their allegiance does so because it taps into their deepest longings. And those longings are, ultimately, religious. In this unit and the next we will contrast the genuine redemption available in Christ with the false offers of redemption that spring from the naturalist worldview.

Hegel and Inevitable Progress

To understand what has happened in our world, we need to go back to nineteenth-century German philosopher George Friedrich Hegel and the idea of the inevitability of progress. Hegel's idea has fueled the great utopian movements traced in the previous section.

Until Hegel's time, the world had been pictured as a static ladder of life. Everything from rocks to plants to animals to humans to angels to God Himself had its niche on a rung on this great ladder. But Hegel did something entirely new, something really breathtaking. He tilted the ladder of life on its side, so that instead of being a list of all the things that exist in the world at any one time, it became a series of *stages* through which the world passes over the course of history. Thus the ladder was transformed into a dynamic series of steps: Everything moves from one rung to the next in an endless progress toward perfection.[2]

How does Hegel's idea seem to correspond with the idea of evolution? _____
_____
_____
_____

If you noted that Hegel applied evolution much more broadly than just to the evolution of biological life, you're on the right track. As a result of Hegel's influence, everything was seen as subject to evolution—not just living things, but also customs, cultures, and concepts. The universe was thought to be in a process of constant change, caught up in a great transformation from primitive beginnings to some exalted future.

You might be saying, "Wow! What an unbelievable leap of faith." Was Hegel's idea a matter of science or religion? Why?

_____
_____
_____
_____

The people who follow Hegel blur the line between science and philosophy. Many believed the inevitability of progress was a genuine scientific discovery.

In every field, from biology to anthropology, from law to sociology, there was a fevered search for "laws of development" that would reveal the pattern of history and the direction of evolution, providing people with guidance on how to live in accord with that great movement toward a better world. There was great optimism that the best human minds could uncover

Christian Worldview Timeline

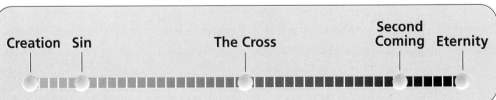

Creation Sin   The Cross   Second Coming Eternity

the laws of progress and lead us forward into utopia—a substitute vision of heaven. Philosophers and thinkers began vying with one another to be the one to unveil the path to the earthly heaven, the means of redemption.

Genesis 11:1-9 shows us a primitive society with lofty ideals and high hopes. According to verses 1-4, to what did these people aspire?

_____
_____
_____
_____

How were the people's goals at odds with God's will? _____
_____
_____
_____

Apart from Hegel's thought, we might picture the time line of life like the timeline on the previous page, but Hegel made a stunning change in the way people viewed life. He gave birth to what we call "the Escalator Myth."

The Escalator Myth

All the liberation ideologies in the marketplace of ideas today are variations on a single theme that has been pervasive in Western thought since the nineteenth century: that history is moving forward toward a glorious consummation. This is sometimes dubbed the "myth of progress," or, in the words of British philosopher Mary Midgely, "the Escalator Myth," and it is a seculariza-

tion of the Christian teaching of the providence of God. Whereas Christianity teaches that history is moving toward the kingdom of God, the Escalator Myth reassures us that we are evolving toward an earthly utopia that is the product of human effort and ingenuity.[3]

STATEMENT The Escalator Myth or myth of progress is the idea that history is moving forward toward an earthly utopia brought about through human means.

With the Escalator Myth, we suddenly picture life like the time line below.

In biblical thought, what is our hope according to the following passages?

Matthew 25:31-33 _____
_____
_____
_____

2 Thessalonians 2:1-8 _____
_____
_____
_____

What do believers in the Escalator Myth substitute for the biblical expectation?

_____
_____
_____
_____

Hegel's Myth of Progress Timeline

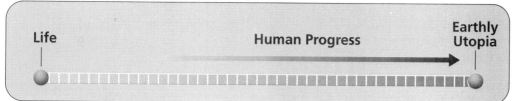

Life   Human Progress   Earthly Utopia

Heavenly Redeemer,
Thank You that while
the world struggles
in vain to save itself,
You have made
redemption possible
through our Lord
Jesus Christ.

Believers in the myth of progress have substituted all sorts of variations, but the theme is always the same. They believe that humanity will save itself working through science or economics or whatever form of liberation seems trendy at the time.

You can always use the three-part worldview grid to evaluate the myth of progress. Rather than believing in the biblical fall, those following the Escalator Myth believe either that we haven't evolved sufficiently or that something else has gone wrong with humanity and society. Then they believe humans can somehow redeem themselves and create a perfect society.

DAY TWO

The False Redemption of Karl Marx

"Jesus answered: 'Watch out that no one deceives you. For many will come in my name, claiming, "I am the Christ," and will deceive many.' " —Matthew 24:4-5

Karl Marx (1818-1883)

Marx was a German social philosopher, economic theorist, and revolutionary. He developed the idea that the material conditions of societies determine the beliefs of those societies. His philosophical system is often called dialectical materialism, and his thought laid the groundwork for the communist movements of the twentieth century.

Hegel's best-known disciple was young Karl Marx, and Marxism (or communism) is best understood as a prime example of the Escalator Myth—an effort by the modern mind to secularize the kingdom of God, to create a purely human heaven here on earth.

STATEMENT Karl Marx is the co-founder of communism. He believed humanity had once lived in a primitive state of communism in which no one owned anything. He believed humanity had been corrupted when people began to own property with the resultant division into rich and poor. He saw history moving toward a communist revolution where the poor would rise up and destroy private ownership, returning humanity to its original goodness.

Marxism as a Religion

While Karl Marx hunched over his books in the British Museum in the mid-nineteenth century, feverishly philosophizing, he came up with a full-blown alternative religion. In the beginning was a creator: namely, matter itself. In Marxism the universe is a self-originating, self-operating machine, generating its own power and running by its own internal force toward a final goal—the classless, communistic society. Marx's disciple, Lenin, stated the doctrine in explicitly religious language: "We may regard the material and cosmic world as the supreme being, as the cause of all causes, as the creator of heaven and earth."[4]

What basic idea of Rousseau formed the foundation for the thought of Marx? (see page 23).

_____
_____
_____
_____
_____
_____
_____

Marxism's counterpart to the Garden of Eden is the state of primitive communism. In this garden, the original sin is the creation of private property and the division of labor, causing humanity to fall from its early state of innocence into slavery and oppression. From this follow all the subsequent evils of exploitation and class struggle.

Redemption, according to Marx, comes through reversing the original sin, destroying the private ownership of the means of production. And the redeemer is the proletariat, who will rise up against the capitalist oppressors. "The savior-proletariat [will] by its suffering redeem mankind and bring the Kingdom of Heaven on earth," wrote historian Robert Wesson.[5]

Fill in the three-part grid to evaluate a worldview. How did Marx see each of the following?

✳ **Creation**

_____
_____
_____

⬡ **Fall**

_____
_____
_____

✋ **Redemption**

_____
_____
_____

The Day of Judgment, in Marx's theology, is the day of revolution, when the evil bourgeoisie will be damned.[6] It is significant that Marx called not for repentance but for revolution. Why? Because, like Rousseau, he regarded humanity as inherently good. Evil and greed arose from the economic structures of society (private property), and

therefore they can be eliminated by a social revolution that destroys the old economic system and institutes a new one.

Again you see Rousseau's ideology at work. Complete the following with Marxist ideas.

✳ **Original innocence is …**

_____
_____
_____

⬡ **The Fall—corruption comes from …**

_____
_____
_____

✋ **The task of the State is …**

_____
_____
_____

so utopia can result …

Finally, like all religions, Marxism has an eschatology (a doctrine of the final events of history). In Christianity, the end of time is when the original perfection of God's creation will be restored, and sin and pain will be no more. In Marxism, the end of history is when the original communism will be restored and class conflict will be no more. Paradise will be ushered in by the efforts of human beings whose consciousness has been raised. Marx looked forward to this inevitable consummation of history as eagerly as any Christian anticipates the Second Coming.

"Marxism is a secularized vision of the kingdom of God," writes theology professor Klaus Bockmuehl. "It is the kingdom of man. The race will at last undertake to create for itself that 'new earth in which righteousness dwells.' "[7] Marxism promises to solve the human dilemma and create the New Man living in an ideal society.

These religious elements explain Marxism's puzzling powers of endurance. Most of Marx's specific theories have failed spec-

Redemption, according to Marx, comes through reversing the original sin, destroying the private ownership of the means of production.

tacularly, and his promise of a classless society has never come to pass, despite countless Marxist-inspired revolutions around the globe.[8]

Knowing the idea of Marxism, why has one dictator after another been willing to murder millions of their own people?

_____
_____
_____
_____
_____
_____
_____
_____

Why, then, is Marxism still so popular? Why do so many liberation movements today adopt Marxist categories and analysis? Why has multiculturalism and political correctness cut a huge swath across the university campus, sweeping up students and teaching them to view the world through the lens of aggrieved self-righteousness? Precisely because Marxism aims at an essentially religious need, tapping into humanity's hunger for redemption.

Marx himself knew he was offering a militantly atheistic counterpart to Christianity. "Marx was confirmed at fifteen and for a time seems to have been a passionate Christian," says historian Paul Johnson. But ultimately he rejected the biblical God, denouncing religion as "the illusory sun around which man revolves, until he begins to revolve around himself."[9]

How does Marx's conclusion compare to what Paul said in 2 Corinthians 10:12?

_____
_____
_____
_____
_____
_____
_____

Autonomy as the Ultimate Goal

Marx's ultimate goal was autonomy. He wrote: "A _being_ only considers himself independent when he stands on his own feet; and he only stands on his own feet when he owes his _existence_ to himself." But a person cannot be independent if he is the creation of a personal God, for then "he lives by the grace of another."[10] So Marx determined to become his own master, a god to himself.

How do the words of Marx resemble the following words from Genesis? " 'You will not surely die,' the serpent said to the woman. 'For God knows that when you eat of it your eyes will be opened, and you will be like God, knowing good and evil' " (Gen. 3:4-5).

_____
_____
_____
_____
_____
_____
_____
_____
_____
_____

This is the root of Marxism, and it is the point where we must begin to critique it. How plausible is this insistence on absolute autonomy? Ironically, Marx himself admitted that it was _im_plausible. Belief in a creator, he acknowledged, is "very difficult to dislodge from popular consciousness." To most people the notion of absolute autonomy is "incomprehensible." Why? "Because it contradicts everything _tangible_ in practical life."[11] In other words, in real life it is obvious that we are _not_ completely autonomous. We do not create ourselves, and we cannot exist completely on our own. We are finite, contingent, dependent beings—tiny specks within a vast universe, a mere eddy within the ever flowing stream of history.

Marx's worldview is fatally flawed; it does not match up with reality. And Marx himself admitted as much when he acknowledged that his philosophy "contradicts everything" we learn in "practical life." Marx is a living example of the apostle Paul's description of unbelievers: They *know* the truth, and still they suppress it (see Rom. 1:18-32).

As a young man, Marx wrote poetry, much of it dwelling on themes of rage, destruction, and savagery. One of his surviving pieces includes these lines:

> Then I will wander godlike and
> victorious
> Through the ruins of the world
> And, giving my words an active force,
> I will feel equal to the creator.[12]

Here he reveals the ultimate religious motivation behind his philosophy: to be equal to the Creator, to give his own words the active force of God's creative words.

Marx's self-deification has had disastrous results for millions of persons, leading to war, massacre, and labor camps—not the promised redemption. "Apply Marxism in any country you want, you will always find a Gulag in the end," says French philosopher Bernard-Henri Levi, himself a former Marxist.[13] For if revolutionaries are confident that the next stage in history will automatically represent progress, that any change will be for the better, they readily tear down and destroy the existing order—which historically has often meant killing off anyone who resists, from rulers to peasants.

Moreover, because Marxism assumes that the reconstruction of social and economic institutions is enough to usher in harmony and peace, it puts no moral restraints on the leaders in the new order. Because it denies the evil in human nature, it does not recognize the need to place checks and balances on the individuals in power. Marxist ideology allows leaders to accrue absolute power, and we all know what absolute power does.

Marxism is a substitute religion that wreaks devastation and death. And today's liberation movements, which depend heavily on the Marxist worldview, are inherently religious as well. They may have dropped Marx's focus on economics in favor of race or gender or ethnicity, but the basic thought forms remain the same—and they are equally flawed and dangerous.

Name one or more revolutions currently occurring on earth. _____
_____
_____
_____
_____
_____
_____
_____
_____
_____

What is the stated motive? _____
_____
_____
_____
_____
_____
_____
_____
_____
_____
_____
_____

How is it like or unlike Marxism? _____
_____
_____
_____
_____
_____
_____
_____
_____
_____
_____
_____
_____

Apply Marxism in any country you want, you will always find a Gulag in the end. (A gulag is a prison camp for political prisoners).

Today's Prayer
Father, I am not comfortable always having to be on guard in order not to be deceived. Yet I know that many come in Your name to do just that. Give me insight to know truth and strength to go outside my comfort zone to take a stand against it when You guide me to.

DAY THREE
The Updated Versions of Marxism

"But the goat chosen by lot as the scapegoat shall be presented alive before the Lord to be used for making atonement by sending it into the desert as a scapegoat."—Leviticus 16:10

When Diane went off to college in 1967, she also went off the deep end. Within weeks she was smoking marijuana, flouting her childhood faith, and mouthing slogans about women's liberation.

Today Diane has returned to her Christian faith and no longer calls herself a feminist. "I got tired of being a victim," she explains. "I used to read feminist books by the armload. Then one day it hit me. All these books were the same! Every problem a woman might have was explained by saying that someone, somewhere had done her wrong—as if women were weak, passive creatures. It was pathetic."

Diane has since changed her mind, but millions still march behind the banner of women's liberation—along with a host of other liberation ideologies. Across the nation, groups gather around ideologies of gender, race, and sexual orientation, seething with rage over alleged oppressions of one kind or another.

The Old Testament concept of the scapegoat provided a visual way of expressing the idea of someone carrying our sin. In Christian theology, who is the ultimate scapegoat? (see Num. 28:30, 1 Pet. 2:24, 1 John 2:2).

_____

_____

_____

_____

_____

How did he carry away our sin?_____

_____

_____

_____

_____

_____

Read Isaiah 53:4-6. How does the prophet describe the man in the verses? _____

_____

_____

_____

_____

We all have a deep inner need to do something with our sin. To understand the appeal liberation theology groups exert, we need to understand their underlying worldview. They too have a scapegoat or rather a list of them. Each group blames the evils of society on their chosen scapegoat.

Good Human Nature

Corrupted by Scape Goat

The State as Savior

Perfect Society Results

What is the human dilemma, the source of suffering and injustice? Rather than seeing the problem within ourselves as in the biblical view, according to these groups the answer is oppression by the wealthy, whites, males, heterosexuals, or some other group. What is the solution, the way to justice and peace?

What is the way to justice and peace in the biblical worldview?

_____
_____
_____
_____
_____
_____
_____
_____

In your opinion, which solution is easier and which solution places the greatest responsibility on the individual?

_____
_____
_____
_____
_____
_____
_____
_____

According to these groups, the way to justice and peace is to raise our consciousness and rise up against the oppressors. Thus, the promise of liberation is ultimately a promise of redemption.

In the Marxist drama of history, the main characters were the capitalists and the proletariat (urban factory workers). In the newer, multiculturalist ideologies, the oppressed people are women, minorities, or homosexuals. In classic Marxism, the proletariat will rise up against their oppressors; in the updated forms, people of various colors and genders are called to harness their rage and do battle against their oppressors—usually white, male heterosexuals.

Why does the "scapegoating" of some groups appeal to our human nature?

_____
_____
_____
_____
_____
_____
_____

The politically correct campus today offers countless variations on this Marxist theme, as evidenced by the way the themes overlap and complement one another. The University of California at Santa Barbara offers a course listed as Black Marxism, linking Marxism and black liberation. Brown University connects black and homosexual liberation in a course called Black Lavender: Study of Black Gay/ Lesbian Plays. UCLA relates Hispanic ethnicity with homosexuality in a course list-ed as Chicana Lesbian Literature. Villanova combines feminism with environmentalism in a course titled Eco-feminism, and Stanford University mixes everything in a single cauldron with Women of Color: The Intersection of Race, Ethnicity, Class, and Gender. As a result, our college graduates are taking Marxist categories into law, politics, education, family studies, and many other fields.

What all this means is that Marxism, though largely discredited as a political ideology, is still very much alive and well in Western intellectual life. Reborn as multiculturalism and political correctness, it remains one of the most widespread and influential forms of counterfeit salvation. Government-mandated group rights and other outgrowths of multiculturalism are even being read into the U.S. Constitution, so that though original Marxism never took over our nation, this reborn Marxism may yet do so.

And for those who really believe in salvation through the Escalator Myth, the sexiest form of liberation around is … sex itself, as we will see in tomorrow's study.

Today's Prayer
God, thank You for providing Jesus as my Scapegoat. He did not deserve to die, yet He chose to die in my place. It's incredible to know that You love me that much.

DAY FOUR
Salvation Through Sex?

" 'Haven't you read,' he replied, 'that at the beginning the Creator "made them male and female," and said, "For this reason a man will leave his father and mother and be united to his wife, and the two will become one flesh"?' —Matthew 19:4-5

Sex is a vital part of God's created order, a sacred part of the marriage covenant; and our sexual nature is a good gift from God. But for many modern thinkers, sexuality became the basis for an entire worldview, the source of ultimate meaning and healing, a means of redemption. Sex has been exalted to the means of raising ourselves to the next level of evolution, creating a new kind of human nature and an advanced civilization. In short, sexuality was tied to another version of the Escalator Myth.

How could thinkers believe that sex holds the key to creating a new kind of human nature? The key is found in the neo-marxist thinking based on Rousseau. Fill in the drawing below.

_____

_____

_____

These near-mystical ideas of sexuality are an updated version of Rousseau. Recall that for Rousseau, human nature was itself good; evil was the result of the constraints of civilization, with its moral rules and social conventions. Freud later applied these ideas to sexuality, tracing all neuroses to moral rules and to the guilt they produce. Then, as science learned more about the physiology of sexuality—for example, the action of the glands—these same ideas were dressed up in scientific garb.

Did you note that moral rules about sexuality become the corrupting influence in this version of the Escalator Myth?

Read Isaiah 5:20. How does liberation through sex turn the world upside down, calling good evil? _____

_____

_____

_____

_____

_____

_____

_____

Do you realize what Freud and his followers have done? They have made biblical morality out to be the source of evil in the world. According to these people the problem that causes evil is not breaking the Ten Commandments; for them the problem *is* the Ten Commandments.

Margaret Sanger

Margaret Sanger pioneered this Neo-Marxist approach. Though generally remembered as an early champion of birth control, Sanger actually taught a much broader philosophy of sexuality, a philosophy reinforced by science. She contended that science had proved sexual restraint suppresses the activity of the sex glands and thus injures health and dulls the intellect. The drama of history, she concluded, consists of a struggle to free our bodies and minds from the constraints of morality, the prohibitions that distort and impoverish human nature.

Which of the following reflects what Margaret Sanger believed?
❏ Sexual restraint is good for you because it builds strength of character
❏ Sexual restraint makes people intellectually weak.
❏ Sexual restraint can lead to a better way of life.

Sanger adamantly opposed "the 'moralists' who preached abstinence, self-denial, and suppression," and described Christian ethics as "the cruel morality of self-denial and 'sin.'" She hoped to replace it with her own morality of sexual liberation, promising that the release of sexual energies was "the only method" by which a person could find "inner peace and security and beauty."[14] It was also the only method for overcoming social ills: "Remove the constraints and prohibitions which now hinder the release of inner energies, [and] most of the larger evils of society will perish."[15]

How would you characterize Sanger's belief?
❏ science ❏ religion Why? _____
_____
_____
_____
_____
_____

Imagine that you wholeheartedly believe in Sanger's theories. How would you feel about Christianity? _____
_____
_____
_____
_____

What Sanger offered was a doctrine of salvation in which morality is the root of all evil and free sexual expression is the path to redemption. She even resorted to religious language, calling on a sexual elite to "remove the moral taboos that now bind the human body and spirit, free the individual from the slavery of tradition, and above all answer their unceasing cries for knowledge that would make possible their self-direction and salvation."[16] Salvation? In another passage, she promises that men and women will literally become geniuses through "the removal of physiological and psychological inhibitions and constraints which makes possible the release and channeling of the primordial inner energies of man into full and divine expression."[17] Divine? Here's a new twist on the serpent's promise in Eden: It's not the tree in the garden that will make us godlike; it's the release of sexual energies.

Looking at our society today, would you say that Sanger's belief system has proved true or false? Why? _____
_____
_____
_____
_____
_____
_____

Sanger's philosophy is simply another version of the Escalator Myth, in which sexual freedom is the means for transforming human nature and creating the New Man. It is in our power to "remodel the [human] race" and create "a real civilization," to "transmute and sublimate the

> Margaret Sanger put a new twist on the serpent's promise in Eden: It's not the tree in the garden that will make us godlike; it's the release of sexual energies.

Margaret Sanger (1879-1966)

Margaret Sanger was born on September 14, 1879 in Corning, New York to Michael Hennessey Higgins, an Irish-born stonemason. The sixth of eleven children, Margaret blamed her mother's premature death on her frequent pregnancies. Margaret became famous as a crusader for birth-control. In keeping with her private views on sexual liberation, she had a series of affairs with several men, including Havelock Ellis and H.G. Wells.

everyday world into a realm of beauty and joy," she wrote euphorically. She resorts again to religious language: "Through sex, mankind may attain the great spiritual illumination which will transform the world, which will light up the only path to an earthly paradise."[18]

Alfred Kinsey

One of Sanger's contemporaries, Alfred Kinsey, was equally influential in shaping sexual mores and sex-education theories, particularly with his books *Sexual Behavior in the American Male* and *Sexual Behavior in the American Female,* published in the 1940s.[19] Kinsey's impact was due in part to the pose he struck as an objective scientist, tabulating what Americans did in their bedrooms. But the truth is that he was neither objective nor scientific. Like Sanger, he was committed to an ideology that defined morality as a harmful force to be opposed and that elevated sexuality into a means of salvation.

How do you feel about ideas like those of Sanger and Kinsey having such an enormous affect on our beliefs, laws, and culture? (Check all that apply and/or express your own feelings).

❑ I'm angry because we've been lied to.
❑ I feel helpless; this is all so overwhelming.
❑ I don't believe this; it isn't true.
❑ I feel like a war has been going on, and we didn't even know we were being attacked.
❑ I feel... _____
_____
_____
_____
_____

To liberate sex from morality, Kinsey reduced sex to the sheer biological act of physical orgasm. He then claimed that all orgasms are morally equivalent—whether between married or unmarried persons, between people of the same or the opposite sex, between adults or children, even between humans and animals. His model was the animal world. Kinsey was a devout Darwinian and believed that since humans evolved from animals, there are no significant differences between them. He liked to talk about "the human animal," and if a particular behavior could be found among animals, he made it normative for humans as well. For example, Kinsey claimed that certain mammals are observed to have sexual contact between males, and even across species; therefore, he concluded, both homosexuality and bestiality are "part of the normal mammalian picture" and are acceptable behavior for humans.[20]

Kinsey's naturalistic approach was so dehumanizing that even the anthropologist Margaret Mead, who herself did much to tear apart American sexual morality, was offended, complaining that the Kinsey Report ripped "sexual behavior out of its interpersonal context" and "suggests no way of choosing between a woman and a sheep."[21]

Kinsey has also been criticized for taking unrepresentative samples in his research, including a disproportionate percentage of sexual offenders and other deviants. It is hardly scientific to use such skewed samples to define "normal" sexuality, and yet, as biographer James Jones documents, Kinsey persistently studied people who were on the margins, or even beyond the pale, in their sexual behavior: homosexuals, sado-masochists, voyeurs, exhibitionists, pedophiles, transsexuals, and fetishists.[22]

Apply the worldview grid to what you know of Kinsey. How did he explain the following?

1. Where we came from and who we are

_____
_____
_____
_____
_____
_____

2. What has gone wrong with the world

_____
_____
_____
_____

3. What must be done to fix it

_____
_____
_____
_____
_____
_____

Kinsey remained undeterred by criticism, however, for his sexual views were not based ultimately on science but on an intensely held personal belief system. In the words of Stanford professor Paul Robinson, a sympathetic critic, Kinsey viewed history "as a great moral drama, in which the forces of science competed with those of superstition for the minds and hearts of men."[23] By "superstition," Kinsey meant religion and its moral prescriptions. Kinsey sometimes spoke as if the introduction of Bible-based sexual morality was *the* watershed in human history, a sort of "Fall" from which we must be redeemed. In Kinsey's mind, sexual expression was the means of saving human nature from the oppression of religion and morality.

In the words of Isaiah:

"Woe to those who call evil good
and good evil,
who put darkness for light
and light for darkness,
who put bitter for sweet
and sweet for bitter"
(Isa. 5:20).

DAY FIVE
The Sexual Crusaders

"This is the verdict: Light has come into the world, but men loved darkness instead of light because their deeds were evil."–John 3:19

Along with Sanger and Kinsey, another major influence was Austrian psychologist Wilhelm Reich, who became something of a cult figure in the 1960s. His contribution was the search for the "ultimate orgasm," which quickly became one of the fads of the human potential movement. Reich taught that nearly everyone is in some degree neurotic and that every neurosis is in turn a symptom of sexual failure. Reich believed that human beings are nothing more than biological creatures and that redemption comes through complete immersion in the sexual reflex.[24]

Are human beings a part of the animal kingdom? Why or why not?_____
_____
_____
_____
_____

The enemy in Reich's sexual Eden is, once again, traditional religion and morality, that "murderous philosophy" that creates guilt, distorts our drives, and gives rise to personality disorders.[25] He insisted that since nature knows nothing of morality, any moral restraints on the sexual impulse work like a slow poison on the entire per-

sonality. In a review aptly titled *Salvation through Sex*, psychiatrist Eustace Chesser says that for Reich, orgasm "is man's only salvation, leading to the Kingdom of Heaven on earth."[26]

If you believed in Reich's philosophy, what would be your attitude toward Christianity?

❏ I would believe Christianity was unimportant.
❏ I would believe Christianity provides answers for effective living.
❏ I would believe Christianity is a curse on humanity.

Reich's ideas were incorporated by Robert Rimmer in his provocative novel *The Harrad Experiment*, published in 1966.[27] The book sold three million copies and helped fuel the sexual revolution. For an entire generation of college-educated Americans, it became recommended reading in college courses on marriage and family, and many people credit the book with being instrumental in the sudden merger of male colleges with female colleges and in the creation of coed dormitories.

In the paragraph below circle the thinking we have now come so clearly to associate with Jean-Jacques Rousseau.

STATEMENT The novel portrays an experimental college where the students are expected to couple up in various combinations and permutations to develop a free and uninhibited approach to sexuality. The philosophy behind this sexual utopia is voiced by the professor who founded the college: "The premise is that man is innately good and can lift himself by his bootstraps into an infinitely better world." How? By sexual liberation. It is the means for taking "one more step up the evolutionary ladder," for "evolving into a new form of man and woman."[28]

Rimmer's view of sex is frankly religious, and he has the professor state openly that intercourse "is actually an act of worship." Or, as he has another character say (quoting philosopher Alan Watts), "What lovers feel for each other in this moment is no other than adoration in the full religious sense. ... Such adoration which is due God, would indeed be idolatrous were it not that, in that moment, love takes away the illusion and shows the beloved for what he or she in truth is ... the naturally divine." Sex is portrayed as the path to divinity.[29]

In a postscript added in the 1990 edition of the novel, Rimmer neatly summarizes his religion: "Can we lift ourselves by the bootstraps and create a new kind of society where human sexuality and the total wonder of the human body and the human mind become the new religion—a humanistic religion, without the necessity of a god, because you and I and all the billions who could interact caringly with one another are the only god we need? I think we can."[30]

How would you refute Rimmer's contention that promiscuous sex is a caring act?

_____

_____

_____

_____

Clearly sexuality is being presented as more than mere sensual gratification or titillation. It is nothing less than a form of redemption, a means to heal the fundamental flaw in human nature. Only when we see these sexual ideologies as complete worldviews, held with religious fervor, will we understand why Christians and moral conservatives find it so hard to reform sex-education courses in public schools. You won't find contemporary sex educators using words like *salvation;* nonetheless, many hold the same basic assumption that free sexual expression is the means to a full and healthy life. To communicate with such people requires the kind of pre-evangelism that gets back to the level of world-views. We must show why their worldview does not match reality and how a biblical worldview provides the hope for an effective life.

Is the Opposition Religious?

Mary Calderone, a major architect of contemporary sex education and former executive director of the Sex Information and Education Council of the United States (SIECUS), said in a 1968 article that the "real question" facing sex educators is: "What kind [of person] do we want to produce" to take the place of human nature as we know it today? And "how do we design the production line" to create this advanced creature?[31]

What in Calderone's language tells you she is talking faith rather than science? _____
_____
_____
_____
_____
_____
_____
_____
_____
_____

The problem, as Calderone sees it, is that human nature is not evolving as quickly as technology. She feels that we must remold human nature itself to fit the modern, ever-changing world. A new stage of evolution is breaking across the horizon, she writes, and the task of educators is to prepare children to step into that new world. To do this, they must pry children away from old views and values, especially from biblical and other traditional forms of sexual morality—for "religious laws or rules about sex were made on the basis of ignorance."[32]

Whenever people start talking about transforming human nature and creating a new type of human, they are talking faith, not science.

In this new stage of evolution, all currently held values will fall by the wayside, making way for new values based on science alone. Therefore, says Calderone, the best thing we can do for our children is to prepare them to view all notions of right and wrong as tentative, changing, and relative. Then, loosed from the old values, they can be inculcated with the values of a scientifically trained elite (consisting of professionals like herself, of course), who know what makes a human being truly healthy.

From the events of the last 30 years, including the rise of AIDS and other sexually transmitted diseases, what would you say to Calderone's idea of what makes a human being truly healthy? _____
_____
_____
_____
_____
_____

Calderone calls on schools and churches to use sex education to develop "quality human beings by means of such consciously engineered processes as society's own best minds can blueprint."[33] Here sexual utopianism takes on almost frightening tones, for it ties sex education to a vision of technological control and social engineering according to a "blueprint" drawn up by a scientific elite.

When we trace the history of ideas about sexuality, it becomes clear that the founders of sex education never did seek simply to transmit a collection of facts about how our bodies work. Rather, they were evangelists for a utopian worldview, a religion, in which a "scientific" understanding of sexuality is the means for transforming human nature, freeing it from the constraints of morality and ushering in an ideal society. It is another form of the Escalator Myth.

When we trace the history of ideas about sexuality, it becomes clear that the founders of sex education never did seek simply to transmit a collection of facts about how our bodies work.

> The tragic results of sexual licentiousness have spread across our entire society.

How Well Does It Work?

If we examine the lives of these self-appointed prophets, we find little grounds for believing their grandiose promises. Margaret Sanger was married twice and was involved in numerous affairs—or, as she put it, "voluntary mates." She was addicted to the painkiller Demerol and was obsessed with numerology, astrology, and psychics in a desperate attempt to find meaning. The sexual liberation that Sanger actually lived out was not the high road to salvation that she had promised in her writing.[34]

Kinsey, too, had a secret life we rarely hear about. His goal was "to create his own sexual utopia," says biographer James Jones, and Kinsey built up a select circle of friends and colleagues who committed themselves to his philosophy of total sexual freedom. Since the results were often captured on film, we know that Kinsey and his wife both had sexual relations with a host of male and female staff members and other people. Kinsey was also a masochist, sometimes engaging in bizarre and painful practices.[35]

But Kinsey had an even darker secret. In *Kinsey, Sex, and Fraud,* researcher Judith Reisman argues convincingly that Kinsey's research on child sexual responses could have been obtained only if he or his colleagues were actually engaged in the sexual molestation of children. How else could "actual observations" be made of sexual responses in children age two months to fifteen years old?[36] And this is the man whose ideas have been so influential in shaping American sex education.

Wilhelm Reich's life likewise reveals the flaws in his own philosophy. Reich demanded complete sexual freedom for himself and conducted multiple affairs, but he couldn't stand the thought that his wife might live by the same sexual philosophy. His third wife writes that he was desperately jealous and forbade her from living life as he did.[37] The test of whether a worldview is true is whether or not it corresponds to reality: Can we live with it? Obviously Reich could not.

What does Proverbs 6:32 tell you about the wisdom of these leaders?

_____
_____
_____
_____
_____
_____
_____
_____
_____

The truth is that sexual liberation has been no high road to salvation for those who have worshiped at its shrine. Instead, the tragic results of sexual licentiousness have spread across our entire society, producing epidemics of abortion, sexually transmitted diseases, and children born out of wedlock, with all the attendant social pathologies, including school problems, drug and alcohol abuse, and crime. Yet for many Americans, sexual liberation remains a cherished right, and the utopian visions planted by Sanger, Kinsey, Reich, and Calderone continue to flourish. Their ideas still form the unspoken assumptions in the sex-education curricula used throughout our public school system.

Match the sexual crusaders with their distinctive ideas below.
a. Sanger, b. Kinsey, c. Reich, d. Calderone

____ 1. reduced sex to a sheer biological act.
____ 2. believed that sexual repression injures health and dulls the intellect.
____ 3. saw sexual liberation as the vehicle to produce a new kind of human.
____ 4. taught that nearly everyone is in some degree neurotic and that every neurosis is in turn a symptom of sexual failure.

We all base our lives on some vision of ultimate reality that gives meaning to our individual existence. If we reject God, we will put something in his place; we will absolutize some part of creation. That's exactly what has happened with those who look to a sexual utopia for fulfillment and salvation. Biology takes the place of God as the ultimate reality, and sex becomes the path to the divine.

The irony is that those who reject religion most emphatically, who insist most noisily that they are "scientific," end up promoting what can only be called a religion. In fact, this seems to be a common malady among those who pride themselves on being scientific. Back in the Age of Reason, science was offered as a substitute for religion. But what few foresaw was that in the process, science would take on the functions of religion. Today science is one of the most popular forms of redemption.

Next week we'll examine salvation through science.

The answers to the activity on page 106 are: 1. b; 2. a; 3. d; 4. c.

[1]Bernard N. Nathanson, "Sounding Board, Deeper into Abortion," *New England Journal of Medicine* 291, no. 22 (November 28, 1974): 1188-90.
[2]Thomas Sowell, *Marxism* (New York: William Morrow, 1985), 17.
[3]Mary Midgley, *Evolution as a Religion: Strange Hopes and Stranger Fears* (New York: Methuen, 1985), 30-35.
[4]Vladimir Lenin, as quoted in Francis Nigel Lee, *Communism versus Creation* (Nutley, N.J.: Craig Press, 1969), 28.
[5]Robert Wesson, *Why Marxism? The Continuing Success of a Failed Theory* (New York: Basic Books, 1976), 30.
[6]Throughout their lives, Marx and his colleague Frederick Engles looked expectantly for the *Dies Irae,* as they themselves called it, when the mighty would be cast down. The *Dies Irae* (literally "day of wrath") is a medieval Latin hymn about the Day of Judgment and is sung in requiem masses.
[7]Klaus Bockmuehl, *The Challenge of Marxism* (Leicester, England: InterVarsity Press, 1980), 17.
[8]Modern historians do not accept Marx's stages of social and economic evolution—from primitive communism to slavery to serfdom to capitalism to communism.
[9]Paul Johnson, *Intellectuals,* (New York: Harper & Row, 1988), 53, 56.
[10]Karl Marx and Frederick Engles, "Private Property and Communism," in *Collected Works,* vol. 3 (New York: International Publishers, 1975), 304 (emphasis in the original).
[11]Ibid.
[12]Karl Marx, as quoted in Thomas Sowell, *Marxism* (New York: William Morrow, 1985), 166.
[13]Bernard-Henri Levi, as quoted in Ronald Nash, *Social Justice and the Christian Church* (Milford, Mich.: Mott Media, 1983), 102.
[14]Margaret Sanger, *The Pivot of Civilization* (New York: Brentanos, 1922), 238-39.
[15]Ibid., 232.
[16]Ibid.
[17]Ibid., 233.
[18]Ibid., 270-71.
[19]Alfred C. Kinsey, *Sexual Behavior in the Human Male* (Philadelphia: W. B. Saunders, 1948); and Alfred C. Kinsey, *Sexual Behavior in the Human Female* (Bloomington, Ind.: Indiana University Press, 1998).
[20]Kinsey, *Sexual Behavior in the Human Male,* 59.
[21]James H. Jones, "Annals of Sexology," *New Yorker* (August 25, 1997): 110.
[22]Alan Wolf, review of *Alfred C. Kinsey: A Public/Private Life,* by James H. Jones, *New Republic* 217, no. 21 (november 24, 1997): 31.
[23]Paul Robinson, *The Modernization of Sex* (New York: Cornell University Press, 1988), 83-86.
[24]Wilhelm Reich, as quoted in Eustace Chesser, *Salvation through Sex: The Life and Work of Wilhelm Reich* (New York: William Morrow, 1973), 44.
[25]Wilhelm Reich, *Ether, God and Devil: Cosmic Superimposition* (New York: Farrar, Strause and Giroux, 1973), 9.
[26]Chesser, *Salvation through Sex,* 67.
[27]Robert Rimmer, *The Harrad Experiment* (Amherst, N.Y.: Prometheus Books, 1990).
[28]Rimmer, *The Harrad Experiment,* 13, 46, 145.
[29]Ibid., 157, 167.
[30]Ibid., 264.
[31]Mary Calderone, "Sex Education and the Roles of School and Church," *The Annals of the American Academy of Political and Social Sciences* 376 (March 1968): 57.
[32]Mary S. Calderone and Eric W. Johnson, *The Family Book about Sexuality* (New York: Harper & Row, 1981), 171.
[33]Calderone, "Sex Education," 59.
[34]Madeline Gray, Margaret Sanger: *A Biography of the Champion of Birth Control* (New York: Richard Marek, 1979), 416-18.
[35]James H. Jones, "Annals of Sexology," *New Yorker* (August 25, 1997): 98.
[36]Judith A. Reisman and Edward W. Eichel, *Kinsey, Sex, and Fraud: The Indoctrination of a People* (Lafayette, La.: Huntington House, 1990), 29-30.
[37]Chesser, *Salvation Through Sex,* 71.

Real Redemption

Our world today presents a bewildering array of offers of redemption–means to achieve truth and meaning in life. In this unit you will evaluate more of those offers.

A Study in Contrasts

At Bernie Nathanson's baptism, my mind flashed back to a day three months earlier when I had joined a group of religious leaders to plead with senators to override the veto of a ban on partial-birth abortions. During the roll call of votes, I sat in the gallery, watching and praying. The atmosphere that day was unusually solemn; the senators seemed to move about the chamber in slow motion. The only sound was the secretary calling the roll, followed by the "yea" or "nay" responses.

Suddenly the shrill cry of a baby pierced the eerie silence… probably the child of a tourist visiting the Capitol building. Was it my imagination, or did some of the senators turn ashen? The sound of a live baby in that chamber was a vivid reminder of what was at stake in this crucial vote.

Yet it made no difference.

The vote to override failed.

Dejected, ashamed for my country, I made my way through the crowds and down to the reception room just off the Senate chambers. There I saw the leaders of the pro-abortion forces celebrating—embracing, cheering, and exchanging high fives. The scene struck me as macabre. Here were well-dressed, professional women celebrating the right to continue an utterly barbaric practice in which a baby is removed from the birth canal backward, all except for its head, the skull is punctured and the baby's brains are sucked out.

That day the supporters of partial-birth abortion had won. But political victories are temporary. The political victory paled in comparison to what Patty and I witnessed three months later at Bernie Nathanson's baptismal service. There before our eyes was the real victory: God's ultimate triumph over sin through Christ's sacrifice on the cross.

After the baptism, our small group gathered to celebrate. Speaking softly and with deep feeling, Bernie thanked everyone for coming.

"All I could think about while I was kneeling at the altar was my bar mitzvah," he said. "That day I was so afraid." He hesitated, then looked up. "Today I felt all that fear fall away. I experienced sheer grace."

Bernard Nathanson had been redeemed. He was a new man, taking his first tentative steps into a new world of faith and hope, his fears relieved, his tormented soul transformed, and the most vexing questions of life answered. As I listened to him speak, I shivered with wonder at the transformation that can take place in the human soul.

Like the transformed prison in Ecuador, Bernard Nathanson's story speaks to more than the immediate situation. His story serves as a parable of our modern dilemma. The two worldviews see life from exact opposite perspectives. The biblical worldview sees life of such value that the Son of God died to save an abortionist. The naturalist worldview makes human life so valueless that a living child can be destroyed at the moment of birth.

DAY ONE
Salvation Through Science

"She will give birth to a son, and you are to give him the name Jesus, because he will save his people from their sins."—Matthew 1:21

When the movie *Independence Day* hit the theaters in the late 1990s, many viewers had the feeling they had seen the story somewhere before[1]. In effect, they had. The film was essentially a remake of the 1953 science-fiction classic *War of the Worlds*—but with one significant difference. In the 1953 movie, the scientists' weapon to kill the invading aliens is destroyed, and the panicking population is forced to turn to God. Churches are jammed with people praying, and their prayers are answered: The aliens contract earthborn bacteria and suddenly die off. "All that men could do had failed," says a final voice-over, and deliverance came from the hand of God alone. The film ends with a scene of people standing on a hillside, singing praise to God.[2]

The contemporary update is quite different—signaling a dramatic change in American culture within only a few decades. *Independence Day* nods politely in God's direction by showing people praying for help. But real deliverance comes through the deployment of advanced military technology: A few strategically placed bombs blow up the aliens and save the world. Indeed, *Independence Day* is a celluloid expression of a widespread belief in science and technology as means of salvation.

What indications have you seen that people today are hoping for redemption through science and technology?

_____

_____

_____

In your opinion, what has brought about the change in American culture reflected in the two movies mentioned above?

_____

_____

_____

_____

_____

_____

_____

The Myth of Science as Savior
The outline of this faith in science as savior is neatly summarized in Daniel Quinn's best-seller *Ishmael,* which gives a series of conversations between a disaffected 1960s idealist and a know-it-all gorilla, who offers to explain what's wrong with the world. The problem, says the gorilla, is that Western culture has bought into the myth of science as savior. The myth goes something like this: The universe started out about fifteen billion years ago with the big bang; our solar system was born about seven billion years ago; eventually, life appeared in the chemical broth of the ancient oceans, evolving first into simple microorganisms, then into higher, more complex forms, and finally into human beings. Humans are the apex of evolution, with the intelligence to control nature and bend it to serve our purposes. The solution to our social problems therefore lies in our own hands, through the exertion of human intelligence and ingenuity. Through our ever-advancing science and technology, we will save ourselves.[3]

The Furniture of the Western Mind

Quinn put his finger squarely on the assumptions that float around in the minds of most Western people, many of whom hold this basic worldview without even realizing that they do. Because the worldview has no name, no label, no church, and no rituals, most people don't identify it as a religion or even as a distinctive belief system. It's simply part of the furniture of the Western mind. Yet it is nothing less than a vision of redemption, a surrogate salvation, a substitute for the kingdom of God, setting up science as the path to utopia.

Look again at the sentence: "Because the worldview has no name, no label, no church, and no rituals, most people don't identify it as a religion or even as a distinctive belief system." What do you understand now about that sentence that you would not have understood before you started this study?

_____
_____
_____
_____
_____
_____
_____

Science as Hero in Popular Culture

The entertainment industry both shapes and reflects the beliefs of a society. Students of films can easily detect a shift in the role of science that has taken place in the past half century. Today popular entertainment portrays science as the savior that will rescue humanity from all manner of evils.

The Origin of Science as Redeemer

Looking back over history, we find some of the first dabbling with this notion in the writings of the sixteenth-century scientist Francis Bacon. Bacon wrote a tale titled *New Atlantis,* depicting an imaginary civilization centered on a gigantic laboratory committed to perpetual progress through science—or, as Bacon quaintly put it, to "the effecting of all things possible."[4]

More influential was Auguste Comte, who is honored today as the founder of sociology. Comte proposed that all societies pass through three stages of social evolution. The most primitive is the theological stage, where people seek supernatural explanations for events; the second is the metaphysical stage, where people explain the world through abstract philosophical concepts; and the highest stage is the scientific stage, where people find truth through scientific experimentation.[5]

Unlike most of his contemporaries, Comte admitted that what he was proposing was essentially a religion. He actually founded the Religion of Humanity, complete with churches, hymns, and calendars listing special days for the "saints" of science and philosophy—with himself as the high priest.[6]

Western culture has recently turned increasingly more to interest in the supernatural. Why do you think people are turning from "science" to belief in such things as beings from other planets?

❏ **The hope for scientific solutions has failed.**
❏ **People have a longing in their hearts that science cannot fill.**
❏ **Looking to "scientific" answers has devalued life and created more problems than it has solved.**
❏ **Your response** _____
_____
_____
_____
_____

The religion of progress through science really took off after Charles Darwin published his theory of evolution by natural selection. By providing scientific sanction for evolution, Darwin's theory gave enormous impetus to the idea of endless, universal progress.[7]

In the following paragraph look for evidence that evolution was seen from the beginning as far more than a scientific theory.

English philosopher Herbert Spencer expanded evolution into a comprehensive philosophy covering all of reality—from stars to societies. In his system, the goal of evolutionary progress is the emergence of human beings, who, in turn, will help produce something new and better for the next stage of evolution. Spencer's gospel of evolution became a secular substitute for Christian hope. As religion and physics professor Ian Barbour writes, "Faith in progress replaced the doctrines of creation and providence as assurance that the universe is not really purposeless."[8]

Was Spencer's philosophy more like science or religion? Why? _____
_____
_____
_____

Even certain strains of Marxism identify science rather than revolution as the source of salvation. In the early part of this century, physicist J. D. Bernal predicted that after the triumph of the proletariat and the rise of the classless society, there was still one more stage before a real utopia would appear—a stage when a new "aristocracy of scientific intelligence" would create a world run by scientific experts. In a burst of enthusiasm, Bernal predicted that scientists would actually evolve into a new, superhuman race that would "emerge as a new species and leave humanity behind."[9]

What evidence can you list to show that humanity is indeed evolving into a higher, "superhuman" species? _____

_____

_____

_____

_____

_____

_____

What evidence do you see that humanity is not evolving to any higher life form?

_____

_____

_____

_____

_____

_____

Match the thinker in the list below with the idea in today's lesson.

____ a. Francis Bacon

____ b. August Compte

____ c. Herbert Spencer

____ d. J. D. Bernal

1. Scientists will become the new superhuman race, the aristocracy or scientific intelligence.
2. He believed in perpetual progress through science.
3. His gospel of evolution became a secular substitute for Christian hope.
4. The founder of sociology, he proposed three stages of social evolution.

Review the day's study to confirm your answers.

DAY TWO
Genetic Salvation

"Fear God and give him glory, because the hour of his judgment has come. Worship him who made the heavens, the earth, the sea and the springs of water."—Revelation 14:7

The idea of creating a new and improved race is a key component in many forms of scientific utopianism. In the early twentieth century, after Gregor Mendel's groundbreaking work on genes was rediscovered, many scientists began to place their hope in a vision of creating the New Man through genetic engineering.

In the 1930s, the great geneticist H. J. Muller divided the history of life into three stages: In the first stage, life was completely at the mercy of the environment; in the second stage, human beings appeared and reversed that order, learning how to reach out and control the environment; and in the dawning third stage, humans would reach inside and control their own nature. Humanity will "shape itself into an increasingly sublime creation—a being beside which the mythical divinities of the past will seem more and more ridiculous," Muller wrote. This godlike being surveys the entire universe, and, "setting its own marvelous inner powers against the brute Goliath of the suns and planets, challenges them to contest."[10]

Muller did his work in the 1930s. What world leader most exemplifies the attempt to implement Muller's vision of a super race?
❑ Joseph Stalin
❑ Adolf Hitler
❑ Franklin D. Roosevelt
❑ Mao Zedong

What philosopher from the 19th century laid the groundwork for Muller's idea of a genetically enhanced super race?
❑ Auguste Comte
❑ Karl Marx
❑ Friedrich Nietzsche
❑ Rene Descartes

Muller was an excellent scientist, but what he is describing here is not science. It is science turned into a myth of salvation. Whether Muller fully understood the source of his ideas or not, Nietzsche originated the vision of a super race. Hitler then took Nietzsche's idea, supported by the so called "science" of men like Muller, and caused the slaughter of 50 million people in World War II.

The apostle Paul warned the young preacher Timothy to avoid "the profane and idle babblings and contradictions of what is falsely called knowledge" (1 Tim. 6:20, NKJV). Could Muller's belief in the promise of genetic manipulation be classified as "falsely called knowledge"?
❑ yes ❑ no ❑ not sure

What does 2 Corinthians 4:3-4 say about those who are perishing?
_____
_____
_____

Muller did not distinguish between genuine science and philosophical or religious ideas. What he called scientific knowledge was really nothing but his fantasy. This same myth motivates much of the research done today in genetic engineering. Nobel prize-winner Francis Crick, codiscoverer of DNA, writes: "We can expect to see major efforts to improve the nature of man himself within the next ten thousand years."[11] Some people even believe genetic science will eventually develop "supergenes" to produce human beings with superintelligence or superstrength. This is salvation by genetics—the creation of the New Man by gene manipulation.

What is the difference between genetic research to improve human health and to alter human nature? Which is science and which is faith in a worldview? _____
_____
_____
_____

The Test of Reality

But will such a salvation really save us? How does this vision of redemption stack up in a test against reality? Not very well.

Science itself gives no moral guidelines for our genetic experimentation. How do we decide which traits we want? Do we want to create a super-Einstein or a super-Mother Teresa? Do we want to create a class of subhuman slaves to do our menial work? These questions presuppose a standard of values, which science itself cannot provide.

Why can science not provide a standard of values? _____
_____
_____

More important, the sheer attempt to remake human nature genetically would strip people of their dignity and reduce them to commodities. With technology offering greater choice and control over the embryo's traits, having a child could become like purchasing a consumer product. And children themselves may come to be regarded as products that we plan, create, modify, improve, and evaluate according to standards of quality control. What happens if the "product" doesn't meet the parents' standard—if they do not think they're getting their money's worth? Will the child be tossed aside, like an appliance that stops working? As one theologian argues, human beings are "begotten, not made," and if we reverse that—if children become products that we manufacture—we do immeasurable damage to human dignity.[12]

We've seen before that our worldview controls how we see reality. In the following paragraph, underline any statement that suggests the peculiar blindness produced by a naturalist worldview.

> **STATEMENT** Unfortunately, objections like these are not likely to be raised in a climate where scientists hold a faith in inevitable progress, for the Escalator Myth creates the expectation that change will always be for the better. This explains why scientists reveal a disturbingly uncritical acceptance of genetic engineering. But clearly, change can be either an improvement or a degeneration. New forms of technology can be used in the service of either good or evil. The faith that we can save ourselves through science can be sustained only if we shut our eyes to the human capacity for barbarism.[13]

Many people in the scientific community believe that "If we can do it, we should" Do you agree or disagree? Why? _____
_____
_____
_____

How can a biblical worldview help address those questions? _____
_____
_____
_____

Look to the Stars

Many thoughtful scientists find it hard to go along with such a blind faith. They see that human progress often results in greater misery and destruction. Yet rather than look for another form of salvation, they simply transfer the Escalator Myth to a different galaxy.

Read the following paragraph carefully. Underline evidence that these ideas are religious rather than scientific.

> **STATEMENT** Because planet Earth is so mired in pollution, war, and other pathologies, they say, we are likely to destroy ourselves before we manage to evolve to a higher stage. For example, Stephen Hawking, author of the bestseller *A Brief History of Time,* warns that evolution will not improve the human race quickly enough to temper our aggression and avoid extinction.[14] Some scientists believe, then, that our only hope is to link up with beings elsewhere in the universe—a civilization of extraterrestrials who have themselves successfully evolved to a more advanced stage and can help us. These are not the rantings of wide-eyed UFO enthusiasts, mind you. Both the federal government and private foundations have poured huge amounts of money into the Search for Extra-Terrestrial Intelligence (SETI), scanning the heavens with powerful radio telescopes in the hopes of picking up signals from another civilization. If we ever do discover another civilization in space, says Frank Drake, who heads up the SETI Institute, "it can tell us what we might evolve to, and how far we might evolve." These friendly extraterrestrials might even pass on their technological knowledge, handing over "scientific data which otherwise might take us hundreds of years and vast resources to acquire."[15]

What in the quotes you just read indicates that these persons search for extraterrestrials is fueled by faith rather than fact? _____

_____

_____

_____

_____

_____

The breathless enthusiasm that often accompanies descriptions of SETI is a dead giveaway that this search for an extraterrestrial solution is at core religious. And no one was a more enthusiastic supporter than the late Carl Sagan. Sagan built an entire worldview out of his vision of the cosmos as our creator and savior. For him, SETI was not just a scientific project; it would be, quite literally, the source of the world's redemption. His reasoning went like this: Any society capable of transmitting messages to us must be far more technologically sophisticated than our own. Therefore, the receipt of a message from space would give us "an invaluable piece of knowledge," telling us "that it is possible to live through [the] technological adolescence" through which we are now passing.[16]

No such message has ever been detected, of course, yet Sagan offered detailed descriptions of the wondrous secrets we might learn if we ever succeed in decoding one. "It is possible," he exclaimed, "that among the first contents of such a message may be detailed prescriptions for the avoidance of technological disaster, for a passage through adolescence to maturity." Sagan never explained how an alien race that has never had any contact with Earth, a race whose chemistry, brains, and language would be completely different from ours, would just happen to know exactly what our problems are, or how they would be capable of giving "detailed prescriptions" for solving them. Still, he seemed certain that they would offer advice for "straightforward solutions, still undiscovered on Earth, to problems of food shortages, population growth, energy supplies, dwindling resources, pollution, and war."[17]

In your opinion, which takes greater faith?

❏ believing in the God of the Bible who has revealed Himself
❏ believing in Sagan's extraterrestrials

Though disguised as science, this is nothing more than a magical vision of heavenly ETs emerging from the unknown to lift us from our misery. A longtime critic of SETI puts the matter bluntly: "It's a dream based on faith—a technological search for God."[18]

So this is where the great promise of science and technology leads us—not to a glorious earthly utopia, but to a fantasy-world escape from this planet and from the horrors that this same technology has created. This view of salvation is no more rational than the demented dreams of the Heaven's Gate cult—thirty-nine intelligent, well-educated people who ingested cocktails of alcohol and drugs in the hope that, by leaving their bodies behind, their spirits would meet up with a comet and move on to the "Level above Human." In their case, the Escalator Myth proved deadly.

Use the three-part worldview grid to evaluate the hope of salvation through science.

✺ **Where do adherents to this view believe we came from?** _____

_____

_____

⬢ **What do they think is wrong with our world?** _____

_____

_____

✋ **What do they believe is to be done about it?** _____

_____

_____

None of this scientific optimism, one should note, involves a change of heart. Humanity's problems are not caused by wrong moral choices but by lack of knowledge. For example, Sagan promises that the longed-for message from outer space will teach us "the laws of development of civilizations," that will enable us to control society, just as knowing the laws of physics and chemistry enables us to control nature. What need is there for an awkward and troublesome thing like morality when we can control society for its own good through inviolable laws of "cultural evolution"?[19]

Yet history offers no evidence that knowledge will save human society. To the contrary, the problem with the Hitlers and Stalins of the world was not that they were stupid or ignorant of the laws of cultural evolution; the problem was that they were evil. Bigger and better technology simply gives people bigger and better means to carry out either good or evil choices.

Having confidence in technology is a misguided form of salvation; some things are simply not amenable to a technical quick fix. It is the human heart that determines how we will use our machines—whether we will fashion them into swords or plowshares. Instead of scanning the skies for messages from other galaxies, it is far more realistic to seek the God who *made* those heavens and who came to reveal the truth by living among us. We don't need radio messages from extraterrestrials; we already have a message from God Himself, and it is found in an ancient book that proclaimed the creation of the cosmos long before there were astronomers around to muse over such questions. The message begins: "In the beginning God created the heavens and the earth" (Gen. 1:1).

Properly understood, science is a wonderful tool for investigating God's world. But science cannot solve the human dilemma, and it cannot give us hope and meaning. And ultimately, those who exalt science into a religion discover this—which is why they finally give in to a profound pessimism, adrift on a space station called Earth, waiting for a beacon from beyond to save us from ourselves.

But for those less inclined to fantasy, there is no escape from the dreadful realization that a world without God can end only in despair.

DAY THREE
The Drama of Despair

" 'Meaningless! Meaningless!' says the Teacher. 'Utterly meaningless! Everything is meaningless.' "–*Ecclesiastes 1:2*

"The more the universe seems comprehensible, the more it also seems pointless." With these startling words, Nobel prize-winning physicist Steven Weinberg ended *The First Three Minutes,* his book about the origin of the universe.[20]

Science reveals that we live in an "overwhelmingly hostile universe," Weinberg explains. It existed long before human beings appeared, and it is not going to remain habitable forever. According to current predictions, the universe is headed for a heat death, and it will take us with it. Nothing we do will outlast our temporary span on this globe. Life is meaningless, purposeless, "pointless."[21]

For many modern thinkers, the alternative to the Christian message of salvation is

Jean-Paul Sartre (1905-1980)

Sartre's father died when Jean-Paul was 15 months old and sick. When Sartre recovered, he and his mother went to live at her parent's house before moving in 1911 to Paris. Sartre taught himself to read at a very early age. Disappointed with his first school day's progress, his grandfather withdrew him the second.

God ceased to be a meaningful object of faith to Sartre. "Failing to take root in my heart," he said, "He vegetated in me for a while, then He died."

not an artificial salvation but a free fall into pessimism and despair. For many people today, there is no transcendent purpose, no expectation of redemption, no answer to life's most wrenching dilemmas. For them the courageous person is the one who faces reality squarely and shakes off all illusory hopes. Yet, ironically, even this pessimism is often held with a fervor that resembles faith. Like the antihero in literature, who is really the hero, this is an antifaith that actually functions as a faith.

If you rule out the existence of God, what would you have left to provide hope for life?

_____
_____
_____
_____
_____
_____
_____
_____
_____
_____
_____
_____

What happened to the utopian dreams of the past two centuries, the vision of endless upward progress? For many people, those dreams crashed in the convulsions of two world wars that left a trail of horrors,

from the blood-soaked trenches of Argonne to the ashes of Auschwitz. From 1918 to 1945, a little more than a quarter century, the world was shocked out of its complacent optimism by the inescapable reality of naked evil.

European intellectuals who experienced the madness firsthand, on their native soil, were the first to preach a philosophy of despair. "There are no divine judges or controllers," proclaimed French philosopher Jean-Paul Sartre. "The world is all there is, our existence is all we have." Thus was born the word *existentialism*. In his play *No Exit,* one character distills the existentialist creed to a catch phrase: "You are your life, and that's all you are."[22] There is no higher purpose, goal, or meaning to life.

Albert Camus, another post-World War II existentialist, probed the problem of meaninglessness in *The Myth of Sisyphus*, based on a classical mythology story in which Sisyphus is punished by the gods who require him to push a boulder to the top of a hill, only to have it roll down again. For Camus, this mythological figure represents "the absurd hero," the person who recognizes the absurdity of existence and rebels against it. Since the universe is "without a master," Camus writes, all that's left for the absurd hero is to exercise his free choice and rebel, thereby becoming his own master.[23]

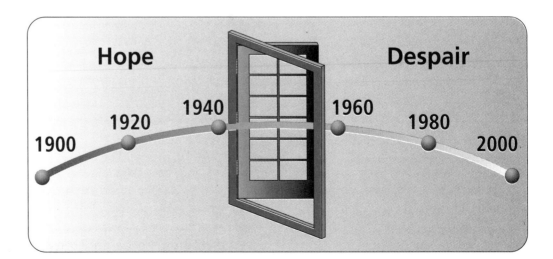

Hope — 1900 1920 1940 1960 1980 2000 — Despair

What is existentialism?
- ❑ the belief that only God exists
- ❑ the philosophy that there is no goal or purpose to life
- ❑ the philosophy that economic factors determine human nature

In the 1960s, Sartre's and Camus' books, which became very popular among American intellectuals and university students, fed into the antiestablishment mood of the Vietnam era. If naturalistic science leads to the conclusion that there is no ultimate meaning to life—that life is absurd—then why not seek alternative sources of meaning in sensual pleasure and mind-altering drug experiences? Existentialism is the philosophy of meaninglessness. Life is absurd. No meaning exists, so you can only create meaning through your own choices.

Make no mistake. The sixties was not just an era of long hair and bell-bottoms. It was an intellectual and cultural upheaval that marked the end of modernity's optimism and introduced the worldview of despair on a broad level. Ideas concocted in the rarefied domain of academia filtered down to shape an entire generation of young people. They, in turn, have brought those ideas to their logical conclusion in postmodernism, with its wholesale rejection of reason and objective truth.

In what ways did existential thinking appeal to the counterculture movement of the 60s?

_____
_____
_____
_____
_____
_____
_____
_____

Of course, modernity has always had its dark underside. Already in the nineteenth century, sensitive people realized that science seemed to suggest an image of the universe that was hostile to human values. The world discovered by science was supposedly a world of mathematical entities: mass, extension, and velocity. Those things that matter most to humans—purpose, meaning, love, and beauty—were relegated to the subjective realm of the mind, while human beings were reduced to an insignificant presence in an unthinking, unfeeling, purposeless world of masses spinning blindly in space. Science teaches us that mankind is no longer "the Heaven-descended heir of all the ages," said Lord Balfour. "His very existence is an accident, his story a brief and transitory episode in the life of one of the meanest of the planets."[24]

Above, review the idea of relegating meaning and purpose to the subjective realm. What concept discussed in unit 1 does this idea describe?
- ❑ the origin of species
- ❑ the fact/value distinction
- ❑ the modernist controversy

The emphasis on only cold, hard, facts presents a gloomy picture, but many have found it all the more attractive for its gloom, shuddering "in delicious horror" before it, writes historian John Herman Randall. In fact, starting in the nineteenth century, "many believed it _because_ it was so dreadful; they prided themselves on their courage in facing facts."[25] The idea that only those things that are "scientifically measurable" are real is the basis for the fact/value distinction we encountered in unit 1. By arbitrarily declaring spiritual truth invalid, we find ourselves left with a meaningless world in which pessimism rules.

Remember the power of ideas. The underlying philosophy shapes a culture, even if the majority of the people do not actively understand or embrace the philosophy. In the following paragraph, look for the practical outcome of the philosophy of meaninglessness.

STATEMENT The creeds of pessimism often take on a distinctly Darwinian cast. Darwin's theory suggests that human beings are merely advanced animals competing in the struggle for existence. All life forms are driven to compete for the next rung on the evolutionary ladder, leaving the weak behind. In the late nineteenth and early twentieth centuries, such ideas were enshrined in social Darwinism—the idea that the rich and corrupt are in power because they've proven themselves the "fittest" in the struggle for survival and that there's nothing we can do about it because it's simply the law of nature. Moral persuasion and spiritual redemption are irrelevant because we are trapped in an endless struggle to reach the top of the heap.

What effect did Darwinist thinking have in the realm of politics in the late nineteenth and early twentieth century?

_____

_____

_____

_____

_____

Darwinist philosophy led to the belief that the fittest reached the top of the heap, so no reason existed to help the poor, or to work for better government. You can see that philosophy powerfully impacts practical life.

What could possibly make such a negative faith appealing? It offers one compensation: It gives adherents a way to debunk conventional religion and morality. It dis-

The Rise of Sociobiology

This dark side of Darwinism remained an undercurrent, causing few ripples in the reigning myth of progress until recent decades, when it burst forth in what is known as sociobiology—today often called evolutionary psychology. Sociobiologists conclude that evolution requires ruthlessly selfish behavior. Even actions that appear to be for the benefit of others are grounded in underlying selfishness: We are nice to others only so they will be nice to us. Love and altruism are illusions, cover-ups for underlying self-interest.

What a ferocious picture of life! Taken at face value, it is a rather ridiculous one. No human society exists without altruism, charity, and cooperation. Yet these can be explained away, says the sociobiologist. According to the theory, the real agents of evolution are the genes, their only interest is in surviving and being passed on to the next generation. When we engage in apparently altruistic behavior, we are being duped by our genes, which are busily stacking the deck in their favor. Thus, the mother's selfless sacrifice for her child is her genes compelling her to take care of the vehicle for her genes to survive.

Edward O. Wilson, founder of sociobiology, said, "The organism is only DNA's way of making more DNA," as if genes were capable of planning and making things. Wilson even argues that the ultimate source of human morality is the "morality of the gene," making genes capable of moral reasoning and choice.[26]

Sociobiology attributes genes with consciousness, will, and choice, while reducing humans to machines that carry out their orders. This is a worldview in which genes become the deity—the ultimate creators and controllers of life.

British science writer Richard Dawkins says, "Like successful Chicago gangsters, our genes have survived ... in a highly competitive world," and "the ultimate rationale for our existence" is to preserve them. "By dictating the way survival machines [that's us] and their nervous systems are built, genes exert ultimate power over behavior." Finally, Dawkins waxes positively lyrical. The gene "does not grow old. It leaps from body to body down the generations, manipulating body after body in its own way and for its own ends, abandoning a succession of mortal bodies before they sink in senility and death. The genes are the immortals."[27]

pels the "illusion" that a loving, sovereign God gives human beings dignity and significance as genuine moral agents.

Why in the world will people believe in such absurd theories while rejecting Christianity? (Check all that apply.)

❏ because the facts support naturalism
❏ because they have adopted an anti-christian worldview
❏ because humans are rebellious and desire to dethrone God

Edward O. Wilson, admits that he left his Baptist tradition at the age of fifteen and transferred his religious longings elsewhere. "My heart continued to believe in the light and the way ... and I looked for grace in some other setting"–which turned out to be science.[28] Having entered "the temple of science," Wilson shifted his faith to the "mythology" of scientific materialism, and then searched for a "single grand naturalistic image of man" that would explain everything "as a material process, from the bottom up, atoms to genes to the human spirit."[29] Wilson is completely candid that his goal is to "divert the power of religion" into the service of materialism or naturalism.[30]

To the question above, you may have noted the thesis of this entire study. A war is raging between two worldviews. Which worldview we embrace then determines how we see all of life. Real science does not compel anyone to adopt a worldview that denies the reality of true redemption and that dramatizes nature as a stage of hostile and perpetual conflict. Indeed, many pessimists engage in circular reasoning: First they banish God and conclude that the universe is meaningless; then they argue that since the universe is meaningless, there cannot be a God. Atheism is presented as the conclusion when it is, in fact, the hidden premise.

If your premise is rejection of the biblical God, then no matter how sophisticated your theories, you will end in despair. These pessimistic myths are right about one thing: A universe without God is purposeless, meaningless, and impersonal. It is, in Weinberg's words, pointless. Ernest Hemmingway then becomes the poster child for the philosophy of meaninglessness.

Ernest Hemingway (1899-1961)

Ernest Hemingway, one of this century's great novelists, held to the existentialist credo that life is "a short day's journey from nothingness to nothingness."[31] To give meaning to that nothingness, Hemingway invented his own code: He would taste life to the fullest—experience everything, feel everything, do everything. Even death could be overcome if he treated it as another experience, the most exciting and interesting experience of all.

And so, at age sixty-one, after a life of notoriety as a big-game hunter, adventurer, and womanizer, Hemingway deliberately embraced death. He could no longer prove that he was master of his own fate by his daredevil adventures or self-indulgent lifestyle, but he could prove it by controlling the time and means of his own death.

On Sunday morning, July 2, 1961, Hemingway loaded his favorite gun, seated himself in the foyer of his Idaho home, braced the butt of the gun on the floor, put the barrel in his mouth, and pulled the trigger.

Neurotic? Sick? Perhaps not. Given his worldview, Hemingway's action was eminently logical. After all, if life is meaningless and despair crouches like a lion at the gate, the best option might be to exit heroically on your own terms. Ernest Hemingway shook his fist at despair one last time by controlling his own death.[32]

In the end, those who deny the God of the Bible and history have only two choices: They can either trivialize death by defying it or control death by embracing it on their own terms. Thus, Hemingway is the perfect icon for the failure of Western science and philosophy: having played out the logical consequences of the Enlightenment's rejection of God, many people are brought to complete despair of any transcendent truth or meaning. The blazing, optimistic hope that humanity is moving ever upward and onward, boldly progressing to a new stage in evolution, has been replaced by bitter cynicism. Marooned on the rocks of reality, science itself now promises only the near comical fantasy that we might be rescued by extraterrestrials from outer space.

One might think that upon hitting the dead end of despair, men and women would be driven to return to the Creator. But, alas, although it is true that "our hearts find no peace until they rest in [God]," the human instinct is to flee Him.[33] For finding God will cost us our cherished autonomy.

So where do many turn? To the East.

DAY FOUR
A Look to the East

"He said to me, 'Have you seen this, son of man? Is it a trivial matter for the house of Judah to do the detestable things they are doing here? ... Therefore I will deal with them in anger; I will not look on them with pity or spare them.'" —Ezekiel 8:17-18

When the bright image of science and progress began to fade, and optimism gave way to disillusionment and despair, many people began to cast about for new answers. Asian religions, especially Hinduism and Buddhism, have always enchanted people from Western cultures to some degree, and now these religions have become popular alternatives to the dominant Western worldview.

In the following paragraph, circle the factors that make Eastern religious thought appealing to people today.

STATEMENT The attraction is powerful. Western secularism is materialistic, limiting reality to what can be tested scientifically. Eastern mysticism is spiritual, opening the consciousness to new levels of awareness. Western thought is analytical, leading to fragmentation and alienation. Eastern thought is holistic, promising healing and wholeness. Western science has destroyed the environment and polluted the air. Eastern pantheism proffers a new respect for nature.

In the 1960s, many young people turned to Eastern religion to fill their spiritual emptiness, giving rise to the New Age movement. Today the movement has become so mainstream that community colleges offer classes in yoga, tai chi, astrology, and therapeutic touch. The New Age movement is also a major commercial success. Local supermarkets offer free copies of slick New Age publications advertising everything from holistic health practices to past-life therapy.

It's obvious why Eastern religion is such an attractive form of salvation for a post-Christian culture. It soothes the ego by pronouncing the individual divine, and it gives a gratifying sense of "spirituality" without making any demands in terms of doctrine or ethical living. To make it even more palatable, the New Age movement reshapes Eastern thought to fit the Western mind, with its hunger for upward progress.

Where traditional Eastern thinking is fatalistic and pessimistic—the cycle of karma is called the "wheel of suffering"—the New Age adaptation is optimistic and utopian. New Age promises that if we get in touch with the Universal Spirit, of which we are all part, we will create a new consciousness and a new world.

How does the New Age movement differ from the Buddhist and Hindu roots from which it sprang?

_____
_____
_____
_____
_____

We are poised on the threshold of a great leap forward into, literally, a new age of "harmony and understanding, sympathy and trust abounding," to quote the musical *Hair*.[34] The massive social upheavals of the past decades are not a warning of imminent disaster but the prelude to evolutionary transformation. As New Age writer Ken Wilber puts it, "Men and women have ultimately come up from amoebas, [and] they are ultimately on their way towards God."[35] Toward *becoming* God, Wilber means. Humanity is about to make a quantum leap forward, to emerge as an entirely new creature, to become divine. This is nothing but the Escalator Myth in spiritualized form.

Roots of the New Age Movement

It may seem that the New Age movement appeared out of nowhere in the 1960s, but the way had been prepared in the Romantic movement of the nineteenth century. At that time, science was creating a picture of the world as a vast machine with no place for beauty, meaning, or purpose. So the Romantics revived an ancient philosophy known as neo-Platonism, a blend of Greek thought and Eastern mysticism. They tossed out the picture of the universe as a machine and replaced it with the idea of the universe as a living thing, animated by a "Life Force."

Everything is alive, the Romantics said. Even matter itself, they thought, has a rudimentary form of life or consciousness. And what is the major characteristic of life? Growth. Development. Just as each organism unfolds in stages according to an inner law of development, so life itself unfolds in definite stages from simple to complex under the direction of the Life Force. The Life Force often took on the trappings of an immanent deity, where God was not the transcendent creator, but a spirit pervading nature. "The world was no machine, it was alive," writes historian John Herman Randall, "and God was not its creator so much as its soul, its life."[36]

Do you notice how biblical and naturalistic thoughts are exact opposites? Where does the biblical worldview see the source of evil in the world?

❏ Internal—evil comes from the bent nature of human beings.
❏ External—evil comes from bad government and social conditions.

Ironically, how does New Age thinking see God?

❏ Internal—we are each part of God, made up of all things.
❏ External—God is transcendent (separate from the created order).

The publication of Darwin's *Origin of Species* gave the concept of spiritual evolution a big boost. Most people who accepted Darwinian evolution were not atheists; instead, many tried to integrate it in some way with religion by identifying God with a force that gives purpose and direction to evolution. But the end result was more akin to pantheism than to orthodox Christianity. This God was completely immanent in the world, compelling evolution to ever greater heights and leading mankind to some far-off divine perfection. As Alfred Lord Tennyson wrote, there is "One God, one law, one element,/ And one far-off divine event, / To which the whole creation moves."[37]

You probably recognized the questions above as involving the second element of a worldview. The biblical worldview sees evil coming from our hearts (Matt. 15:19), while naturalism, including the New Age form, see evil outside of us. Ironically, the biblical view sees God as transcendent, beyond and independent of the created order, while New Age naturalism is pantheistic. It sees the created order as God.

For a long time, in the arts, philosophy, and even theology, the Western world has been embracing ideas compatible with Eastern pantheism. All it took was a widespread disillusionment with Western culture to send these ideas hurtling into the mainstream.

Here with a Vengeance

New age thinking is permeating much of Western society, spawning a host of techniques used in medicine, business, education, the military, and even—tragically— churches. Various meditation exercises are sold as means for resolving conflict and for enhancing relaxation, creativity, self-esteem, and even physical health. For example, at Stanford University's Graduate School of Business, a seminar listed as Creativity in Business includes meditation, chanting, "dream work," tarot cards, and a discussion of "the New Age Capitalist."[38] Government agencies as well as private businesses spend millions of dollars in contracts with consulting companies that use New Age techniques for management training.[39]

The New Age in Schools

These New Age programs have even permeated our elementary and secondary schools. A mother in Atlanta, Georgia, was concerned when her second-grade daughter failed to respond to her one day when they were driving in the car. The mother called her daughter's name repeatedly and finally turned around to look in the back seat. Her daughter's eyes were closed and her head drooped forward. Alarmed, the woman stopped the car, opened the back door, and shook her daughter's arm. The girl jerked awake, as if startled out of a trance.

"What's wrong?" the mother asked anxiously. "You wouldn't answer when I called."

"Don't worry, Mom," the little girl replied. "I was with my friend Pumsy."

Questioning her daughter further, the mother discovered that the girl had been learning meditation techniques from the school's guidance counselor through a program called PUMSY In Pursuit of Excellence. Pumsy is a cute, fairy-tale dragon who discovers a wise guide named Friend, who teaches Pumsy (along with the children in the program) basic concepts of the Eastern worldview. For example, Friend tells Pumsy that her mind is like a pool of water: When she is tempted to think negative thoughts, her mind is muddy. But when she thinks positive thoughts, she can tap into a Clear Mind, which will help her solve her problems.[41]

Naturally, these programs rarely use overtly religious language. For example, the Universal Spirit (Brahma, in classic Hindu thought) is often called the Higher Self or some similar term. Yet beneath the secular rhetoric, these programs embody the basic Hindu doctrine that the individual human mind or spirit is part of a Universal Mind or Spirit, and that by relaxation and guided imagery exercises, we can tap into that Mind as a source of wisdom and creativity.[40]

Read "The New Age in Schools" on page 124.

Clear Mind is capitalized because it's another term for Brahma, the god of Hinduism. One clue is the quasi-religious language used to describe it. For example, Friend tells Pumsy, "Your Clear Mind is the best friend you'll ever have … It is always close to you, and it will never leave you." This sounds suspiciously close to biblical language: "I will never leave you nor forsake you" (Josh. 1:5). A few pages later in the story, we read, "You have to trust [your Clear Mind] and let it do good things for you." Through this program, children are essentially being taught to place religious trust in a Hindu notion of God as a Universal Mind.[42]

Of course, such New Age techniques are not sold to teachers as religion. They are marketed as a way to increase creativity and boost self-esteem. PUMSY teaches youngsters to chant slogans like, "I can handle it," "I can make it happen," and "I am me, I am enough." Once again, we hear echoes of biblical themes: "I AM WHO I AM" (Ex. 3:14). This program is teaching self-worship, not self-esteem. It's teaching that we are saved not by a transcendent God who reaches down to us in grace but by realizing that God is within us, that *we* are God. Salvation is not a matter of recognizing our sin; it's a matter of raising our consciousness until we recognize our inner divinity.[43]

Even Christians can be disarmed by the subtleties of the New Age. "You must read this book," an enthusiastic friend told Nancy, handing her a copy of *The Secret Garden* by Frances Hodgson Burnett, first published in 1911. The friend was a thoughtful Christian mother, and the book is a children's classic, but Nancy was jolted by what she read—for the book is Hindu philosophy dressed up in a charming children's story.

In the words of ten-year-old Colin, one of the book's main characters, the world is made of a single spiritual substance, which he calls Magic (always capitalized). "Everything is made out of Magic, leaves and trees, flowers and birds, badgers and foxes and squirrels and people," says Colin.[44] "The Magic is in me. … It's in every one of us."[45] This is classic pantheism, and Burnett entwines it with language right out of the Christian creeds. "Magic is always … making things out of nothing," says Colin.[46]

The difference between this pantheistic deity and the biblical God is that this is an impersonal force that can be tapped, like an electric current. As Colin says, we need to learn how to "get hold of it [Magic] and make it do things for us—like electricity and horses and steam."[47] This is not a Lord to be obeyed but a force to be manipulated. And the way to do that is through spells and incantations. Thus, Colin chants, "The Magic is in me … Magic! Magic! Come and help!"[48]

By what means is New Age thinking making its way into our society?

_____
_____
_____
_____
_____
_____
_____

Clearly, the New Age movement should not be laughed off as a silly fad. It is the vehicle for a complete worldview, offering an answer to all three major life questions.

✵ Where did we come from and who are we? We are somehow fragmented off from the Universal Spirit.

✡ What has gone wrong with the world? We have forgotten our true nature, forgotten that we are part of God.

✋ What is the source of our salvation? We must rediscover our true nature and link up to the God within.

Like all forms of the Escalator Myth, this one starts with utopian premises. There is no real evil, only ignorance: We have forgotten who we are. And by the same token, there is no real redemption, only enlightenment: We must recover a mystical knowledge of our inner divinity. This we do by various techniques, such as meditation, relaxation exercises, guided imagery, visualization, and use of crystals—all aimed at producing a state of consciousness in which the boundaries of the self dissolve and we gain a sense of unity with the divine. Through this higher consciousness, a person is said to tap into divine power and become more creative, more energetic, and even capable of healing illnesses through the power of the mind.

But like all forms of utopianism, this offer of salvation is hollow. By denying the reality of sin, it fails to address the crucial truth of our existence—that we are fallen creatures prone to evil. Proponents of the New Age reassure us that alienation and strife exist only on the superficial level of existence; at the deepest level, we are one with each other in God. As we become aware of this unity, they assert, we will begin to treat each other with kindness and charity.

Why is the New Age god unable to provide us genuine salvation? (Check all that apply).

❏ **New Age thinking begins with a false idea that we are basically good.**

❏ **This imaginary god is no greater than we are.**
❏ **The New Age god provides the power of a god who is greater than we are.**

The New Age view of human nature simply doesn't stack up against reality. Mere knowledge is not enough to undercut the evil in the human heart. Simply *knowing* what is right doesn't enable us to *do* right.[49] This is the dilemma the apostle Paul wrestled with: The good that I want to do, I don't do (see especially Rom. 7:14-25). We don't need to raise our consciousness; we need to be saved.

In the next four paragraphs, underline every weakness of the New Age religion.

The New Age god cannot save us. It is an impersonal spiritual substratum of energy underlying all things. He—or rather, it—is more akin to electricity than to a deity. It is a power people try to plug into, not a personal God people can love and with whom they can communicate.

Moreover, for all its promises about raising self-esteem, the New Age gospel does nothing to affirm the worth of the individual; it offers no basis for human dignity and meaning. On the contrary, the goal of all meditation techniques is to lose the individual self, to dissolve it in the Universal Spirit, just as a drop of water dissolves in the ocean. How utterly unlike the biblical God, who created us as individuals, who watches over each of us and numbers "even the very hairs of [our] head" (Matt. 10:30).

Furthermore, New Age philosophy gives us no basis for morality. If God is in everything, God is in both good and evil; therefore, there is no final difference between them. Morality is only a method for purifying the soul from desires so that it can attain mystical consciousness, like the eight-fold path of Buddhism.[50]

But the ultimate failure of New Age thinking is its sheer implausibility. How many of us are capable of insisting, with a straight face, that we are perfect? Yet New Age proponents actually claim that "we are perfect exactly the way we are. And when we accept that, life works."[51] People who can swallow that have to be deliberately oblivious to their own failures, shortcomings, and sins.

From the words you underlined, explain why the New Age solution is a hollow hope.

_____
_____
_____
_____
_____
_____
_____

In short, spiritual evolutionism is not merely an error, a mistaken idea; it is religious rebellion against reality—against the sheer fact that God is the Creator and we are creatures. It is the empty boast of the pot that claims to make itself without the need of a Potter.

In the final analysis, any religious worldview must pass the most crucial test: Can it make sense of the human predicament? Does it provide a true source of redemption? Is it true? Applying this test to the New Age worldview, we detect its fatal weaknesses. It fails to correspond to reality as we experience it.

And if there is no answer in the West and no answer in the East, where does one turn?

DAY FIVE
Real Salvation

"Salvation is found in no one else, for there is no other name under heaven given to men by which we must be saved."—Acts 4:12

The glaring inadequacy of all the Western, rational offers of salvation has led many people to embrace exotic religious movements from the East. But Eastern methods of spirituality propose to dissolve the individual in the Cosmic Spirit, thus failing to answer the cry of the individual heart for meaning and spiritual significance.

This smorgasbord of ideas, this buffet of belief systems, led Catholic scholar Ronald Knox to quip, "The study of comparative religions is the best way to become comparatively religious."[52] Sadly, that is often the effect. Yet a genuinely objective comparison of various belief systems ought to lead to exactly the opposite effect: By lining up the Christian faith against other worldviews and religions we see with astonishing clarity that Christianity offers the only real answers to the most basic questions of life and the best understanding of how we can be saved.

First, Christianity begins with an accurate diagnosis of the human dilemma. God created us and established the moral dimensions for our lives. But we have sinned, every one of us; we have all fallen short of God's perfect standard (see Rom. 3:23). We have defied the moral order of the universe, and, as a result, we are alienated from God.

What is the human dilemma according to the biblical worldview? _____
_____
_____
_____
_____

Admittedly, people often do not *feel* guilty before God, since we are indoctrinated with the belief that guilt is merely a subjective feeling, a neurosis to be cured, and that we really ought to feel good about ourselves. As a result, many people come to Christianity on grounds other than guilt: a longing for inner peace and purpose, an attraction to the quality of love practiced in a local church, or a need to resolve some life crisis. But no matter what initially attracts us to Christianity, at some point each of us must confront the truth of our own moral condition: Guilt is objectively real, and we *are* guilty. We are sinners in the hands of a righteous God. The Holy Spirit can penetrate the hardest heart to convict us of our sinfulness. I know, because that is exactly what the Spirit did in my life.

How did you come face to face with the truth of your own sinfulness and need to be forgiven? _____
_____
_____
_____
_____

Second, Christianity also provides the only answer to the problem of sin. God Himself reaches across the moral chasm that separates us from Him, and He brings us back. In His great love for His creation, God devised a way that He could pay the punishment; He satisfied the demands of divine justice, yet He spared us. God Himself became a man, lived a perfect life in obedience to the moral order, and in His death suffered the blow of divine justice and paid the penalty we rightly deserve for our sins. With that substitutionary atone-

ment, God can justify the sinner and yet remain just—to be both "just and the one who justifies" (Rom. 3:26). God can forgive sin without turning a blind eye to the moral law that flows from His own holy character. God's righteousness is vindicated, and yet He can also bestow mercy on those who call on Him.

But death of the God-man is not the end of the story, for Jesus was resurrected from the dead. He overcame death (the effect of sin), making it possible for us to be free from sin and death. By receiving His salvation, we become new men and women—a restored creation.

What does Christianity present as the solution to humanity's basic problem? _____
_____
_____
_____
_____

All the ideologies we've examined in this section are but pallid imitations of the Christian Gospel. These ideologies promise to free people from oppression (or neurosis, or whatever else enslaves us) and create the New Man, build the New Society, usher in the New Age. Clinging to the beauty of the gospel's hope, but wanting none of the Gospel's requirements, they recast it in the Escalator Myth, the myth of progress. They promise that we can create a new life through politics, sex, science, or Eastern spirituality. But all of these worldviews are defective, inadequate substitutes for the real needs of real people for real redemption.

Third, Christianity's offer of salvation is based on historical truth. Christianity is based not on some evolutionary projection millions of years into the future or on some extraterrestrial fantasy. It is based on an historical event at a specific time and place: the crucifixion of Christ during the Jewish Passover in Jerusalem and His resurrection three days later.

Why is it important to stress that Christianity's solution is rooted in historical fact?

_____

_____

_____

_____

_____

Over the past two thousand years, the historical validity of this event has withstood every imaginable assault, ranging from the charge of "a cover-up" (by religious leaders of Jesus' day) to modern claims that it was a "Passover plot" or a "conjuring trick with bones." What skeptics overlook is that the empty tomb was an historical fact, verified by a number of people, including the soldiers who guarded the tomb (why else did they need to concoct an alternative explanation?). The resurrected Christ also appeared to five hundred eyewitnesses—too many to explain away as mass hysteria or the power of suggestion (1 Cor. 15:3-7).

Another powerful piece of evidence is the refusal of the original disciples to renounce Jesus, even though they were persecuted, tortured, and martyred. This defeated band of men, who had already returned to their jobs, would never have been transformed into bold preachers of the gospel and defenders of the faith had they not seen Jesus' resurrected body and known Him to be the living God. Furthermore, no Passover plot could ever have been kept secret. (I know how impossible it is for a group of people, even some of the most powerful in the world, to maintain a lie. I saw this firsthand in the unraveling of the Watergate cover-up. The actual cover-up lasted only a few weeks before the first conspirator broke and turned state's evidence.[53]) People will die for something they _believe_ to be true, but they will never die for something they _know_ to be false.

Another common stance, especially among theological liberals, is that the historicity of Jesus' death doesn't matter. They say that even if the events didn't happen, Jesus is an important moral teacher, and the death and resurrection are interesting religious symbols.

But historical truth _does_ matter. It is not enough to see Jesus' life and death as a purely subjective idea that can be "true for me," even if others do not believe it. The Christian message is the good news about what God has actually done. _But if the gospel is a myth, then God has not done anything._ "If religion be made independent of history, there is no such thing as a gospel," wrote the great Christian scholar J. Gresham Machen. "For 'gospel' means 'good news,' tidings, information about something that has happened. A gospel independent of history is a contradiction in terms."[54]

The next several paragraphs present evidence that Jesus' life, death, and resurrection are historical facts. In the margin note the different types of evidence as if you were preparing a legal case.

Jesus' resurrection is much _more_ than an historical fact, but it is nothing _less_ than one. Historical scholarship supports the gospel's claims. Critics used to argue that the New Testament wasn't written until hundreds of years after Jesus lived, by which time myth and legend had grown up and distorted the original events. But we now know that the New Testament books were originally written within a few decades after Christ's resurrection.

Today Jesus' life is more thoroughly validated than is the life of virtually any other ancient figure. Of the New Testament record alone, we have several thousand copies that date from only a few years after Jesus lived on earth. By contrast, we have only 20 copies of the works of the Roman writer Tacitus, the earliest manuscript dated one thousand years after he lived. The earliest manuscript we have of the work of Aristotle is dated fourteen hundred years after he lived. The earliest copy of Caesar's *Gallic Wars* is dated one thousand years after he wrote it. Yet no one questions either the historicity of Tacitus or Aristotle or Caesar, or the authenticity of their writings.[55]

The salvation attested to in the New Testament is the culmination of a long process of preparation in the Old Testament, which is also historical, as archeological discoveries continue to verify. For example, there was a time when critics said Moses could not have written the Pentateuch because writing had not yet been invented. Then archaeologists discovered writing was well developed thousands of years before Moses' day. Egypt and Babylonia were highly literate cultures, with dictionaries, schools, and libraries.[56]

I hope you noted that the New Testament books were written soon after the events, many copies of the manuscripts exist, and the validity of the Old Testament supports the New Testament. Next underline the evidences that support the Old Testament.

The sharpest criticism was once reserved for the early chapters of Genesis, where the stories of the patriarchs were considered legends. But in recent years, archaeological discoveries have repeatedly confirmed the accuracy of names, places, trade routes, and customs of patriarchal times found in Genesis. Archaeologists have found cuneiform tablets containing references to names such as Abraham and his brothers Nahor and Haran. Tablets also explain puzzling customs, such as Abraham's and Jacob's practice of having children by a servant girl; records show this was a common practice at the time. Yet, only a few centuries later these patriarchs lived, many of these names and practices and even some cities had completely disappeared, making it impossible that these stories were invented later, as the critics once claimed.

Furthermore, the discovery of the Dead Sea scrolls has vindicated much of the Old Testament—even its supernatural character. Take Psalm 22, which contains details that bear an uncanny resemblance to Christ's crucifixion. Skeptics, rejecting the reality of divinely inspired prophecy, insisted that it must have been written in the Maccabean Era, just before the birth of Christ, since before then the practice of crucifixion did not exist in the Roman Empire. But when the Dead Sea scrolls were discovered, they included copies of the Psalms dated centuries *before* the Maccabean Era.

Read Psalm 22. Note below the specific details that seem to describe the crucifixion.

_____

_____

_____

_____

_____

_____

And the evidence continues to mount. In the 1970s, archeological excavations confirmed the unique design of Philistine temples, with the roof supported by two central pillars about six feet apart. This gives historical plausibility to the story of Samson, who grasped two pillars in the Philistine temple and brought it down.

The stories in the Old and New Testaments are not made-up fables; they are accounts of real people and real events in history. As British journalist and historian Paul Johnson concludes, "It is not now the men of faith, it is the skeptics, who have reason to fear the course of discovery."[57]

Paul Johnson's quote applies to the following areas we have studied: (Check all that apply.)

1. What do the skeptics have to fear about recent findings in science?

❏ **Studies in biology demonstrate the complete impossibility of life having begun by natural processes.**

❏ Studies in astrophysics demonstrate that the universe had a specific beginning, as the Bible teaches.

❏ Studies in archaeology show consistent gaps in the fossil record, demonstrating that one species does not evolve from another.

2. What do skeptics have to fear about recent findings in archaeology?

❏ The arguments that have been used against the Old Testament have been disproved.

❏ The evidence shows that the New Testament was written soon after the life of Jesus.

❏ The human evidence from the lives of the apostles shows they told the truth.

All of the above evidences point powerfully to the truth of the gospel record, but Christianity did not end with the historical record of Christ's resurrection. For at Pentecost, the risen Christ sent forth the Holy Spirit into the lives of believers, to work out His purposes in their lives.

Write the reference to the appropriate Scripture before the aspect of the Christian life the passages describe: John 1:12; 2 Corinthians 3:18; 1 Peter 2:1-9.

_____ 1. Christians are being transformed and restored to our true nature, people created in the image of God.

_____ 2. Every believer receives the power to become a child of God.

_____ 3. We live as the community of hope, in eschatological expectation, knowing that Christ will return and establish his rule over all.

God's redemption, then, does not change us into something different so much as it *restores* in us the image of God, the image that was broken at the Fall. Virtually all of the words describing salvation in the Bible imply a return to something that originally existed. To *redeem* means to "buy back," and the image evokes a kidnapping: Someone has been seized and is being held for ransom; a second person pays the ransom and buys the captive back, restoring the person to original freedom. *Reconcilia-tion* implies a relationship torn by conflict, then returned to its original friendship. The New Testament also speaks of *renewal,* implying that something has been battered and torn, then restored to its pristine condition. *Regeneration* implies something returned to life after having died. "All these terms suggest a *restoration* of some good thing that was spoiled or lost."[58]

Read Psalm 8. What purpose for humanity does verse 6 express?

_____

_____

_____

Being justified before God is a wonderful gift, yet it is just the beginning. Salvation empowers us to take up the task laid on the first human beings at the dawn of creation: to subdue the earth and extend the Creator's dominion over all of life.

Only Christianity provides true redemption—a restoration to our created state and the hope of eternal peace with God. No other worldview identifies the real problem: the stain of sin in our souls.

Only Christianity can set free a tormented soul like Bernard Nathanson. Only Christianity can set free a sinner like me—and like you. Only Christianity liberates us from the ruins of our lives. And having been liberated from sin, only Christianity empowers us to help bring Christ's restoration to the entire created order.

[1]*Independence Day,* Twentieth Century Fox (1996).
[2]*War of the Worlds,* Paramount Pictures (1953).
[3]Daniel Quinn, *Ishmael* (New York: Bantam Books, 1992).
[4]Francis Bacon, as quoted in John Herman Randall, *The Making of the Modern Mind* (New

Today's Prayer
Thank You, God. You have provided real salvation and hope through the reality of the death and resurrection of Your Son. Help me to share Your love with others around me who do not know You.

York: Columbia University Press, 1976), 204.

[5]See Auguste Comte, *Religion of Humanity: The Positivist Calendar of Auguste Comte, and other Tables* (London: The London Positivist Society, 1929); and Auguste Comte, *The Religion of Humanity: Love, Order, Progress, Live for Others, Live Openly* (Liverpool, England: Church of Humanity, 1907). See also T. R. Wright, *The Religion of Humanity: The Impact of Comtean Positivism on Victorian Britain* (Cambridge: Cambridge University Press, 1986).

[6]Ibid.

[7]Mary Midgley, *Evolution as a Religion: Strange Hopes and Stranger Fears* (New York: Nethuen and Co., 1985), 34. Ironically, Darwin himself admitted that he could see "no innate tendency to progressive development."

[8]Ian Barbour, *Issues in Science and Religion* (New York: Harper Torch books, 1966), 94.

[9]J.D. Bernal, as quoted in Mary Midgley, *Evolution as a Religion,* 35.

[10]H. J. Muller, as quoted in Mary Midgley, *Evolution as a Religion,* 34.

[11]Francis Crick, *Life Itself, Its Origin and Nature* (New York: Simon & Schuster, 1981), 118.

[12]Oliver O'Donovan, *Begotten or Made?* (London: Oxford University Press, 1984).

[13]Beyond this, when you consider that the supposed evolutionary process requires several million years to accomplish even minor changes, the idea that we can predict anything at all about the end result is preposterous. This is utter pie-in-the-sky, blind faith.

[14]Stephen Hawking, *A Brief History in Time* (New York: Bantam Books, 1988).

[15]Frank Drake, interviewed by Bob Arnold in "Frank Drake Assesses the NASA Search," *SETI News* (first quarter, 1993).

[16]Carl Sagan, *Broca's Brain* (New York: Random, 1979), 276.

[17]Ibid.

[18]Cited in Terence Dickinson, "Critics Scoff but Cool ET Hunt Carries On," *Toronto Star,* 24 August 1997.

[19]Sagan, *Broca's Brain,* 276.

[20]Steven Weinberg, *The First Three Minutes: A Modern View of the Origin of the Universe* (London: André Deutsch, 1977), 155.

[21]Ibid., 1-2.

[22]Jean-Paul Sartre, *No Exit and Three Other Plays* (New York: Random, 1949).

[23]Albert Camus, *The Myth of Sisyphus and Other Essays* (New York: Alfred A. Knopf, 1955).

[24]Lord Balfour, as quoted in John Herman Randall, *The Making of the Modern Mind* (New York: Columbia University Press, 1940), 581-82.

[25]Randall, *The Making of the Modern Mind,* 581-82 (emphasis added).

[26]Edward O. Wilson, *Sociobiology: The New Synthesis* (Cambridge, Mass.: Harvard University Press, 1975), 3.

[27]Richard Dawkins, *The Selfish Gene* (London: Oxford University Press, 1976), 2, 64 (emphasis added).

[28]Edward O. Wilson, as quoted in Howard L. Kaye, *The Social Meaning of Modern Biology* (New Haven: Yale University Press, 1986), 169-79.

[29]Ibid.

[30]Ibid.

[31]"Hero of the Code," *Time* (July 14, 1961): 87.

[32]See chapter 2 in Colson's *Kingdoms in Conflict* (New York: William Morrow; Grand Rapids: Zondervan, 1987).

[33]Saint Augustine, *Confessions, book 1,* paragraph 1, trans. R. S. Pine-Coffin (New York: Penguin, 1961), 21.

[34]Hair opened off Broadway in 1967, then made its Broadway debut in 1968.

[35]Ken Wilber, as quoted in Robert Burrows, "New Age Movement: Self-Deification in a Secular Culture," *Spiritual Counterfeit Project Newsletter* 10 (winter 1984-1985).

[36]John Herman Randall, *The Making of the Modern Mind* (New York: Columbia University Press, 1976), 419.

[37]Alfred, Lord Tennyson, *In Memoriam,* LV-LVI.

[38]Robert Lindsey, "Spiritual Concepts Drawing a Different Breed of Adherent," *New York Times,* 29 September 1986.

[39]Martha M. Hamilton and Frank Swoboda, "Mantra for a Company Man: New Age Approaches Increasingly Popular in Management Training," *Washington Post,* 30 June 1996.

[40]For example, yoga is sold as a means of relaxation or physical exercise. Yet the word yoga literally means "yoke," and the actual purpose of the exercise is to yoke, merge, or unite the individual spirit with the Cosmic Spirit.

[41]Jill Anderson, *PUMSY in Pursuit of Excellence* (Eugene, Ore.: Timberline Press, 1987.

[42]Ibid.

[43]Deborah Rozman writes in *Meditating with Children:* "Meditation takes us back to the Source of all Life. We become one with ALL." What PUMSY teaches coyly, Rozman teaches openly: that we all are God, that salvation consists in realizing our divine nature. She even encourages children to apply biblical phrases to themselves, such as "I and my Father are one," "Before Abraham was, I am," and "I am that I am." Deborah Rozman, *Meditating with Children: The Art of Concentration and Centering* (Boulder Creek, Calif.: Planetary Publishing, 1994), 143.

[44]Frances Hodson Burnett, *The Secret Garden* (New York: Dell, 1987), 230.

[45]Ibid., 233.

[46]Ibid., 230.

[47]Ibid., 229.

[48]Ibid., 233.

[49]See also Charles Colson and Nancy Pearcey, "Creating the Good Society," *How Now Shall We Live?,* (Wheaton: Tyndale House, 1999), 373-382.

[50]Peter Kreeft, *Fundamentals of the Faith: Essays in Christian Apologetics* (San Francisco: Ignatius Press, 1988), 90.

[51]*Spiritual Counterfeit Project Newsletter* 10 (winter 1984-85).

[52]Ronald Knox, as quoted in Peter Kreeft, *Fundamentals of the Faith,* 74.

[53]For a fuller explanation of this argument, referring to the Watergate cover-up, see Colson, "Watergate and the Resurrection," chapter 6 in *Loving God* (Grand Rapids: Zondervan, 1983).

[54]J Gresham Machen, *Christianity and Liberalism* (New York: Macmillan, 1923), 121.

[55]Paul Johnson, "A Historian Looks at Jesus," (a speech first presented at Dallas Theological Seminary in 1986), *Sources,* no. 1 (1991).

[56]Joseph P. Free, "Archaeology and Biblical Criticism," *Bibliotheca Sacra* (January 1957): 23. See also Joseph P. Free, *Archaeology and Bible History* (Grand Rapids: Zondervan, 1992).

[57]Johnson, "A Historian Looks at Jesus," *Sources,* no. 1 (1991).

[58]Al Wolters, *Creation Regained: Biblical Basics for a Reformational Worldview* (Grand Rapids: Eerdmans, 1985), 58 (emphasis in the original).

The Church and Culture

*The church has a great heritage as the creator of culture
to the glory of God. Through the past century the evangelical
church has largely forsaken that heritage. In this unit you will
examine the cultural mandate.*

Danny's Wake-Up Punch

Danny Croce couldn't settle into sleep. He couldn't even come close. He watched and listened as his fellow inmates muttered and the Plymouth County Correctional Facility's old pipes complained. Danny had boxed professionally, but now the scenes from that night hit him like short punches with plenty of leverage—a pounding he couldn't fend off.

He felt again the horrible stab of recognition. The man on the ground was police officer John Gilbert, the same John Gilbert who played pool with him and teased him about keeping in shape for the ring. Danny's car had carried John Gilbert thirty yards, they said. Through the nights, the scene played over and over in Danny's head. It was his own hell, which he knew he deserved.

When Danny turned in his bunk to stare at the opposite wall, he saw Gilbert's family—his wife, his two kids, the empty chair at their dinner table. He had wanted to apologize to Jeanie Gilbert a thousand times before the sentencing, but his lawyers had said no. So he remained their ghost…and they remained his nightmare.

One night, about three months into Danny's sentence, an inmate named John Dunn poked his head into Danny's cell just before lockdown. Danny was not overjoyed to see him. He knew Dunn thought of himself as spiritual.

"We're starting a vehicular-homicide group," Dunn said. "You get 'good time' for it—time off your sentence," he added. "A day for an hour."

Danny thought about the eighteen-month stretch still ahead of him. "I guess you'll be seeing me, then," he said.

Eventually Danny told his story to the group. Several men told him in one way or another, "It was his time." The process was supposed to provide some relief, but Danny felt none. It *wasn't* John Gilbert's time. That was the whole point.

Afterward, a longhaired hippie type came up to him. "Have you ever prayed to God?"

Danny hadn't prayed since he was a kid. But later that night, back in his cell, he found himself begging, more out of desperation than anything else: "Please, God, let me sleep."

That was the last thing he remembered. Suddenly it was morning, and for the first time in months, he had an appetite for breakfast.

The insomnia returned, though. He waited it out for several nights, then prayed once more, just as simply. "Please, God, let me sleep."

Again, the next thing he knew, it was morning.

This occurrence was so curious that he felt compelled to talk with the longhair. Danny asked the hippie if he had a Bible, and the man loaned Danny his New Testament. As Danny read the Gospels, he discovered that the Jesus they described really appealed to him. Jesus was straight with everyone, and although He was always being set up, He stood His ground.

Lying on his bunk at night, Danny began to review his whole life, horrified by the person he had become. He saw himself living for his next drink, his next coke party; he saw himself using women.

That next Sunday, when the guard called out for people who wanted to be let out of their cells to attend chapel, Danny shouted, "Cell 16." But he sat like a stone through the service, hearing little. He was there to ask a question. Afterward, he approached Chaplain Bob Hansen, wanting to make sure the passages he had read about outer darkness were really about hell.

"Yes," said the chaplain.

"Then I'm in big trouble," Danny said.

"When you get back to your cell, get on your knees by your bunk," said the chaplain. "Confess your sins to God, and pray for Jesus Christ to come into your heart."

Danny did just that. In his cell, he knelt, confessed that he was a sinner, and asked for Christ to be his Lord. As he did, he kept remembering horrible things he had done, and the memories brought both pain and an eagerness to be forgiven. Talking to God seemed like carrying on a conversation with someone he had missed all along without knowing it. He could almost hear God replying through a silence that echoed his sorrow and embraced it. Danny not only felt heard, he also felt understood, received.

He slept that night. And every night afterward.

Ten years after his release, Danny Croce once again entered Plymouth Correctional. He stood in the lock, between the double doors operated by security.

"Who are you?" a voice said over the intercom.

For a panicky moment he wondered. He remembered being in the old prison. Was he the man who had killed John Gilbert? Yes.

Who else was he? Faces and events rushed through his memory like a video in fast-forward. The day he was released from prison. His marriage. His five children. The years working with troubled kids in Boston. Then the big break: being accepted at Wheaton College and receiving the Charles W. Colson scholarship for ex-offenders. His graduation. His ordination. Yes, he remembered. Both who he had been and who he now was.

"Who are you?" the voice repeated.

"I'm the new prison chaplain," Danny answered.

DAY ONE
Culture Can Be Renewed

"Then God said, 'Let us make man in our image, in our likeness, and let them rule over the fish of the sea and the birds of the air, over the livestock, over all the earth, and over all the creatures that move along the ground.'"—Genesis 1:26

Danny Croce's wake-up punch is the perfect punch line for this study. Not because it's a heartwarming conversion story—though it is—but because of what Danny did *after* his broken life was redeemed. It's the kind of wake-up punch that contemporary Christians urgently need, as well as an apt metaphor for the theme that will be woven through the rest of our study.

When Danny Croce became a Christian, he embarked on an adventure to change the world. First to be transformed was his own life: He cleaned up his act, got out of

> Our purpose in this final section of this study is to show how to make genuinely biblical choices in various areas of life.

prison, married, settled down into a respectable life, and earned a college degree. Changing his own life wasn't the end of things for Danny. After graduation, he didn't head off for the comfortable life that his education might have given him. No, he set out to transform the world he had known. He went back to prison.

In each prison unit, Danny located an on-fire Christian believer, or he preached and witnessed until God converted someone. Danny appointed these men to help and lead others. To equip them, he disciples and teaches them, giving courses on theology and doctrine, often using seminary-level materials. He also holds weekly Bible studies throughout the prison, assisted by Prison Fellowship volunteers. Every day Danny talks with inmates one-on-one, teaching, encouraging, and helping them solve personal problems.

Yes, cultures can be renewed—even those considered the most corrupt and hopeless. If we are to restore our world, we first have to shake off the comfortable notion that Christianity is merely a personal experience, applying only to one's private life.

One of the great myths of our day is that our decisions are personal and that no one has a right to tell us what to do in our private lives. We easily forget that every private decision contributes to the moral and cultural climate of our society.

What have you learned in previous units that explains why Christians have turned inward, making their faith only a personal matter?

_____

_____

_____

_____

Every decision contributes to the culture around. Every choice, every action, either expresses a false worldview and thus contributes to a disordered and broken world, or expresses God's truth and helps build a world that reflects His created order.

To the question above you could think of such things as our having bought into the fact/value distinction and our retreat because the naturalist worldview seemed to have facts behind it. Christians in the past century have responded to these forces by "privatizing" their faith—making faith merely a personal matter involving God and the believer.

Restoration of Culture

Our purpose in this final section is to show how to make genuinely biblical choices in various areas of life. The three worldview categories—*creation, fall,* and *redemption*—provide a framework to identify what is wrong with non-Christian ways of thinking and then formulate a Christian perspective on every subject.

The first essential task, then, is to be discerning, examining the worldviews by measuring how well they answer the fundamental questions of life:

⚛ **Creation—Where did we come from, and who are we?**

🛡 **Fall—What has gone wrong with the world?**

✋ **Redemption—What can we do to fix it?**

Trace out the way any worldview answers these three questions, and you will be able to see how non-biblical ideas fail to fit reality while the biblical worldview provides answers that are internally consistent and really work.

When we apply this three-part analysis, we learn how to put biblical principles into practice in every area of life. We call putting those biblical principles to work the *cultural mandate*. Saving souls is not sufficient. God does not just want people to go to heaven. He intends to reclaim the world for His purposes. As we have seen with Danny Croce and Jorge Crespo, transformed people transform cultures—not through coercion but through sacrificial service as worldview missionaries.

Understanding the Cultural Mandate

The scriptural justification for culture building starts with Genesis. At the dawn of creation, the earth is unformed, empty, dark, and undeveloped. Then, in a series of steps, God did the work of creation.

Until the sixth day, God did the creating directly, but then He changed His strategy. On the sixth day, God created the first human beings, and He ordered them to carry on where He left off: to live in His image and to have dominion (Gen. 1:26). From then on, creation would be primarily social and cultural; it would be the work of humans as they obey God's command to fill and subdue the earth (Gen. 1:28).

How is the role of humans as having "rule" (NIV) or "dominion" (KJV) over the creation similar to God's role as creator?

_____

_____

_____

How is it different?_____

_____

_____

_____

God proclaimed creation "very good," but He gave the task of building a civilization to His image bearers. "By being fruitful they must fill it even more; by subduing it they must form it even more," explains Al Wolters in *Creation Regained.*[1] Sometimes called the "cultural commission" or "cultural mandate," God's command is the culmination of His work in creation. The curtain has risen on the stage, and the director gives the characters their opening cue in the drama of history.[2]

If you struggle with the notion that the cultural mandate is an outdated Old Testament concept, here's an exciting assignment. Read Revelation chapters 4 and 5. Both chapters contain a majestic hymn of praise.

1. What is the basis of the praise in chapter 4 (especially 4:11)? _____

_____

_____

2. What is the basis of the praise in chapter 5 (especially 5:9)? _____

_____

_____

Revelation reflects teaching consistent with all of Scripture. The cultural mandate is still binding on us today. Though the Fall introduced sin and evil into human history, it did not erase the command to build a culture to the glory of God. The generations since Adam still bear children and build families. They still construct cities and governments. They still make music and works of art. Sin introduces a destructive power into God's created order, but it does not obliterate that order.

When we are redeemed, we are not only freed from the sinful motivations that drive us but also restored to fulfill our original purpose: to build societies and create culture—and, in doing so, to restore the created order.

STATEMENT It is our contention that the Lord's cultural commission is inseparable from the Great Commission. That may be a jarring statement for many conservative Christians, who, through much of the twentieth century, have shunned the notion of reforming culture, associating that concept with the liberal social gospel. The only task of the church, many evangelicals have believed, is to save as many lost souls as possible from a world literally going to hell. But this implicit denial of a Christian worldview is unbiblical and is the reason we have lost so much of our influence in the world. Salvation is not simply freedom from sin; salvation also means being restored to the task we were given in the beginning— the job of creating culture.

When we turn to the New Testament, we do not find it specifically commanding believers to be engaged in political issues or the law or education or the arts. It doesn't need to, because the cultural mandate given to Adam still applies. Every part of creation came from God's hand, every part was drawn into the mutiny of the human race, and every part will someday be redeemed. This is the apostle Paul's message to the Romans, in which he promises that "creation itself will be liberated from its bondage to decay" (Rom. 8:21). Redemption is not just for individuals; it is for all God's creation.

Compare Romans 8:21 to Matthew 6:10. What do the passages suggest about God's attitude toward restoration of His dominion on earth?_____

_____

_____

Paul made the point most strongly in Colossians 1:15-20, where he described the lordship of Christ in three ways: (1) *everything was made by and for Christ:* "By him all things were created: things in heaven and on earth, visible and invisible ... all things were created by him and for him"; (2) *everything holds together in Christ:* "He is before all things, and in him all things hold together"; (3) *everything will be reconciled by Christ:* "For God was pleased to have all his fullness dwell in him, and through him to reconcile to himself all things, whether things on earth or things in heaven."

Redemption covers all aspects of creation, and the end of time will not signal an end to creation but the beginning of a new heaven and a new earth: *God will make all things new* (Rev. 21:5).

The lesson is clear: Christians are saved not only *from* something (sin) but also *to* something (Christ's lordship over all of life). We are meant to proceed to the restoration of all God's creation, which includes private and public virtue; individual and family life; education and community; work, politics, and law; science and medicine; and literature, art, and music.

DAY TWO
Holy Ground

"Do not come any closer," God said. "Take off your sandals, for the place where you are standing is holy ground."—Exodus 3:5

God told Moses the ground was holy because of His presence, but for Christians all ground is holy. The goal of building a culture to the glory of God permeates everything we do, for there is no invisible dividing line between sacred and secular. We are to bring "all things" under the lordship of Christ, whether in the home or the corporate boardroom, the movie screen or the city council.

Because all ground is God's ground, a Christian must have a comprehensive worldview. Since God created with purpose, every aspect of the world was created with a structure, a character, a norm. These underlying principles are God's "laws"—God's design and purpose—for creation and can be known through both *special revelation* (God's Word given in Scripture) and *general revelation* (the structure of the world He made). They include both laws of nature and norms for human life.

We must press this point, because most people today operate on a fact/value distinction, believing that science uncovers "facts," which they believe to be reliable and true, while morality and religion are based on "values," which they believe to be subjective and relative to the individual.

Unfortunately, Christians often mirror this secular attitude. We tend to be confident about God's laws for nature, such as gravity, motion, and heredity; but we seem far less confident about God's laws for the family, education, or the state. Yet a truly Christian worldview draws no such distinction. It insists that God's laws govern all creation. Just as we have to learn to live in accord with the law of gravity, so, too, we must learn to live in accord with God's norms for society.

Think of the last time you know you broke one of God's moral laws. Would you have as readily disregarded a natural law such as gravity? ❏ yes ❏ no

Why do you suppose we ignore God's moral laws? _____
_____
_____
_____
_____

These two types of laws seem quite different—perhaps because only the latter are in a sense "voluntary." Stones fall, planets move in their orbits, seasons come and go, and the electron circles the nucleus—all without any choice in the matter—because God rules directly in the physical world. But in culture and society, God rules indirectly, entrusting human beings with the task of making tools, doing justice, producing art and music, educating children, and building houses. Though a stone cannot defy God's law of gravity, human beings *can* rebel against God's created order—and

they often do so. Yet that should not blind us to the fact that there is a single objective, universal order covering both nature and human nature.

All major cultures since the beginning of history have understood this concept of a universal order—all, that is, except postmodern Western culture. Despite the differences among them, all major civilizations have believed in a divine order that lays down the law for both natural and human realms. In the Far East it was called *Tao;* in ancient Egypt it was called *Ma'at;* in Greek philosophy it was called *Logos.*[3]

Read Psalm 147:15-20. How does the psalmist combine God's law of nature and His law of society?

_____
_____
_____
_____
_____

In almost a single breath, the Old Testament psalmist speaks of God's spreading the snow like wool and revealing His laws and decrees to Jacob, suggesting that there is no essential difference between God's laws for nature and those for people (see Ps. 147:16-19). Both types of law are part of a single universal order.

John's Gospel borrows the Greek word for this universal plan of creation *(logos)* and, in a startling move, identifies it with a personal being—Jesus Christ Himself. "In the beginning was the Word *[Logos],*" which is the source of creation (John 1:1). "Through him all things were made; without him nothing was made that has been made" (John 1:3). In other words, Jesus Himself is the source of the plan or design of creation.

As a result, obedience to Christ means living in accord with that plan in all aspects of life. Family and church, business and commerce, art and education, politics and law are institutions grounded in God's cre-

di·chot·o·my
\di-kät-e-me\ *n, pl* -mies
[Gk *dichotomia,* fr. *dichotomos]* (1610)
1: a division or the process of dividing into two esp. mutually exclusive or contradictory groups

Today's Prayer
Dear Father, Thank You for those heroes of the faith who made our world and communities a better place to live. Help me to make a difference in the places where I live, work, and worship.

ated order; they are not arbitrary in their configuration. A school is not a business and shouldn't be run like one; a family is not a state and shouldn't be run like one. Each has its own normative structure, ordained by God, and each has its own sphere of authority under God.[4]

For the Christian, there must be no dichotomy between the sacred and the secular because nothing lies outside of God's created order. Our task is to reclaim that entire created order for His dominion.

Read 2 Corinthians 10:4-5. In what arena did Paul indicate the battle takes place?

❏ government
❏ thought
❏ business

Christians need to be involved citizens. We need to represent Christ in every area of life, but Paul reminded us where the real battle rages. The world is a spiritual battleground, with two powers contending for the same territory. That territory is ultimately the minds and hearts of people.

What would you say to those who think Christians want to take over and "force their beliefs down the throats" of nonbelievers?

_____
_____
_____

God's adversary, Satan, has invaded creation and now attempts to hold it as occupied territory. In Christ, God launched a counteroffensive to reclaim His rightful domain, and we are God's soldiers in this ongoing battle. Redeemed, we are armed for the fight to extend that kingdom and push back the forces of Satan. The fighting may be fierce, but we must not lose hope, for what we are waging is essentially a mop-up operation. Because of the Resurrection, the war has been won, the victory is assured.[5]

We must show a skeptical world that Christians are here to serve and bear witness to the Truth. Our power comes from truth, not coercion. The history of Christianity is filled with glorious demonstrations of the truth and power of the gospel. Believers have renewed, restored, and, on occasions, even built new cultures.

DAY THREE
The Cost of the Cultural Mandate

"They overcame him
by the blood of the Lamb
and by the word of their testimony"–Revelation 12:11

A group of Jewish dissidents spread a preposterous message about a condemned felon who rose from the dead. From ignoble beginnings, Christianity grew into a force that dominated Western culture and then the world. How? By believers' dramatic testimony under persecution.

Why do you think the testimony of believers during times of persecution has such a powerful impact? _____
_____
_____
_____
_____

In the second century, the church father Tertullian reproached the secular authorities for the failure of their harsh policies: "Your cruelty [against us] does not profit you, however exquisite. Instead, it tempts people to our sect. As often as you mow us down, the more we grow in number. The blood of the Christians is the seed [of the church]." As a result of their striking witness, Christians soon filled every corner of ancient society. Tertullian mocked the Romans "We have filled all you have—cities, islands, forts, towns, assembly halls, even military camps, tribes, town councils, the palace, senate, and forum. We have left you nothing but the temples."[6]

What one Christian martyr or group of Christian martyrs has made the greatest impact on your life? _____
_____
_____

Even as Christians were growing in number, however, they were also working to transform the culture from within. Another second-century saint, Justin Martyr, showed the way.

As a young man, Justin decided to become a philosopher and studied with teachers of the various philosophical schools of the ancient world, from Stoicism to Aristotelianism to Platonism. Finally he realized that the truth he sought was found in Scripture, and he became a believer, but he did not abandon philosophy. By becoming a Christian, he argued, he had simply become a *better* philosopher: He was now able to gather all the individual truths discovered by various philosophers and make sense of them within the framework of the one perfect truth provided by divine revelation. "Whatever things were rightly said by any man, belong to us Christians," he wrote.[7]

Which of the following do you think more nearly reflects Justin's statement?

❑ **All religions are just different paths to God.**
❑ **All truth is God's truth.**
❑ **All truth is contained in the Scriptures.**

Justin wasn't urging Christians to be complacent relativists, as if all paths lead to God. He was resolutely opposed to the paganism of his day, and when he was put on trial for being a Christian, he refused to renounce his faith and was executed. No, Justin wasn't one to compromise the truths of Christianity. Yet he did believe that pagans perceive reality in part, and he taught that Christ is the fulfillment of all the partial truths embodied in pagan philosophy and culture. He recognized that all truth ultimately is God's truth. It derives from God and the structure He built into the universe.

Justin demonstrates that a Christian can have a great impact in a "secular" career. Philosophers had great influence in the ancient world. We are all called to be a testimony for Christ in the job setting. What are some specific (non-religious) careers today in which Christians can have a great influence professionally as well as personally?

_____
_____
_____
_____

Following Justin, the early church sought to fulfill both the Great Commission and the cultural mandate, to redeem both souls and society. And when the Roman Empire fell, it was Christians who saved civilization in one of the most inspiring chapters of Western history.

How the Church Saved Civilization

The Dark Ages began with a cold snap. In A.D. 406 the Rhine River froze, forming a bridge of ice that allowed a band of barbarians to cross from the Germanic territories into Roman territory. Successive waves of Vandals and Visigoths, Sueves and Alans then overran the rest of the Roman Empire and Europe, reducing cities to rubble and decimating populations. The entire substructure of Roman civilization was destroyed, to be replaced by small kingdoms ruled by illiterate, barbaric warrior-kings.

As the shadow of the Dark Ages fell over Western Europe, who emerged from the rubble? Who rebuilt Western civilization? The Christian church.[8]

Patrick the Slave

One of the most exciting episodes started in 401 A.D, when a 16-year-old British boy named Patricius was seized by a raiding Irish war party, abducted from his Romanized homeland, and sold to a petty Irish chieftain named Miliucc, who sent the boy out to shepherd his flocks. Patricius spent months alone in the hills, hunger gnawing at his innards and the clammy cold biting into his limbs, until finally he sought help from the only source left: He began to pray.

Before this time, Patricius had not really believed in the God his Christian parents had taught him about, and he thought priests were fools. But he found in God a source of strength that helped him endure six long years of bitter isolation and deprivation. "Tending flocks was my daily work, and I would pray constantly during the daylight hours," he wrote later. "The love of God and the fear of him surrounded me more and more—and faith grew and the Spirit was roused."[9]

Has a time of loss or deprivation ever caused you to turn to God?
❏ yes ❏ no   If so, describe the situation.

_____
_____
_____

Then one night, Patricius was awakened by a mysterious voice telling him that he was going home. "Look, your ship is ready," said the voice. Although uncertain of the direction or distance, Patricius set out for the sea. More than two hundred miles later, he found a ship bound for England.

When he reached his homeland, however, Patricius discovered that he no longer fit in with his people. "Hardened physically and psychologically by unsharable experiences, hopelessly behind his peers in education, he cannot settle down," wrote Thomas Cahill.[10] Then, one night, the former slave boy heard Christ's voice again, this time telling him to return to Ireland. He entered theological training and eventually returned as Patrick, missionary to the Irish.

Patrick the Missionary

This was no romantic return, set to the tune of Irish ballads. When St. Patrick began his mission, he faced pagan Irish priests (druids) who still practiced human sacrifice to their monstrous Celtic gods (often portrayed eating people). The fierce Irish warriors, believing that the human head was the seat of the soul, hung their enemies' skulls from their belts as trophies.

Into this bloodthirsty culture St. Patrick brought the Christian message of love and forgiveness, and established monasteries throughout the land. Whereas in earlier centuries the monastic movement had been a way to retreat from the world, in Ireland it became a way to revolutionize the world, replacing the old values of a warrior society with the new values of Christianity. Within St. Patrick's lifetime, warriors cast aside their swords of battle, intertribal warfare decreased markedly, and the slave trade ended. A culture of battle and brute power was transformed by an ethic that sanctified manual labor, poverty, and service. A culture of illiteracy and ignorance became a culture of learning.

Read Colossians 3:10. How has knowing Christ changed how you value work?

_____
_____
_____
_____

Today's Prayer

Lord, Thank You for the opportunity I have to be Your ambassador in the place where I do my daily work. Help me live out the values of my Christian faith so that as others watch my life and listen to my words, their hearts will turn to You.

The Legacy of St. Patrick

"I will make rivers flow on barren heights,
and springs within the valleys.
I will turn the desert into pools of water,
and the parched ground into springs."—Isaiah 41:18

After Rome fell, the Irish monasteries also became refuges for vast numbers of Christian scholars and monks fleeing the barbarians, streaming in from all across Europe, and as far away as Egypt, Armenia, and Syria. As a result, says historian Kenneth Clark, "for quite a long time—almost a hundred years—western Christianity survived by clinging to places like Skellig Michael, a pinnacle of rock eighteen miles from the Irish coast"[11] And survive it they did. Eventually a flood of missionaries from Ireland fanned out across Scotland, England, and the Euro-pean continent. All along the way the monks established monasteries and carried on their tradition of copying and preserving the Bible, along with every other book they could get their hands on—including the great classics of the Greeks and Ro-mans, some of which had not been seen in Europe for centuries. They also taught their converts Latin, music, and painting.

To give some idea of their success, by the early 600s nearly seven hundred monastic communities had been established along the rocky coasts and mountains of Scotland alone, and between A.D. 650 and A.D. 850 more than half of all known biblical commentaries were written by Irishmen. Everywhere they went, the Irish monks carried their Bibles and books around their waists, just as the Irish pagans had once tied their enemies' skulls to their belts.

If you were to display your trophies—those items of greatest value to you and of which you are most proud—around your waist, what would those trophies be?

_____
_____
_____
_____
_____
_____

This is "how the Irish saved civilization," to use Cahill's words, for it was the disciplined labor of the monks that stanched the tide of barbarism, preserved the best of Western culture, and infused new life into the decadent monasticism of the continent. Instead of being a refuge from the world, as it had been, the monastery became the center of culture, replacing the dying cities and expanding into a vast complex populated by monks, workers, servants, and dependents. Gradually, "the woody swamp became a hermitage, a religious house, a farm, an abbey, a village, a seminary, a school of learning, and a city."[12]

How did the monks defeat the forces of barbarism? (Check all that apply.)

❑ **an example of sacrificial service**
❑ **force of arms**
❑ **spiritual conversion**
❑ **political strength**
❑ **hard work**
❑ **education**

The Church and Culture

As we began this study, on day 1 we studied what power?

❑ the power of political organization
❑ the power of the military
❑ the power of ideas

Write a phrase or sentence from each of the following Scriptures that illustrates the power God gave the monks to transform their world.

Proverbs 16:32 _____
_____
_____
_____
_____

Matthew 5:5 _____
_____
_____
_____
_____

John 19:11_____
_____
_____
_____
_____

2 Corinthians 10:4 -5 _____
_____
_____
_____
_____

1 Thessalonians 2:7 _____
_____
_____
_____

What's more, this astonishing feat was accomplished again and again throughout the Dark Ages. From the north, Vikings repeatedly swooped down on the coasts or sailed deep inland on the rivers to loot and destroy, murdering people, ruining fields, plundering wealth, and burning cities across Europe. From the east, the Magyars and Avars, the Huns and Mongols, swept successively across the steppes, leaving similar devastation and death in their wake. Each time, Christianity showed its unquenchable, supernatural power of spiritual regeneration. Each time, the monastic communities arose from the rubble to become islands of peace and spiritual order.

What Scriptures would you add to the list?

_____
_____
_____
_____
_____
_____
_____
_____
_____
_____

The monks' first concern was to nourish the inner life of faith. But spiritual reform inevitably led to social change as they fulfilled the call to defend the oppressed and speak boldly against evil in high places. In the monks, says historian Christopher Dawson, "the lawless feudal nobles, who cared nothing for morality or law, recognized the presence of something stronger than brute force—a numinous supernatural power they dared not ignore."[13]

Lasting peace could not come to Europe, however, until the barbarians themselves were evangelized, and one of the most exciting chapters in the history of the Christian church is the transformation of the barbarians from bloodthirsty warriors into peace-loving farmers, determined to live by the work of their own hands instead of by theft and plunder.[14] As the barbarians were converted and the destructive invasions ceased, European society began to flourish. Cities grew, guilds emerged to protect the interests of the crafts and professions, and ideas of representative government took root.

In this setting, Christianity gave birth to a new institution, the university, which developed from schools attached to the great cathedrals in places such as Paris and Bologna, eventually replacing the monasteries as centers of learning and culture. Later, the Reformation would spark a quantum leap in culture formation, inspiring a new work ethic that would fuel the industrial revolution and create a political climate that made free democracies possible.

Much of the secular world sadly believes Christians are ignorant and the enemies of education and science. In outline form describe how you would explain that Christianity is actually the father of science and education. _____
_____
_____
_____
_____
_____
_____
_____
_____

This is how Christianity is meant to function in society—not just as a private faith but as a creative force in the culture. The inner life of faith must shape our actions out in the world. In every choice and decision we make, we either help to overcome the forces of barbarism—whether medieval or modern—or acquiesce to those forces; we either help build a life-giving, peace-loving ethos or we fan the flames of egoism and destruction.

In what practical ways can you respond to the information you have been studying?

❏ I can prepare myself and defend the faith in the intellectual arena.
❏ I can get positively involved in my local school or government.
❏ I can express appreciation to believers I know who are serving Christ in secular jobs.
❏ Your response: _____
_____
_____
_____
_____

DAY FIVE
A Creative Force in the Culture

"I will remain in the world no longer, but they are still in the world, and I am coming to you. Holy Father, protect them by the power of your name —the name you gave me—so that they may be one as we are one."—John 17:11

At the dawn of the new millennium, we face the same challenge and opportunity that the early church and the medieval monks faced: to build a culture of individuals informed by a biblical worldview. People everywhere today are searching for answers that make sense of the world. We have an opportunity to present the gospel and see a new revival of Christianity throughout the world. Is this false optimism? On all sides I hear battle-weary evangelicals say that we have lost the culture war and that we might as well turn back to building our churches instead. But in light of our historical heritage, we dare not give in to despair. That would be not only a sin (lack of faith in God's sovereignty) but also a misreading of our times. To leave the cultural battlefield now would be to desert the cause just when we are on the threshold of a great opportunity.

From all that you have studied in this course, what reasons can you list to show that now is an historic moment of opportunity?

_____
_____
_____
_____

In recent years, all the grand propositions advanced over the past century have fallen, one by one, like toy soldiers. The twentieth century was the age of ideology, of the great "isms": Communism, socialism, Nazism, liberalism, scientism. Everywhere, ideologues nursed visions of creating the ideal society by some utopian scheme.

Today all the major ideological constructions are being tossed on the ash heap of history. All that remains is the cynicism of postmodernism, with its bankrupt assertions that there *is* no objective truth or meaning, that we are free to create our own truth as long as we understand that it is nothing more than a subjective dream, a comforting illusion.

As the reigning ideologies crumble, people are caught in an impasse: Having believed that individual autonomy was the holy grail that would lead to liberation, they now see that it has led only to moral chaos and state coercion. The time is ripe for a message that the social peace and personal fulfillment people really crave is available only in Christianity.

The church has stood unshaken through the ebb and flow of two millennia. It has survived the persecutions of the early centuries, the barbarian invasions of the Middle Ages, and the intellectual assaults of the modern era. Its solid walls rise up above the ruins littered across the intellectual landscape. God forbid that we, heirs of saints and martyrs, should falter at this pivotal moment.

Of all the reasons we have written in this study, none is more important than this: take time to pray that we, the body of Christ, will rise to the challenge before us. Pray that the new century may become a "springtime" of Christianity.

The dawn of the new millennium is a time for Christians to celebrate, to raise our confidence, to blow trumpets, and to fly the flag high. This is the time to make a compelling case that Christianity offers the most rational and realistic hope for both personal redemption and social renewal. We must take our stand, united in Christ, making a conscious effort among all true believers to come together across racial, ethnic, and confessional lines, just as Jesus commanded (John 17).

Christian Unity

Jesus prayed fervently that we would be one with one another, as He is one with the Father. Why? So that the world will know that He is the Christ. Christian unity is the key to evangelism. I truly believe that much of the church's weakness can be traced to its inability or unwillingness to obey the command to strive for unity in Christ.

Carefully read the great high-priestly prayer of Jesus in John 17. What requests did Jesus make repeatedly in the prayer?_____

_____
_____

Jesus' words show the extreme value He placed on Christian unity. His repeated requests were for protection and unity of believers. This fact is difficult for many evangelicals (as well as Catholics and Orthodox) to accept, and understandably so. The bloody wounds inflicted in the Reformation and Counter-Reformation remain raw and painful, and deep doctrinal differences continue to divide believers. Conservative believers are distrustful of ecumenism because of the danger of glossing over those differences. Focusing on worldview, however, can help build bridges. We share a biblical worldview that forms the basis for our united front in the face of secularism.

Review again the three-part grid of worldview. How much common conviction do conservative evangelicals, Catholics, and Orthodox believers share on the issues of:

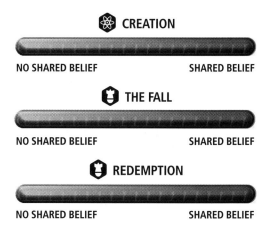

Abraham Kuyper, a committed Calvinist, saw more clearly than any other modern figure that the battle of our times is worldview against worldview, principle against principle, and that in this battle against the forces of modernity, Catholics and Protestants must stand side by side on worldview issues. More than a hundred years ago in his famous Stone Lectures at Princeton, Kuyper argued that when we understand Christianity as a worldview, we "might be enabled once more to take our stand by the side of Romanism in opposition to modern pantheism." For "what we have in common with Rome … are precisely those fundamentals of our Christian creed now most fiercely assaulted by the modern spirit."

As evangelical believers, we clearly do not endorse or accept the sacramental theology of Catholicism regarding salvation.

We do, however, recognize with Kuyper our common ground concerning creation and the fallen nature of humanity. The naturalistic worldview constitutes a common enemy to both Evangelicals and Catholics.

Kuyper was only echoing themes expressed back in 1541. In the very midst of the Reformation battles, a group of Catholic and Protestant leaders, including a cardinal from the Vatican, met at Regensburg, Germany, in the Colloquy of Ratisbon. The group reached agreement on the doctrine of justification, which had been the great opening wedge of the Reformation (though discussions foundered on other issues, such as the Mass). One of the Protestant participants wrote a letter to a friend, in which he said, "You will be astonished that our opponents yielded so much … [they] have retained the substance of the true doctrine."[15] The writer of that letter was a young aide to the Protestant negotiators. His name was John Calvin.

Today we need the kind of stand Calvin sought and Kuyper so powerfully urged on us. We need what C. S. Lewis called *Mere Christianity:* believers standing together, rallying around the great truths of Scripture. Only when such unity is visible in the world will we truly experience the power of the gospel.

Have you experienced a time when denominational differences faded and believers came together because you shared a common worldview?
❏ yes ❏ no ❏ I'm not sure.

If so, describe the situation.

_____
_____
_____
_____
_____
_____
_____
_____
_____

Different believers have described times when a shared worldview overcame the differences that separate believers.

- Bill described his family reunion. Most of the family members are not Christians. Those who are Christians share a common goal to share Christ with their lost family members.
- Annette shared about her work in an interdenominational home for unwed mothers.
- Cheryl served in international mission work. She shared how Christians come together to witness to a lost society.

Standing together as the people of God, we must obey the great commission and the cultural mandate: first to win the lost, and then to build a culture. Christians must seize this moment to show the world, just as the Irish did centuries ago, that Christianity is not only true … it is humanity's one great hope.

---

[1]Al Wolters, *Creation Regained: Biblical Basics for a Reformational Worldview* (Grand Rapids: Eerdmans, 1985), 36. The following discussion relies heavily on Wolters, who in turn popularized Dutch philosopher Herman Dooyeweerd. See Dooyeweerd, *A New Critique of Theoretical Thought* (Lewiston, N.Y.: Edwin Mellen Press, 1997).

[2]Critics sometimes contend that Genesis gives two creation accounts, the second one beginning in Genesis 2:4, but this is a misunderstanding of the literary structure. The first chapter of Genesis and the first few verses of chapter 2 function as a prologue, setting the cosmic stage and raising the curtain. The drama itself actually begins in chapter 2 as Adam and Eve, the first husband and wife, begin societal life. Their tasks of tending the Garden and naming the animals mark the beginning of cultural life. True, the author uses a flashback technique to give more details on how Adam and Eve were created, but that does not make this a second creation story. Instead, this passage relates how the cultural mandate begins to be fulfilled in actual history.

[3]C.S. Lewis, *The Abolition of Man* (New York: Touchstone, 1975).

4Dutch theologian and statesman Abraham Kuyper developed this argument of the spheres of authority. See Abraham Kuyper, *Christianity: A Total World and Life System* (Marlborough, N.H.: Plymouth Rock Foundation, 1996). One of the most striking passages in Scripture on the God-given character of the order of creation is Isaiah 28:23-29, where we learn that the Lord teaches the farmer his business. There is a right way to plow, to sow, and to thresh, depending on the kind of grain the farmer is growing. A good farmer knows that, and this knowledge is from the Lord, for the Lord teaches him. This is not a teaching from the Scripture, from special revelation, but a teaching through the structures of creation, from general revelation. It comes to us by experience with soil, seeds, and plow.

[5]See Wolters, *Creation Regained,* chapter 4; and Charles Colson with Ellen Santilli Vaughn, *Kingdoms in Conflict,* (New York: William Morrow; Grand Rapids: Zondervan, 1987), chapter 7.

[6]Tertullian, as quoted in Henry Chadwick, *The Early Church* (New York: Penguin, 1993), 65.

[7]Justin Martyr, as quoted in *Chadwick, The Early Church,* 74-83.

[8]This dramatic story is told in Christopher Dawson's *Religion and the Rise of Western Culture* (New York: Doubleday, Image Books, 1991) and Thomas Cahill's *How the Irish Saved Civilization: The Untold Story of Ireland's Heroic Role from the Fall of Rome to the Rise of Medieval Europe* (New York: Doubleday, 1995).

[9]Saint Patrick, as quoted in Thomas Cahill, *How the Irish Saved Civilization,* 102.

[10]Cahill, *How the Irish Saved Civilization,* 105.

[11]Kenneth Clark, *Civilization: A Personal View* (New York: Harper & Row, 1969), 8.

[12]John Henry Newman, as quoted in Christopher Dawson, *Religion and the Rise of Western Culture,* 53-54. Newman explains how the monks accomplished all this: "Silent men were observed about the country, or discovered in the forest, digging, clearing, and building; and other silent men, not seen, were sitting in the cold cloister, tiring their eyes and keeping their attention on the stretch, while they painfully copied and recopied the manuscripts which they had saved."

[13]Dawson, *Religion and the Rise of Western Culture,* 126.

[14]An eyewitness account describes the transformation of Scandinavian culture imbued with better principles and have now learned to love peace and truth and to be content with their poverty. … Of all men they are the most temperate both in food and in their habits, loving above all things thrift and modesty" (Dawson, *Religion and the Rise of Western Culture,* 98).

[15]Letter from John Calvin to William Farel written from Ratisbon, 11 May 1541. See John Calvin, *Letters of John Calvin,* ed. Jules Bonnet, vol. 1 (Philadelphia: Presbyterian Board of Publication, 1858), 260.

Transforming Our Culture

God has called us to be worldview missionaries, to both carry the message of Christ and be the hands of Christ, touching earthly needs. In this unit you will consider practical actions to transform our world.

Anything Can Happen Here

The first day at Special Post 1 on DeKalb Avenue, Bed-Stuy in Brooklyn, Officer Salvatore Bartolomeo keeps his eyes open, watches, gives himself time to learn the beat. He passes an abandoned car, its stripped carcass halfway out into the street. The whole neighborhood looks similarly scavenged. Twenty dilapidated, garbage-strewn, pot-bunkered blocks. Anything can happen here. Anything does. Daily.

The Lafayette Towers, the high-rise projects, loom ahead. First-day jitters tell him that galleries of thousands are watching his every move as three teenagers in army fatigue jackets and baggy pants approach.

"Hello," says Officer Sal. "How you doing today?" The kids look down and keep walking. *I'm Brooklyn just like you,* Sal wants to say. *I grew up here.* For the rest of the morning he walks DeKalb Avenue, says hello, and learns his beat. Sentries for drug dealers are stationed at various locations around the precinct. They've all got a good long view, and they'd be long gone before he could get to them.

He could have that abandoned car towed, though. It would be a start at cleaning up the neighborhood. His assignment here is part of New York City's experiment with a new theory of crime reduction, and his job is to start with the simple things, the first steps in restoring public order. He'll figure out how to bring down the dealers later.

Sal walks the streets close to one of the neighborhood schools. The grade-schoolers begin to come up and hold his hand and are soon calling him "Officer Sal." The middle schoolers, hanging back on street corners, start threading their way toward their homerooms when he shows up. The high schoolers are sometimes more stubborn about standing their ground, but then he has a chance to go up and ask them, "How's it going?" He quickly becomes a celebrated pain in the neck, a favorite target for the put-down artists. Sal always gives as good as he gets. In a few weeks he can call dozens of the kids by name, and sometimes his greetings are actually returned.

The first time Sal posts himself by the check store, he sees a panhandler. "Step off, or I'll run you in for panhandling." The man rises slowly to his feet, "You miss your chance to join the gestapo or what? This is America."

"Yes, it is. A country where people can go into a store without fear of being knocked over the head when they come out."

Sal not only patrols the streets but also conducts "vertical searches," climbing the stairs of the walk-up tenements. On one such venture he finds the body of a young woman, sexually abused, then shot in the back of the head. She is only one of the many young people who will die by violence on his beat. In Sal's years on DeKalb Avenue, the funeral home becomes almost another stop on his rounds. He always goes in, says a prayer. It doesn't matter what kind of gangster the young man or woman might have been. He kneels down and prays.

People habitually run the stoplight at DeKalb and Tenth, even when Sal is right there, blowing his whistle. So Sal hops into the back of a cab and the chase is on. At the next light Sal gets out and strolls over to the rusted-out Chevy. The driver can't go anywhere, so now he's "awfully sorry." Then he's even sorrier because his registration has expired. Sorrier still because his outstanding tickets have resulted in a warrant for his arrest. And truly distraught when he steps out of the car and Sal sees the bag of marijuana on the floor.

Before long, Sal finds cabs nearly as useful as his old cruiser. Nabbing people who run red lights is netting him drug dealers and muggers.

One of Sal's jobs is to work at reducing crime by destroying its protective surroundings, so he goes to work with the sanitation department. One day, the neighborhood sees a transformation. The sanitation department arrives with a regular mechanized army. With the assistance of a crane and wrecking ball, the giant earthmovers raze the abandoned buildings. The wrecked cars are towed at the same time. The users and abusers have no place to hide anymore.

Anything *can* happen here! Sal thinks.

In the spring of 1993, Sal receives an invitation to a block party. The Neighborhood Watch Association is cooking for the community. This is the first time anyone has dared to hold such an event.

The first party is quickly followed by others. People are no longer frightened to be out on the streets, at least in the daytime. The neighborhood has gone from a living hell to at least a borderline place. Now anything truly *can* happen here, including community events.

By 1994, Sal's hips and legs are telling him that his days as a street cop have come to an end. He applies to go back into a cruiser, and the transfer comes through. His beat will be close to DeKalb, though, so he'll be able to roll back through and see his friends.

On his last day, a group of people come up to him. An elderly woman to whom he gave CPR. Two block-association presidents. The tough kid who mouthed off at him the first day on the job. About forty people in all. They are, almost to a person, his favorites, and he wonders how they know about each other.

The Towers security guard steps forward. He's carrying a trophy, a loving cup. "Officer Sal," he says, "we know you're being reassigned. But before you go, we want to say thanks. We got you this trophy. You won a lot of battles here, and you helped us win back our neighborhood."

Everyone cheers, applauds.

Sal looks at the inscription on the cup: "To Officer Salvatore Bartolomeo. 'Robo Cop.' Six Years' Dedicated Service."

Yes, something good *is* happening here.

DAY ONE
There Goes the Neighborhood

"I will listen to what God the Lord will say;
he promises peace to his people, his saints —
but let them not return to folly."—Psalm 85:8

Salvatore Bartolomeo's policing of the streets of Brooklyn illustrates an exciting approach to crime prevention. As Officer Sal pounded his beat, he dealt, of course, with serious crimes. But he also helped clear out the things that attract crime to a neighborhood: the signs of social disorder and decay, such as loitering,

> The crumbling of order and resulting self-destruction of the community start with broken windows not being fixed; next prostitutes and vagrants are allowed to loiter; soon delinquents and youth gangs realize they can act with impunity; and by then the neighborhood is well on its way toward disintegration.
>
> —Andrew Peyton Thomas[1]

panhandling, graffiti, abandoned cars, vacant buildings, and littered lots. The success of this form of policing in New York City suggests that it may well be the key to restoring America's crime-ravaged inner cities. And significantly, it builds on the classic Christian understanding that civil peace comes only from a just and responsible social order—something sorely needed in our culture.

Over the past few decades, both crime and public disorder have risen sharply. One significant cause is the misguided policies of the 1960s and 1970s, shaped by the assumption that the cause of crime is poverty, an approach that seemed to excuse crime by blaming it on the environment.[2]

If the assumption that poverty causes crime is false, then what is the real cause of crime?

As drug use was soaring, causing a domino effect of crime, Great-Society welfare programs were weakening family structure. As a result, gangs of poorly parented juveniles roamed the streets. The resulting social chaos turned America's inner cities into combat zones, and nothing seemed able to stop the downward spiral. Violent crime (per 100,000 persons) grew from 161 in 1960 to 758 in 1992, a 470 percent increase. Property crimes (per 100,000 persons) grew from 1,726 in 1960 to 4,903 in 1992, a 284 percent increase.[3]

Many people blame our inability to respond to crime effectively on the fact that in many cities the police were outnumbered and outgunned. But it wasn't just in-

sufficient manpower and firepower that allowed crime to flourish. It was also a flawed worldview.

The Supreme Court's Contribution

In the 1970s and 1980s, the courts introduced a novel concept of civil liberties that transformed disorderly and disruptive public behavior into a civil right. Most significant were two Supreme Court cases, one in 1972 and the other in 1983, striking down statutes against vagrancy and loitering. In the 1972 case, Justice William O. Douglas waxed colorful about the rights of "rogues and vagabonds" to roam the countryside as "loafers or litterers," as if drunks and panhandlers were merely romantic wanderers. The real culprits, the Court suggested, were the uptight, middle-class moralists who were trying to force all dissenters to conform.[4]

In throwing out laws against vagrancy and loitering, however, the high court departed from a legal tradition that extended as far back as the Middle Ages, and even to ancient Athens. Historically, these laws were designed to discourage "the extreme individualistic license" that marks people who flout social convention and disrupt social order, explains attorney Andrew Peyton Thomas. The laws especially targeted those once referred to as "hobos," "tramps," or "bums"—drifters and transients who "rebel against family and career commitments" and prefer a rootless, roaming existence, sleeping in public places and begging from responsible citizens. "Vagrancy laws sought to uphold public order and personal responsibility by encouraging gainful employment and stable ties to family and neighbors."[5]

In the two landmark cases cited above, the court abruptly abandoned the historical attempt to "uphold public order." Vagrants and drifters were no longer regarded as a danger to social stability but were considered a persecuted class deserving protection. It was civilized society that the Court condemned for shirking its obligations to misfits and miscreants.

What thinker we have studied laid the groundwork of thought behind the supreme court's ruling?

❑ Descartes
❑ Rousseau
❑ Freud
❑ Marx

A domino effect followed from these cases, as lower courts overturned state and municipal laws that had given police authority to restrain behavior in public places. Before long, the streets, parks, and subways of our major cities were filled with panhandlers, prostitutes, drunks urinating on the sidewalks, and people sleeping on heating grates. We maintain that this process can be traced to the thoughts of Rousseau.

The Mental Health Profession

The same concept of civil liberties captured the mental-health profession, as psychiatrists such as R. D. Laing began to argue that there is no generally applicable standard of normalcy and that the mentally ill simply hold a different perspective on life that is equally valid.[6]

The idea that all perspectives of reality are equally valid came from

❑ Plato
❑ Aristotle
❑ postmodernism
❑ idealism

Civil libertarians began to portray the mentally ill as just another oppressed group and to champion the absolute right of everyone, sane or insane, to live by their own perceptions of reality. The American Civil Liberties Union pressed the point home with several lawsuits. The result was a massive movement to de-institutionalize the mentally ill, unleashing a flood of mentally unstable, disoriented people onto the streets of the nation's cities. Many promptly became homeless, often acting in ways that were menacing or intimidating to ordinary citizens. Only in an America influenced by postmodernist thought would such blatant disregard for common sense be enshrined in law.

So at the same time that crime was soaring and the mentally ill were taking over parks and other public spaces, the police were being handcuffed by the courts in their ability to curb antisocial and disorderly behavior. The symbol of the times was "The Wildman of 96th Street," a crack-addicted veteran who for years stalked women, pushed people in front of cars, and generally terrorized people on Manhattan's Upper West Side because authorities were unable either to jail or institutionalize him. Repeated across the country, such incidents sent a clear signal that authorities were unable or unwilling to prevent minor forms of disorder and therefore were unlikely to prevent major crimes as well. As a result, law-abiding citizens began to move out of the cities, while lawbreakers moved in.

How did the Supreme Court add to the problem of crime in the neighborhoods of America? _____
_____
_____
_____

If we hope to restore our cities, we must understand and critique the worldview that unleashed this disorder. This novel view of civil liberties was the direct result of rejecting the biblical doctrine of creation and replacing the Garden of Eden with a hypothetical "state of nature." In this secularized myth of human origins, individuals are the only ultimate reality, and individual rights trump all others; the requirements of public order are outweighed by the imperious demands of individual autonomy. Thus civil liberties came to be defined in excessively individualistic terms, denying the right of communities to promote their values or to insist on standards of public behavior. This definition was adopted by sociologists, aggressively promoted by civil-liberty organizations, enshrined in court decisions, and finally even accepted by the police themselves.

Toward a Solution

The solution, therefore, cannot consist of simply building more prisons and incarcerating more criminals. Indeed, America has tried that route. The 1970s saw the biggest prison-building boom in our nation's history. Speeches sprinkled with slogans about "law and order" and "getting tough on crime" were sure winners on the campaign trail. Arrests rose, prisons became overcrowded, and crime continued to rise.

Then, in the early 1980s, a breakthrough came when social scientists George Kelling and James Q. Wilson advanced what became known as the broken-window theory. They discovered that if a broken window in a building is left unrepaired, soon all the windows are knocked out.[7]

Why do you suppose the broken-window theory works? _____

_____

_____

_____

_____

Damage left untended sends a message that no one cares, that no one is in charge, and that further vandalism will incur no penalty. Hence, a single broken window soon attracts the kind of people who will smash more windows. Likewise, a city that allows pockets of public disorder, starting with graffiti and litter, sends a message that authorities are either unwilling or unable to enforce standards of behavior—to control their space and their citizens. Once a city sends that message, law-abiding citizens leave and the criminal element is attracted—exactly the cycle that has ravaged America's major cities.

In the early 1990s, New York Police Chief William Bratton took the broken-window theory to heart and persuaded New York's newly elected mayor and tough ex-prosecutor Rudolph Guiliani to give the theory a try. The order went out to police in Precincts 69 and 75 and to Brooklyn, where Officer Sal was stationed, to "fix broken windows"—that is, to arrest petty offenders and clean up the neighborhoods.[8] The police adopted a policy of zero tolerance for any violation of public order, and in the process they soon discovered that there is indeed a "seamless web" between controlling petty crime and restraining major crime.

- Whereas before they had ignored turnstile jumping at subways, officers now nabbed the offenders, who, often as not, turned out to be muggers.
- Whereas before they had turned a blind eye to minor traffic violations, they now stopped all traffic violators, which often led to the discovery of drugs and guns in the cars.
- They chased away loiterers and panhandlers, many of whom were drug dealers looking for a sale.

In three years, in Precinct 75, once one of the most dangerous places in America, homicides dropped from 129 to 47.[9]

Civil libertarians attacked Bratton's crime-prevention program repeatedly and even sued the New York Police Department, citing the earlier Supreme Court decisions and arguing that the program targeted people simply because they were poor or homeless. But Bratton had framed his policies carefully to penalize behavior, not status (e.g., homelessness), and the courts denied the challenges of civil libertarians.[10] (One might suspect that judges were also responding to public clamor to end the chaos.)

Cities around the country began imitating New York, with equally dramatic results. Politicians were quick to trumpet their successes anywhere they could find a camera or microphone. It was as if they had discovered the Holy Grail, the long-sought answer to crime. Yet all that Guiliani and the others have "discovered" is well-established, fundamental biblical truth.

Thousands of years before the broken-window theory, the Jewish people had already captured the idea in *shalom.* Although popularly translated "peace," the connotations of the term are actually much broader than the absence of hostilities. *Shalom* refers to peace in a positive sense, the result of a rightly ordered community.

When people live together according to God's moral order—in *shalom*—there is civility and harmony. The best way to reduce crime is not to react after the fact with punishments and rehabilitation but to discourage it before it happens by creating an ordered and civil community life.

How is the "broken window" theory an expression of shalom? _____
_____
_____
_____
_____
_____

DAY TWO

What Can We Do?

"When the foundations are being destroyed, what can the righteous do?"–Psalm 11:3

The biblical basis for creating *shalom* is the doctrine of creation, which tells us we were created for community. Contrary to the notion of a "state of nature," with its war of all against all, the Bible teaches that we are not autonomous individuals. Instead, we are created in the image of the One who in his very essence is a community of being—that is, the Trinity. God's very nature is reciprocal love and communication among the persons of the Trinity. God has created us as beings who need relationships, and the God-ordained institutions of society make rightful demands we are morally obligated to fulfill.

These institutions are not impositions on our freedom but expressions of our inherently social nature. "God might have created men as disconnected individuals," wrote Kuyper. Instead, He created an original couple, with the result that, by birth, each of us "is organically united with the whole race."[11] This social nature is expressed through our social institutions, and these institutions need some kind of authority structure to direct their activities to the common good. Thus to create and maintain order in our political communities, God has ordained the state. All of us have a moral imperative to obey proper authority and to work for justice and *shalom.*

What does Romans 13:1 teach concerning our responsibility to governing authorities?
_____
_____
_____
_____

In the fourth century, Augustine taught that peace (*shalom*) is "the tranquillity produced by order" (*tranquillitas ordin-is*). A political community can enjoy peace and harmony only by following the moral order, he wrote; for only an ordered civil life allows fallen human beings to "live and work together." Therefore, the primary role of the state is not to chase down criminals after the fact but to nurture the *tranquillitas ordinis*, using its unique powers of coercion to that end. *Tranquillitas ordinis* is also the duty of every Christian, for though our sights are set ultimately on the "City of God," as long as we live in the "City of Man," it is morally imperative for us to work for the peace of that city. This is not optional; it is the only way to keep evil in check.[12]

What do each of the following passages contribute to the Christian's responsibility for the tranquillitas ordinis?

1 Thessalonians 4:11-12 _____

_____

_____

_____

_____

Ephesians 4:28 _____

_____

_____

_____

_____

Matthew 22:37-40 _____

_____

_____

_____

_____

_____

1 Peter 2:11-15 _____

_____

_____

_____

_____

Obviously the Scripture has a great deal to say about Christians's behavior in society. What verses would you add to the list?

_____

_____

_____

_____

For centuries this biblical view of communal order dominated Western thought. In the last century, William Wilberforce, the great evangelical and British statesman, noted that "the most efficient way to prevent the greater crimes is by punishing the smaller, and by endeavoring to repress the general spirit of licentiousness, which is the parent of every kind of vice."[13] The same philosophy influenced the original principles of policing laid out by Sir Robert Peel in 1829. The first job of the police, said Peel, is not fighting crime but keeping the peace.[14] Seventy years later, in the first New York City charter, the same principles were repeated: "It is hereby made the duty of the police department to especially preserve the public peace, … remove all nuisances in the public streets, … restrain all unlawful and disorderly conduct."[15] As a result, at the turn of the century it was the police who developed the first food and soup lines; they built police stations with extra space where migrants could stay until they found work; they referred beggars to charitable agencies; and yes, they even helped lost children find their way home. Officer Sal would have been right at home.

The success this approach has exhibited in restoring America's major cities underlines the wisdom of the classic biblical view and provides powerful evidence that it is, in fact, true—true to our nature, true to who we are. The chaos of the last few decades attests to the disastrous consequences of living by a false philosophy of human nature, one that denies the biblical teaching of creation and substitutes a secular myth of our origins and our nature. The secular view has been tried and found wanting, and its failure opens a wonderful opportunity for Christians to make a case for a biblical view of human nature and community.

The good news is that we have positive evidence that the biblical worldview really works. As you read the following case studies, underline specific actions people have taken to restore their communities.

CASE STUDY 1 In Newport News, Virginia, a run-down housing project was scheduled for demolition after police grew weary of constantly answering calls about burglars and drug dealers. The officers decided to clean up the area in preparation for new construction. They carted away trash, removed abandoned cars, filled in potholes. To everyone's surprise, burglary rates suddenly dropped by 35 percent. The police had inadvertently stumbled on the broken-window theory. Restoring order really does create "the tranquillity of order."[16]

CASE STUDY 2 In Charleston, South Carolina, Police Chief Reuben Greenberg decided to fight crime by cleaning up inner-city neighborhoods. Soon formerly crime-ridden areas were clean and neat, signaling that disruptive and disorderly behavior would not be tolerated.

Greenberg then went after open-air drug dealing. He simply placed uniformed police officers on every corner where drugs were being sold. The officers didn't question anyone; they just stood there. Yet the impact on business was immediate. No one came near the drug dealers. They were forced to leave the area or go out of business altogether.

Next Greenberg revived the original 1930s vision of public housing as a refuge for the poor, not a haven for crime. The housing authority began to screen tenants, refusing to accept violent criminals, and today public housing is one of the safest places to live in the entire city.

Finally, to fight soaring juvenile crime, Greenberg reintroduced truant officers. If school-age children were spotted anywhere in the city during school hours, a truant officer was dispatched to pick them up and return them to school. Results were immediate: a 24 percent permanent decrease in such daytime crimes as purse snatching, car theft, and shoplifting.[17]

CASE STUDY 3 Even kids can get in on the act. A few years ago, in Alabama, 50 Christian teenagers armed with hedge clippers and weed whackers descended on a neighborhood of mostly elderly people, determined to tackle the overgrown bushes that provided hiding places for vandals, burglars, and muggers. The kids trimmed towering hedges, thinned low-hanging tree branches, even replaced burned-out lights and installed peepholes in doors. The project, called Youth Cutting Down on Crime, was organized by Neighbors Who Care, a Prison Fellowship ministry that mobilizes churches to help crime victims.

A Method that Works

Why does establishing order work so well as a crime preventive? Because it expresses an underlying moral order and shows that the community is willing to enforce it. Such is the finding of one of the largest studies ever undertaken into the causes of crime and delinquency. Harvard University, the Kaiser Institute, and the University of Chicago joined together to survey 382 Chicago neighborhoods, all with different ethnic, racial, and economic characteristics. They could find no common thread in traditional demographics. In some minority communities crime was high, while in others it was low. The same was true with poverty. The only common pattern researchers found was that rates of violence were lower in areas that had a strong sense of community values and willingness to impose those values on the public space—where neighbors, for example, felt free to step in and discipline kids who skip school, scribble graffiti on the walls, or hang out on the streets. In other words, even disadvantaged communities can overcome adverse conditions if they have common values and are willing to enforce them, especially among the young.[18] As a reporter for the *Boston Globe* put it, somewhat tongue in cheek, the level of violence is mostly influenced by "such things as being willing to look after other people's children and mind others' business."[19]

The "Mrs. Greene" Syndrome

Looking after others' children and minding others' business is what Roberto Rivera calls the "Mrs. Greene syndrome." Rivera grew up in a racially mixed, big-city neighborhood presided over by an imposing woman named Mrs. Greene. She had three children of her own, but she considered it her business to watch out for everyone else's kids, too. "If she saw you doing something stupid or dangerous, she would not hesitate to call you on it," Rivera recalls. "Even worse, you could count on her telling your parents. It was almost impossible to get away with anything when Mrs. Greene was around."

Social science is proving that it's the Mrs. Greenes of this world who enforce community values and keep neighborhoods safe. And values, in turn, derive ultimately from biblical religion. Several recent studies show a direct connection between the influence of Christian faith and crime reduction. Independent studies have shown that crime is highest in neighborhoods with the most bars and liquor stores, and lowest in areas with the most churches.[20]

A landmark study by Richard Freedman of Harvard found that young people who are active in church are more likely to finish school, avoid out-of-wedlock pregnancies, keep a job, and stay out of trouble with the law. In preventing crime, church attendance rates even higher than family structure, a highly significant finding, given that growing up in a fatherless home has also been proven to have a severely negative impact. The power of religion comes from the fact that it instills a sense of purpose and value to life; it also teaches a standard of morality that acts as a restraint on antisocial and criminal behavior.[21]

The same effect has been proven historically as well. James Q. Wilson found that crime fell dramatically in the latter half of the nineteenth century despite rapid industrialization. He traced the cause to a widespread revival (the Second Great Awakening), when Christians created an extraordinary number of associations to help the poor, the needy, unemployed men, and abandoned women.[22] Their success in transforming society gives persuasive evidence that Christians can do the same today.

We Hold the Answers

"if you do not oppress the alien, the fatherless or the widow and do not shed innocent blood in this place, and if you do not follow other gods to your own harm, then I will let you live in this place, in the land I gave your forefathers for ever and ever."
—Jeremiah 7:6-7

Only Christians have a worldview capable of providing workable solutions to the problems of community life. Thus, we ought to be in the forefront, helping communities take charge of their own neighborhoods. Whether it's mobilizing efforts to paint over graffiti and clean up vacant lots, or whether it's political activism to pass laws enforcing standards of public behavior, we should be helping to restore order in these smaller areas as the first step toward tackling major social ills.

Go back and read aloud the first sentence of the paragraph above. Repeat the line. We have spent years researching and writing this study to substantiate that one conclusion. Do you believe that only Christians have a worldview capable of providing the answers on which to build a good society? ❑ Yes ❑ No

Why do you believe the biblical worldview is (or is not) the answer to building the just society?

_____

_____

_____

_____

We can take our lead from the stunning successes of inner-city churches that have assumed an active role in recapturing their neighborhoods. Take, for example, the Reverend Eugene Rivers who leads Azusa Christian Community, a Pentecostal congregation in Boston's impoverished Dorchester area. The churches started offering after-school tutoring ("latchkey learning") and Bible studies; they formed neighborhood patrols to offer kids safe conduct to and from school; they counseled juveniles on probation; and they made contacts with Christian businessmen to help teens get jobs.[23]

You may respond that you are not a pastor and you do not live in an inner-city setting. What needs can you identify in your community? What practical ministry acts could contribute to the *shalom* of your area?

_____

_____

_____

_____

Princeton professor John DiIulio describes such ministries in dramatic terms. Carrying the bold message that "God loves you and has something better for you," church volunteers "go right on the street, right to the gangs, right to the heart of the action. Kids are stunned. Police don't even go in there." But committed Christians go where police fear to tread.[24] DiIulio was so impressed that he reduced his teaching load at Princeton and created an organization called PRRAY (Partnership for Research on Religion and At-Risk Youth) to research and help fund faith-based programs.

Christians can be powerful forces for community, beginning in their own congregations. Read Acts 6:1-6 and summarize the problem.

_____
_____
_____
_____

What steps did the individual church members take to resolve the situation and what steps did the leaders take? _____
_____
_____
_____
_____

According to verse 7, what resulted from this direct effort at restoring _shalom_ in the Christian community? _____
_____
_____
_____
_____

"It was the soccer ball and the Bible that worked," says Kathy Dudley who, with her husband, founded Voice of Hope to restore neighborhoods in West Dallas. "We would go to a street, gather up all the kids, take them to a playground and play ball," she says. "Then we would tell them Bible stories." From that first soccer ball, Voice of Hope has grown into a successful community-development program with after-school tutoring, job training, housing rehabilitation, a dental clinic, a thrift store, and a gift shop.[25]

Kathy Dudley built a ministry with a soccer ball. Take a few minutes to pray about ways you could serve in the name of Christ. As you pray, below jot down any ministry ideas for further prayer or action.

_____
_____
_____
_____

Similar efforts are underway in Chicago under the leadership of Carey Casey, who was pastor of a comfortable, middle-class church until he sensed a call to leave it and revive one of the city's toughest inner-city neighborhoods. Casey's new church, Lawndale Christian Center, has become a safe refuge for kids, with a gymnasium and after-school tutoring. In the College Opportunity Program, eighth-graders commit themselves to a five-year program of twice-weekly study sessions at the church's learning center. If they maintain a 2.5 grade-point average, they receive a $3,000-per-year, four-year college scholarship. If the kids or their family members get sick, they can go to the church's full-service medical center for a minimal fee, and Lawndale's job-training program helps the unemployed find work. The church also has a housing ministry to rehabilitate abandoned buildings and give the poor an opportunity to become homeowners.[26]

Baltimore's Sandtown was once a neighborhood of boarded-up row houses and littered alleys, with drug dealers on every corner—that is, until New Song Community Church was founded. Now the church reaches people like Torey Reynolds, mother of four, who was addicted to crack and on welfare. With the church's help, she went through job training and is now employed as a community health-care worker. Her children attend New Song's Learning Center, and when they're sick, she takes them to New Song Family Health Center. Torey and her husband are also proud first-time homeowners of a home rehabilitated through the local Habitat for Humanity.

What do each of the following Scriptures suggest about our responsibility to minister to the broken and hurting?

Leviticus 23:22 _____
_____
_____
_____

Leviticus 25:35 _____
_____
_____
_____
_____

Deuteronomy 10:17-18 _____
_____
_____
_____
_____
_____

Isaiah 1:17 _____
_____
_____
_____
_____
_____

James 1:27 _____
_____
_____
_____
_____
_____

In Memphis, Tennessee, the biblical vision for restoring social and moral order inspires the members of Mississippi Boulevard Christian Church. The church runs a housing-rehabilitation ministry, a Christian school, the Manna Food Center for distributing food to the poor and elderly, and the Family Life Center with everything from youth basketball and volleyball teams to roller skating, a handball court, and a bowling alley. The church also has a clothing pantry, a job-placement program, a bookstore, and counseling services.

All of these examples were originally inspired by a vision for Christian community development that was first born in the hearts of my friends John and Vera Mae Perkins. John grew up picking cotton in Mississippi, suffered beatings during the civil rights movement, and then founded Voice of Calvary ministry in Mendenhall

and Jackson, Mississippi. Today these ministries have grown to include housing rehabilitation, a thrift store, job training, a school, day care, a food co-op, and a medical center. The Perkins's model of Christian community development is now being imitated across the country.

In recent years, John and Vera Mae have taken their vision to the drug-infested northwest corner of Pasadena, California. The first time I visited the Perkins's new home, I saw drug dealers on the street outside, pulling up in their limousines to do deals amid the garbage and litter. I prayed with John and Vera Mae in their living room, sitting by a window that still had a bullet hole from a drive-by shooting.

Within months, the Perkinses had turned their backyard into a play area where neighborhood kids could play safely and listen to Bible stories. Soon they bought up adjoining properties and renovated them; they opened a youth center and additional family services. They encouraged other Christians to buy properties close by and open related ministries. Over time, the drug dealers disappeared, crime abated, and children were playing in their front yards once more. When I returned for another visit, I could not believe the transformation.

What is happening in Boston, Dallas, Chicago, Baltimore, Memphis, Mendenhall, Jackson, and Pasadena is what Christians should be doing everywhere: converting chaos into the _tranquillitas ordinis_, one house at a time, one block at a time, one neighborhood at a time, one community at a time. Although our citizenship is in the "City of God," we know that God has placed us in our cities and neighborhoods to reflect His character and to restore His righteous dominion in the midst of a fallen world. We begin with our personal lives and habits, move out from there to our families and schools and then into our communities—and from there into our society as a whole.

Today's Prayer
God, I know You are at work in my community. Direct me to what You have for me to do there.

Inside Out

"For out of the heart come evil thoughts, murder, adultery, sexual immorality, theft, false testimony, slander."—Matthew 15:19

How do we redeem a culture? How do we rise to the opportunity before us at the start of a new millennium?

The answer is simple: from the inside out. From the individual to the family to the community, and then outward in ever widening ripples. And we must begin by understanding what it means to live by Christian worldview principles in our own behavior and choices. Unless we do, we will interpret the biblical commands according to the spirit of the age and will therefore be conformed to the world rather than to God's Word.

Read the following story in light of the previous sentence. Then explain why we Christians must live in obedience to a value system based on a biblical worldview.

Some years ago, in the middle of a doctrinal discussion, a young man differed with Nancy over a point the apostle Paul makes in 1 Corinthians.

"I disagree with you," he said.

"No, you disagree with Paul," Nancy corrected him gently.

"Okay, then, I disagree with Paul," he shrugged.

He went on to explain that as he saw it, the Bible was written long ago for a different age, and that today the Holy Spirit could reveal new truth—truth that might even contradict what the Bible teaches.

What makes a Christian's faithfulness to a biblical worldview so important? _____

_____

This young man was a sincere Christian, president of a Christian campus group, and a leader among his peers, but he had absorbed the mental framework of a secular culture and was reinterpreting Scripture in the context of that framework. He had lost his understanding of truth and revelation, of a worldview that roots Scripture in the God who is ultimate reality.

His worldview carried over into his personal choices, evidenced by the fact that he was sleeping with his girlfriend. He was not untaught in biblical ethics, and he was not deliberately backsliding. His honest convictions told him that the Bible consists of human documents and, therefore, is not normative for his life. Whenever he read Scripture, it was filtered through a mental grid set by a non-Christian worldview, resulting in a distorted understanding of doctrine and personal ethics.

Begin with Ourselves

If we want to convert our pagan culture as the monks did in the Middle Ages, we must start with ourselves, understanding what a Christian worldview means for our moral and lifestyle choices. Such a realization is more important than ever because individual moral choices determine the health of the entire society. Polls consistently show that what people worry about most are social and moral decay—crime, family breakdown, drug abuse, sex and violence in the entertainment media—all results of moral choices made ultimately by individuals.[27]

Given these facts, one might expect the nation's bully pulpits would be devoted to encouraging people to take responsibility for their lives, to exert the self-discipline needed to change their behavior. Instead, for the past few decades, the dominant cultural voices have argued that individuals have a right to live in any way they choose and that *society* has a responsibility to pick up the tab for any negative consequences that result.

This attitude was cleverly illustrated in the comic strip "Outland" during the controversial healthcare debate in 1993. In the opening frame, the penguin Opus and his friends are perched precariously on a tricycle at the edge of a precipice. Posted all around are warning signs: Danger! Stop! A surgeon general's warning says "Plummeting down cliffs is hazardous to one's health." But the characters ignore the signs and go careening down. The tricycle topples over, of course, and they all fly off. From the mud, Opus reaches out his hand and demands, "Quick! Free unlimited health care!"[28]

Exercise your creativity. In some way create your own version of the comic strip from Opus and friends. Write a story, song lyrics, or draw a cartoon illustrating the message of the comic strip.

Sadly, the comic strip reflects the attitude many Americans have taken toward the pathologies plaguing both our personal lives and society at large: that our behavior is our own business and that society has a duty to compensate for any negative consequences of our autonomous choices.

Sexual behavior is a prime example. Sexual relationships outside marriage are responsible for the spread of sexually transmitted diseases (STD), for most abortions, for fatherless homes, and for chronic welfare dependency. But did this social wreckage cause sex educators to teach young people to refrain from sex outside marriage? Hardly. From the 1960s through the 1980s, public school sex-education programs and their advocates were adamant that sexual activity was entirely a matter of the student's personal choice. When the inevitable consequences followed, these same educators pressed for government solutions to bandage the negative effects.

- To avoid STDs, the government supplied condoms in the schools.
- When homosexual promiscuity led to fatal diseases, the government was blamed and shamed into picking up the tab for more research.
- When sex led to pregnancy, the government was expected to pay for abortions or supply welfare support to fatherless families.

This attitude began in the 1960s when a new concept of public morality took hold, stated baldly in the words of sociologist Christopher Jencks. Speaking of fatherless families, Jencks argued that if people "truly prefer a family consisting of a mother, children, and a series of transient males, then it is hardly the federal government's proper business to try to alter this choice." What *is* the government's business then? It "ought to invent ways of providing such [single-parent] families with the same physical and psychic necessities of life available to other kinds of families."[29]

How would you respond to Jencks' idea? (Choose one of the following or state your own response.)

❏ **I agree. The government's job is to insulate us from the results of our own behaviors.**
❏ **The idea is foolish because it denies reality. Behaviors have consequences. Those consequences cannot be avoided.**

❑ Such attempts, even if successful in the short term, are destructive because they reinforce additional irresponsibility.

❑ Your response: _____
_____
_____
_____

Note carefully what Jencks is saying: the government *must not* seek to help shape the nation's moral climate or discourage irresponsible behavior. Instead, its job is to "invent ways" to compensate for any disadvantages created by the bad choices people make. As psychiatrist David Larson puts it, the government is supposed to make sure people had their cake and eat it, too![30]

This attitude is not confined to the government. It's amazing how many ordinary Americans have fallen into the trap of expecting someone else to pick up the costs of their own irresponsibility. The American Medical Association says the growth in health-care expenses can be traced largely to "lifestyle factors and social problems." Some studies indicate that up to 70 percent of all diseases result from lifestyle choices.[31]

People know they should stop smoking, cut out junk food, and get regular exercise. But how many take these basic steps in preventive care? When their unhealthy habits give them heart disease or lung cancer, they expect the health-care system to protect them from the consequences of their own bad habits.[32] The Opus cartoon is uncomfortably close to the truth.

Rooted in Worldview

Where did this idea of value-free lifestyle come from? What are its worldview roots? How do the categories of *creation, fall,* and *redemption* help us to diagnose what's wrong with the predominant secular view—and to see how a Christian worldview leads to a better, healthier, and more rational way of living?

The following paragraph summarizes all we have studied in "How Now Shall We Live?" Number the steps that have led to our modern impasse. I have begun by putting a "1" by "reject the biblical teaching about creation."

In a nutshell, if **(1)** we reject the biblical teaching about creation, we end up with nature as our creator. Morality then becomes something humans invent when they have evolved to a certain level. There is no transcendent source of moral standards that dictates how we should live. Each individual has the right to chart his or her own course. If we reject the idea of sin and the Fall, nothing is objectively wrong and there is no real guilt; there are only false guilt feelings that result from social disapproval. The logical conclusion of this thinking is that redemption means freeing ourselves from false guilt and restoring our natural autonomy by eliminating the stigma from all lifestyles. The role of public authorities is to mobilize resources to make sure that no negative consequences follow from the choices individuals may make.

Now write a phrase to restate each of the steps you identified above.

_____
_____
_____
_____
_____
_____
_____

Number the parts of the biblical plan in the following paragraph.

By contrast, Christianity claims that God created the universe with a definite structure—a material order and a moral order. If we live contrary to that order, we sin against God, and the consequences are invariably harmful and painful, on both a personal and a social level. On the other hand, if we submit to that order and live in harmony with it, then our lives will be happier and healthier. The role of public authorities is to encourage people to live according to the principles that make for social health and harmony.

Over the past three decades, these biblical concepts have receded while our public discourse has been dominated by the value-free model. Today the disastrous consequences of that model are becoming abundantly clear. Even determined secularists have begun to see that society simply can't keep up with the costs of personal and moral irresponsibility: the welfare system is overloaded; crime rates are shockingly high, especially among juveniles; health-care costs climbed so fast that the government keeps threatening to take over. We can increasingly see that the welfare state has *not* been able to "invent ways" to give fatherless families "the same physical and psychic necessities of life available to other kinds of families," as Jencks put it.[33] Instead, welfare has helped create a permanent underclass that is disordered and demoralized. Government's compensation of irresponsible behavior has, essentially, subsidized and encouraged more of it.

The Modernist Impasse

Americans have reached "the modernist impasse": They have been told they have a right to be free from the restrictions of morality and religion, yet as unrestricted choices lead to social breakdown, they begin to long for the protection that morality once provided. After all, we didn't *have* epidemics of crime, broken families, abortion, or sexually transmitted diseases when Americans largely accepted biblical morality.

That's why, after decades of public rhetoric about individual rights, we now hear cultural leaders struggling to find some common secular language to revive a sense of civic duty and virtue.

The time is ripe. The old philosophies are bankrupt. People are hungry for meaning and purpose. And only Christians have a worldview capable of providing workable solutions to the problems of community life. Will we continue to retreat into our churches, or will we claim our culture for a new springtime of Christianity?

DAY FIVE
The Opportunity Before Us

"Great and marvelous are your deeds, Lord God Almighty. Just and true are your ways, King of the ages."—Revelation 15:3

New openness to moral arguments gives Christians an extraordinary opportunity to make our case that living according to the biblical moral order is healthier for both individuals and society. And there's a growing body of scientific evidence we can use to back up our argument. Medical studies are confirming that those who attend church regularly and act consistently with their faith are better off, both physically and mentally. Consider a few recent findings.

- *Alcohol Abuse:* Alcohol abuse is highest among those with little or no religious commitment.[34] One study found nearly 89 percent of alcoholics said they lost interest in religion during their youth.[35]
- *Drug Abuse:* The importance of religion is the single best predictor that youth will avoid substance abuse.
- *Crime:* A strong correlation also exists between participation in religious activities and the avoidance of crime.
- *Depression and Stress:* Several studies have found that high levels of religious commitment correlate with lower levels of depression and stress.[36]
- *Suicide:* Persons who do not attend church at all are four times more likely to commit suicide than are frequent church attenders.[37]
- *Mental Disorders:* Armand Nicholi, professor of psychiatry at Harvard Medical School and a deeply committed believer, argues from his lifelong experience that Christians are far less likely to experience mental disorders than are their secular counterparts.[38]
- *Family Stability:* One study found that church attendance is the most important predictor of marital stability.[39]
- *Physical Health:* Church attendance even affects men's physical health and mortality rates. For men who attend church frequently, the risk of dying from arteriosclerotic heart disease is 60 percent of that for men who attend infrequently.[40]

Mark these statements either true or false according to the information you just read.

___ Religion is simply wish-fulfillment to make people feel better.

___ Practicing your faith contributes to better physical health, mental health, and family life.

___ Religious people are more subject to depression and stress than their secular counterparts.

Why do these practical indicators show the benefit of Christianity? _____

_____

_____

_____

_____

This does not mean that every person of faith is healthy and happy, but the statistics do "make a powerful statement about the typical human condition," writes Patrick Glynn in *God: The Evidence.* Both clinical experience and research data suggest that "among the most important determinants of human happiness and well-being are our spiritual beliefs and moral choices."[41]

The data is so compelling that even a confirmed secularist ought to be convinced that religion is good for society. In fact, that's exactly what Guenter Lewy concludes in his recent book *Why America Needs Religion.* Lewy started out to write a book defending secularism, but after surveying the data, he ended up arguing, to his own surprise, that belief in God makes people happier and more fulfilled. "Whether it be juvenile delinquency, adult crime, prejudice, out-of-wedlock births, or marital conflict and divorce, there is a significantly lower rate of such indicators of moral failure and social ills among believing Christians."[42] In short, a person *can* live a moral and healthy life without God, but statistically speaking, the odds are against it.

Furthermore, the benefits of Christianity are not solely a matter of attitude and lifestyle. It is impossible to dismiss the frankly supernatural. Dr. Dale Matthews has documented experiments in which volunteers prayed for selected patients with rheumatoid arthritis. To avoid a possible placebo effect from knowing they were being prayed for, the patients were not told which ones were subjects of the test. The recovery rate among those prayed for was measurably higher than among a control group, for which prayers were not offered.[43]

It is time for the medical profession to recognize the healing potential of the spiritual dimension, says Harvard professor Herbert Benson. Though not a professing Christian himself, Benson admits that humans are "engineered for religious faith." We are "wired for God. ... Our genetic blueprint has made believing in an Infinite Absolute part of our nature."[44] That is about as close as a nonbeliever can get to confirming the biblical claim that the human spirit was made by God in order to live in communion with Him.

This doesn't mean, however, that just any kind of religion is beneficial. Gordon Allport, the great psychologist of religion, determined that the benefits go to those who genuinely believe, not to those who use religion for ulterior purposes.[45] Benefits accrue only to those who practice their faith, not to those who merely profess it. The inconsistent Christian suffers even more than the consistent atheist. The most miserable person of all is the one who knows the truth yet doesn't obey it.

Which of the following Scriptures teach the idea in the previous paragraph?

❏ Luke 15:7
❏ James 1:22
❏ Ephesians 2:4-5
❏ 1 Peter 1:3

The David Larson Story

The growth in scientific evidence validating the Christian worldview has been greatly inspired by the work of one man, David Larson. His story illustrates not only how Christians should persevere in their convictions but also what we can achieve when we do.

When Larson began his training in psychiatry, one of his professors tried to discourage him. "Tell me, Dave," the professor said. "Your faith is important to you, isn't it?"

"Yes," said Larson.

"Then I think you should put aside the idea of becoming a psychiatrist. For psychiatric patients, religion can only be harmful."[46]

Remember all that you've studied. Why did the professor consider religion harmful?

_____
_____
_____
_____
_____
_____

Larson's professor was stating the conventional wisdom among psychiatrists and psychologists, handed down from Sigmund Freud, the founder of psychoanalysis, who defined religion as "a universal obsessional neurosis," an "infantile helplessness," and "regression to primary narcissism." The terminology has changed since Freud, but most psychologists and psychiatrists retain the assumption that religion is a negative factor in mental health and that it is associated with mental pathologies.[47] If you answered that the professor's worldview made him consider religion harmful, you were right on target.

Yet David Larson refused to be deterred. As he continued his studies, he noticed a very interesting pattern: Religion was not associated with mental illness after all. In fact, quite the opposite: Religion actually helped protect *against* mental disorders.

This insight spurred Larson to conduct his own research, and today his work has begun to turn around an entire profession. "Growing numbers of psychologists are finding religion, if not in their personal lives, at least in their data," reports the *New York Times*. "What was once, at best, an unfashionable topic in psychology has been born again as a respectable focus for scientific research."[48] The data is showing that religion, far from being a mental illness, is actually beneficial to mental health, physical health, family strength, and social order.

Why has it taken the mental health community most of a century to begin seeing the benefits of religious belief?

❑ The data was so difficult to interpret.
❑ The facts are unclear.
❑ A false worldview blinds people to truth.

This new scientific data provides a wonderful tool for apologetics, for it shows clearly that if we ignore biblical principles, we end up living in ways that run against the grain of our being, creating stress, depression, family conflict, and even physical illness. Rather than being an arbitrary set of rules and restrictions that repress and distort our true nature, Christianity actually describes our true nature and shows us how to live in accord with it. We pay a heavy price for denying this reality. When we live in accord with God's truth, we enjoy the fruits of operating the way we were made to. "The fear of the Lord is the beginning of wisdom. ... For through me your days will be many, and years will be added to your life" (Prov. 9:10-11). The evidence is a powerful validation of Proverbs; a biblical view of human nature does indeed conform to reality.

We cannot escape the consequences of our own choices. In our bodies, we flesh out either the biblical worldview or a worldview that is in opposition to the Bible. And when we incarnate the truth of God in our lives and families, we help bring new life to our neighborhoods and churches, our cities and nation, in an ever widening circle.

Conclusion: the Challenge Before Us

From Jorge Crespo in Ecuador to Officer Sal in New York, we see a common pattern: Christians who understand biblical truth and have the courage to live it out can indeed create a new culture in the midst of a dark world. And that is the challenge facing all of us.

As we have sought to demonstrate in these pages, the Christian worldview is more consistent, more rational, and more workable than any other belief system. It beats out all other contenders in giving credible answers to the great questions that any worldview must answer:

• Where did we come from? *(creation);*
• What has gone wrong? *(fall);*
• What can we do to fix it? *(redemption).*
• As a result, the way we *see* the world will lead to changing the world *(restoration).*

No worldview is merely a theoretical philosophy; worldview is intensely practical. It affects the way we live our lives, day in and day out, as well as the way we influence the world around us. If we adopt a false worldview, we will inevitably find ourselves going against the grain of the universe, leading to consequences that we cannot live with—as millions of Americans are discovering. On the other hand, if we order our lives in accord with reality, we will not only find meaning and purpose but also discover that our lives are healthier and more fulfilled. Christianity is that road map of reality, and it is the answer we must be ready to give as those around us grow increasingly aware of the futility of all other worldviews.

Ao we come full circle, back to the questions with which we began this study. Can Christians really make any difference in the world? Does the Christian worldview give us the map we need for living? Can a culture be rebuilt so all the world see in its splendor and glory the contours of God's kingdom? Can we really make the world "a new creation"? Those we have met in these pages show us that the answer is emphatically yes.

Every day you and I are making decisions that help construct one kind of world or another. Are we co-opted by the faddish worldviews of our age, or are we helping to create a new world of peace, love, and forgiveness?

How now shall we live?

By embracing God's truth, understanding the physical and moral order He has created, lovingly contending for that truth with our neighbors, then having the courage to live it out in every walk of life. Because of Christ, we can live boldly and, yes, joyously.

[1]Andrew Peyton Thomas, *Crime and the Sacking of America: The Roots of Chaos* (Washington, DC: Brassey's, 1994), 54.

[2]Ramsey Clark, the attorney general under Lyndon Johnson, wrote, "the crowding of millions of poor people with their cumulative disadvantage society not only offers the easy chance for criminal acts—it causes crime" (Clark, *Crime in America: Observations on Its Nature, Causes, Prevention and Control* [New York: Simon & Schuster, 1970], 29). Similarly, when widespread looting occurred in the late 1970s during a blackout in New York City, then President Jimmy Carter explained it as the result of poverty, though later studies showed that most looters were employed and stole things they didn't need.

[3]These figures from the Federal Bureau of Investigation; the Bureau of Alcohol, Tobacco, and Firearms; and the National Center for Health Statistics were cited in Ted Gest, Gordon Witkin, Katia Hetter, and Andrea Wright, "Violence in America," *U.S. News and World Report* 116, no. 2 (January 17, 1994): 22.

[4]George L. Kelling and Catherine M. Coles, *Fixing Broken Windows: Restoring Order and Reducing Crime in Our Communities* (New York: Free Press, 1996), 55-56.

[5]Andrew Peyton Thomas, "The Rise and Fall of the Homeless," *Weekly Standard 1,* no. 29 (April 8, 1996): 27. See also Andrew Peyton Thomas, *Crime and the Sacking of America: The Roots and Chaos* (Washington, D.C.: Brussey's, 1994).

[6]To read more about this, see Rael Jean Isaac, *Madness in the Streets: How Psychiatry and the Law Abandoned the Mentally Ill* (New York: Free Press, 1990).

[7]James Q. Wilson and George L. Kelling, "Broken Windows," *Atlantic Monthly* (March 1992): 29.

[8]John Carlin, "How They Cleaned Up Precinct 75," *The Independent,* 7 January 1996.

[9]Ibid.

[10]See Kelling and Coles, *Fixing Broken Windows,* chapter 4.

[11]Abraham Kuyper, *Lectures on Calvinism* (Grand Rapids: Eerdmans, 1983), 79.

[12]Saint Augustine, *The City of God* (New York: Modern Library, 1950), 690. In the Middle Ages, Thomas Aquinas gave Augustine's insight a more positive interpretation, arguing that the state is not only a remedial institution established to curb sin, but that it is also a good thing in itself, an expression of our social nature. Living within social institutions is essential to fulfilling our own nature.

[13]William Wilberforce, as quoted in Garth Lean, *God's Politician: William Wilberforce's Struggle* (London: Darton, Longman & Todd, 1980), 74.

[14]Robert Peel, as quoted in Fred Siegel, *The Future Once Happened Here: New York, D.C., L.A., and the Fate of America's Big Cities* (New York: Free Press, 1997), 192.

[15]Eric Monkkonen, *Police in Urban America: 1860-1920* (Cambridge: Cambridge University Press, 1981), as quoted in Siegel, *The Future Once Happened Here,* 192.

[16]James Q. Wilson and George L. Kelling, "Beating Criminals to the Punch," *New York Times,* 24 April 1989.

[17]Reuben Greenberg, "Less Bang-Bang for the Buck," *Policy Review* (winter 1992): 56.

[18]Robert J. Sampson, "Neighborhoods and Violent Crime: A Multilevel Study of Collective Efficacy," *Science 277,* no. 5328 (August 15, 1997): 918.

[19]Delores Kong, "Study Shows Cohesiveness Curbs Neighborhood Violence," *Boston Globe,* 15 August 1997.

[20]John J. DiIulio, "Broken Bottles: Liquor, Disorder, and Crime in Wisconsin," *Wisconsin Policy Research Institute Report 8,* no. 4 (May 1995).

[21]Richard R. Freeman and Harry J. Holzer, eds., *The Black Youth Employment Crisis* (Chicago: University of Chicago Press, 1986), 353-76.

[22]James Q. Wilson and Richard J. Herrnstein, *Crime and Human Nature* (New York: Simon & Schuster, 1985), 432. In the early 1980s, Wilson sought to discover why crime decreased in the middle of the last century and then, after some fluctuations (up in the 1920s, down in the 1930s), shot up dramatically in the 1960s and has been climbing ever since. He checked all the standard explanations of criminal behavior but found that none correlated with the historical pattern. Poverty, for example. If poverty causes crime, why was crime so low during the Depression, when more than a quarter of the population had no income at all? And why did it rise during the affluent 1960s and 1970s?

Then Wilson stumbled on the fact that the decrease in crime in the last century followed the Second Great Awakening. As repentance and renewal spread across the country, church membership rose steeply, Christians formed voluntary associations devoted to education and moral reform, and American society as a whole came to respect the values of sobriety, hard work, and self-restraint—what sociologists call the Protestant ethic. And as the Protestant ethic triumphed, the crime rate plummeted.

Beginning in the 1920s through the late 1930s, however, the Protestant ethic began to fall out of favor among the educated classes. "Freud's psychological theories came into vogue," explains Wilson, and the educated classes began to view religion and ethics as oppressive. Their cause was no longer freedom for religion—a classic American liberty—but freedom from religion.

The attitude of these educated classes was restrained by the Depression and two world wars, but in the 1960s it finally percolated through to popular consciousness, resulting in a widespread cultural shift away from an ethic of self-discipline toward an ethic of self-expression. The result was a sudden and dramatic increase in crime. See James Q. Wilson, "Crime and American Culture," *Public Interest* (winter 1983): 22.

[23]John Leland, with Claudia Kalb, "Savior of the Street," *Newsweek* (June 1, 1998): 20.

[24]Leslie Scanlon, "From the PEWS to the Streets: More Churches Are Going beyond Their Walls to Fight Drugs and Crime," *Courier-Journal,* 27 July 1997.

[25]Roy Maynard, "Voice of Hope," *Loving Your Neighbor: A Principled Guide to Personal Charity,* ed. Marvin N. Olasky (Washington, D.C.: Capital Research Center 1995), 57.

Today's Prayer
God, You have set a challenge before Your children to live out Your love in every walk of our lives. I marvel that You can communicate Your love through imperfect vessels such as myself. Thank You for Your love for me. Help me to show that love to everyone I meet.

[26]This story about Chicago and the following stories about Baltimore, Memphis, and Montgomery are told in John Perkins, with Jo Kadlecek, *Resurrecting Hope: Powerful Stories of How God Is Moving to Reach Our Cities* (Ventura, Calif.: Regal Books, 1995).

[27]For example, a 1996 poll showed that 59 percent of Americans were worried about "our country's ethical and moral condition" (James Davison Hunter, *The State of Disunion: 1996 Survey of American Political Culture, vol. 2* [Ivy, Va.: In Medias Res Educational Foundation, 1996], table 46 F).

[28]Berkeley Breathed, "Outland," 17 October 1993.

[29]Christopher Jencks, as quoted in William Voegel, "Poverty and the Victim Ploy," *First Things* (November 1991): 37.

[30]David Larson, personal interview with Nancy Pearcey (March 1999). We are not denying that government has a role to play in providing a safety net to families in trouble. What is objectionable is the value-free assumption that all family forms are morally equal and that the government's role is to make them equal in all other respects as well.

[31]Louis W. Sullivan, "foundation for Reform," (Washington, D.C.: Department of Health and Human Services, 1991): 15.

[32]Judy Mann, "Going Up in Smoke," *Washington Post,* 26 February 1993.

[33]See note 29 above.

[34]D.B. Larson and W. P. Wilson, "Religious Life of Alcoholics," *Southern Medical Journal 73,* no. 6 (June 1980): 723-27.

[35]David B. and Susan S. Larson, *The Forgotten Factor in Physical and Mental Health: What Does the Research Show?* (Rockville, Md.: National Institute for Healthcare Research, 1992), 68-69. The Larsons have collected and/or conducted a host of studies on the impact of religion on mental and physical health.

[36]Ibid., 76-78.

[37]Ibid., 64-65.

[38]Armand Nicholi Jr., "Hope in a Secular Age," *Finding God at Harvard: Spiritual Journeys of Thinking Christians,* ed. Kelly K. Monroe (Grand Rapids: Zondervan, 1996), 117.

[39]Larson and Larson, *The Forgotten Factor,* 64-65.

[40]Ibid., 110. These findings show a positive association between religious commitment and physical health. This does not appear to be merely a correlation but an actual causal relationship. As Larson and Larson point out, in discussing lower blood pressure among smokers with a high religious commitment: "These findings are striking because the benefits of religion on health are often assumed to be the result of religious motivation for following healthier practices, such as not smoking, avoiding alcohol, and abstaining from harmful dietary practices. In this study, however, it was among the smokers that religious importance made the biggest difference in blood pressure. Consequently the health benefit of religious commitment was beyond avoiding health-risk behavior" (116, emphasis in the original). What was the connection then? Larson and Larson quote the authors of the study as saying, "this may reflect a preferentially greater moderating effect for religion on blood pressure among more tense or nervous individuals who may also be more likely to smoke" (116). In short, religious commitment itself appears to be the cause of the health benefits.

[41]Patrick Glynn, *God: The Evidence: The Reconciliation of Faith and Reason in a Postsecular World* (Rocklin, Calif.: Prima Publishing, 1997) 67.

[42]Guenter Lewy, *Why America Needs Religion: Secular Modernity and Its Discontents* (Grand Rapids: Eerdmans, 1996), 112.

[43]Dale A. Matthews with Connie Clark, *The Faith Factor: Proof of the Healing Power of Prayer* (New York: Viking, 1998), 77-80.

[44]Herbert Benson, *Timeless Healing* (New York: Scribner, 1996), 197, 208.

[45]Larson and Larson, *The Forgotten Factor,* 86.

[46]David B. Larson, "Physician, Heal Thyself!" *Guideposts* (March 1993): 41-43.

[47]Ibid.

[48]Daniel Goleman, "Therapists See Religion As Aid, Not Illusion," *New York Times,* 10 September 1991.

A Matter of Life

Worldview greatly impacts practical living. Nowhere is that importance more graphic than the value we place on human life.

From their hovering position 1500 feet above the ground, the men in Colonel Yarborough's Command & Control (C&C) helicopter kept watch. For the past two weeks, the Ghost-rider division had been shuttling in troops and supplies for a big push in the central highlands at Plei Merong, Vietnam.

As the (C&C) ship circled slowly over the jungle, the crew watched another helicopter rotor into position above the steep hillside landing zone, hovering close to the ground to pick up support personnel returning to base. The men on the C&C ship could see men scurrying below, disappearing in and out of the scrub trees and bushes. The mechanical dragonfly wigwagged, impatient to leave.

Kaboom!

Suddenly the air burst with rockets. Puffs of white smoke from small firearms rose in dozens of places over the hillside. The copter near the ground recoiled left, as if stabbed in its side. A curling plume of gray scorpioned the back rotor, and the machine began to pitch wildly. The smoke grew black and full.

As the wounded machine continued to yaw and heave, Ken McGarity watched the scene from his right-gunner position. He saw the other helicopter fall, slamming down onto the landing zone, its main rotor shattering. Then he spotted two helmets pop out. Then another. The three men ran for cover, one of them on fire.

"We're going down!" screamed the C&C pilot. He shouted at Ken to watch his side as they spiraled down.

The colonel pushed his way to the open door, beside Ken, ready to throw out an extinguisher for the burning soldier on the ground. Their C&C copter had cleared the high bamboo and would soon be down to the scrub trees, but Ken still couldn't see where their guys were hiding. He couldn't see the enemy either.

Soon they were right over the landing zone. Why didn't the colonel throw out the extinguisher? They weren't supposed to be here more than seven seconds. They had been here at least twenty. Throw the thing!

No one saw the B-40 rocket coming. Half the ship exploded on contact. Ken was catapulted into the air and fell from the height of the scrub trees onto the bare ground.

When he regained consciousness, Otto Mertz, a buddy from the first downed copter, was dragging him through the mud to safety.

"My legs!" Ken screamed.

"They're broken," someone said.

His arms had been crossed over his chest. They must be broken, too," McGarity thought.

He passed in and out of consciousness several times before he was finally hoisted onto a medevac helicopter. When he was secured into a transport stretcher, a woman's voice asked, "What's your name?"

"McGarity," he said. "Ken McGarity. Am I hurt bad?"

"We're going to take care of you," the nurse shouted as the thrashing blades lifted them away.

When the wounded men arrived at the Army's 71st Evacuation Hospital at Pleiku on September 21, 1968, Dr. Kenneth Swan was surgeon of the day. The 33-year-old doctor had been in Vietnam only a month.

Two men had died at Plei Merong. All the others could be classified as "walking wounded," having sustained only minor injuries—all except the soldier identified as Army Specialist 4 Ken McGarity. The man was covered with dirt and bloodied mud. One leg hung by a thin strip of skin; the other was broken so badly that the femur protruded from what was left of his thigh. Shoelace tourniquets stopped the arterial bleeding, but the wounds were plastered with mud and sticks. Both arms were badly fractured and pitted with shrapnel wounds. The man's right pinkie finger was gone, and one testicle had been blown away. Blood oozed from both eyes; the left eyeball was shattered. The eye injuries indicated shrapnel wounds, which could mean brain damage.

As Swan assessed the devastation before him, he had two choices. He could classify the soldier as "expectant," medicate him, and leave him to die, or he could devote the full resources of the hospital to treating him. Which call should he make?

By all rights, this soldier should have bled to death already. He had been in the field almost two hours before he had been airlifted out. But he was not only alive, he was conscious.

"How am I doing?" the man asked.

"You're in the hospital."

"I feel like I left my legs back on the copter. They're broken, aren't they?"

Dr. Swan knew the soldier's joke was closer to the truth, but the short exchange made up Swan's mind. Swan, who was a Christian and a churchgoer, reacted instinctively. How could he refuse to treat a man who was talking to him?

"We're going to take care of you," he promised.[1]

X rays revealed what the surgeon already knew: the soldier's legs had to come off. As Swan worked on the amputations—both legs above the knee—he coordinated the activities of the team of doctors he had called in. The orthopedist treated the shrapnel wounds in McGarity's arms. The ophthalmologist removed the man's left eye and cleaned the wounds to the right eye, hoping to save it. When the orthopedist had done all he could on McGarity's arms, Swan amputated the

ragged stump of his right pinkie finger. A urologist worked to limit the damage of the "shrapnel vasectomy."

Then, in a final delicate and involved surgery, the neurologist performed a craniotomy, cutting through the top of the soldier's forehead and lifting away the skull so that he could extract the shrapnel from the brain's frontal lobes—damage that might have a lobotomizing effect—or worse.

For eight hours, the six surgeons stood in their muddy boots on the concrete floor and did the best they could in repairing Ken McGarity. When the surgeries ended, Dr. Swan felt his team had done well. Their patient had a chance.

Later that day, however, Kenneth Swan's commanding officer sat down with him in the mess hall and asked why he had decided to treat last night's casualty so aggressively.

"There was no other way to treat his injuries," Swan replied.

His superior looked him square in the eye. "Look, Ken, why send blind, double amputees with significant brain damage back to their parents? What were you thinking?"

Swan found himself responding from his gut. "I was trained to treat the sick. It's not up to me who lives and dies. That's God's decision."

"As the surgeon on duty, it was up to you," said his commanding officer. "The next time you make a call, ask yourself what kind of life you're condemning someone to." He paused. "Of course, he may die yet." He sounded grimly hopeful.

By the time Ken McGarity reached Walter Reed Army Medical Center in Washington, D.C., three weeks after being wounded, the nightmares had started. As more surgeries followed to repair the ligament damage in his right arm and his amputation

wounds, pain exploded at every level of his consciousness.

In his dreams he saw North Vietnamese regulars run down the middle of the base's airstrip ... the bodies were being picked up after Tet ... He leaned out of the copter once more, desperate to identify his own men. ... He was running down a road in the middle of a firefight wearing only a T-shirt, fatigues, and boots.

When Ken arrived at Hines Veterans Hospital outside Chicago to begin his rehabilitation on the blind ward, orderlies wheeled his 80-pound body into the hospital. In transport, he had sweated out every toxin his infection-riddled body could produce.

"He sure needs to be cleaned up," said the nurse during his intake.

"What am I supposed to do with him," complained the psychiatrist. "Why didn't they let this guy die?"

Why did people assume that because he was blind he was also deaf, Ken wondered. They not only spoke past him, they talked as if saving his life had been a mistake.

On the blind ward at Hines, however, Ken discovered a new power. He didn't have to do anything he didn't want to do. He had always been independent to a fault. Now he could play out rebellion with abandon.

Medical personnel told him he needed to begin learning to live his new life. He needed to exercise his arms, develop upper body strength.

Ken needed only to have the pain go away. So he decided to lie in his bed and let them take care of him until the pain diminished enough for him to think about such things as upper body strength.

Ken hadn't allowed for Nurse Early. She never handed his water cup to him; she always placed it on the table that pivoted in front him. She wanted him to learn to feel for a glass without knocking it over.

Once, he was so frustrated that he knocked a glass across the room with a sweep of his forearm. He heard the water's splat and the plastic cup's skip and bounce with great satisfaction.

But Nurse Early came back every day. During the morning hours, she stretched his arms, working first for mobility, then strength, letting him use a half-pound dumbbell.

"Give me more weight," he demanded. He wanted to exercise like a man. Early wouldn't allow it, so he quit lifting her half-pounder.

Their running battle continued for weeks. Secretly, Ken liked the nurse's perfume. Just to know he had a woman around him, just to smell her scent—he liked that.

One day, feeling particularly lousy, Ken refused to attend occupational therapy. "I ain't no basket weaver!" he complained.

"Oh yeah?" said Early, and plopped him down hard in his wheelchair. "You're going to physical therapy!" she said. "And I'll tell you what else you're going to do. You're going to act like a soldier. Your injuries don't entitle you to anything more than the U. S. Congress is willing to pay for. And it's not paying me to pity you!"

She kept up this harangue during the struggle of getting him belted into his chair and wheeling him out of the ward. She kicked the door open for emphasis. Then she hung a fast right into a room that smelled of freshly washed towels and linen.

"We're in the laundry room, Ken; we're alone." Now her voice was calm, lower. "I want to tell you something."

You've told me enough already, he thought.

"I know you're hurting," she said, her voice warming with compassion.

"I know that's why you don't want to do any of this, but you have to try. You have to try now while it still hurts. When the pain's gone, the opportunity's gone. You won't be able to regain any mobility if much more time passes. Ken, put all that stubbornness to use. I know you can do anything you put your mind to. From now on, it's just going to take a whole lot more effort. You're going to have to find your own way to do things, but you can. You will. If you were a quitter, you would be dead by now. I need you to show me the courage that kept you alive."

"Nurse Early?" said Ken.

"What?"

"What size do you want your stupid basket?"

Ken's ward contained all the worst cases. He didn't need his eyes to know that. He was the only one among the half-dozen in the room who could scoot himself out of bed into a wheelchair. Still, he and his ward mates entertained themselves. On Friday nights, they called a fried chicken delivery service and ordered in buckets and beer.

One Friday afternoon they were kidding each other, feeling high, anticipating their big night of chicken and suds, when Dave Crowley suggested, "Hey, Ken, why don't you get us some munchies? You can get in that chair now. Go on down to the PX and buy out the store."

"Yeah, what else can we do with our money?" said another.

Ken had never been able to turn down a dare. "I'll do it," he said.

He was in his wheelchair and nearly past the nurse's station when the nurse on duty called, "Where you going, Ken?"

"To the PX. Going to get my friends some munchies."

"That's good," she said absently, as if talking to a three-year-old who said he was flying to the moon.

Ken kept rolling. He would show them all.

By the time he reached the end of the first hall, he was wondering how he would ever make it. He waited until he heard the familiar scraping slide of a doctor's surgical booties.

"Can you tell me how to get to the PX, sir?" Ken asked.

"Turn left here, then down this corridor, a right at the next, two more, another left, another right, and then you had better ask again."

"Okay, thanks."

Powering his wheelchair with his left hand and scraping the wall for guidance with his right, he worked his way past and around all the doorjambs, heating ventilators, abandoned IV stands, and laundry carts. The way down to the PX had steep ramps that gave him more than a thrill. As he descended, he wondered how he ever would wheel his chair up these ramps on his way back.

He remembered instructions for one or two corridors at a time, then found another person to ask again. Finally, after asking directions of the last technician, he turned into an open space and smelled hamburgers and fries. A few more hand-pumps, and he hit a table and chair and knew he had arrived.

But how would he make his way along the cafeteria rail? How would he know what was in front of him? He was swiveling his head around, trying to take in as much as he could through his useful senses, when he heard someone talking close by.

"Soldier?"

"Yes, sir?"

"I'm Colonel McDermott. Are you supposed to be here?"

"I'm doing rehabilitation on the blind ward, sir. My buddies asked if I would go to the PX and get them some munchies. I'm the only one who can get in a chair, so I came down."

"That ward's up on level 9, isn't it?"

"Yes, sir."

"Level 9. That's a long way. Did somebody bring you down?"

"No, sir. I came down by myself."

"What's your name, soldier?"

"Specialist 4 Ken McGarity, sir. I was a door gunner with the Ghostriders."

"Would you like me to help you find your snacks?"

"Yes, sir. Appreciate it, sir. I was wondering how I was going to manage."

"You don't mind if I wheel you through the line, do you?"

"No, sir. It's a long way down from level 9."

As Colonel McDermott wheeled Ken past the candy bars, pretzels, potato chips, pies, and cakes, the room grew quiet. So quiet that when the cash register chinged on Ken's purchases, it sounded like a symphonic ta-da!

"How are you going to get that bag up to level 9 with you, private?" the colonel asked.

"Easy." Ken tucked his change in the front pocket of his hospital gown, then grasped the top of the grocery bag between his teeth. He couldn't hold the bag in his lap because his leg stumps were too short to balance anything. He took a big breath through his nose, preparing to roll.

"Private McGarity?" said the colonel.

Ken let loose of the bag to answer. "Yes, sir?"

"I'm saluting you, private."

"Yes, sir."

Suddenly, the quiet was broken as applause rang out around him.

"Carry on," said the colonel.

Outside the PX, Ken powered up the first ramp, a new energy in his hands and arms. He could do it. He had found his way down here; now all he had to do was find his way in life. Nurse Early had said he could do anything he put his mind to; now, for the first time, he was sure that he could. He hadn't realized how tightly his doubts and fears had been gripping him, trying to suffocate the life that remained.

Relief teared in his eyes. He was truly going to make it!

Twenty years later, in 1989, Peter McPherson, a young freelance journalist, called Dr. Kenneth Swan, then a professor of surgery at the University of Medicine and Dentistry of New Jersey. McPherson was writing about trauma care in Vietnam versus present trauma care in the States, and Swan was an ideal interview candidate. Besides his experience in Vietnam, he was chief of surgery for trauma care at his university hospital; he also remained in the army reserves as a full colonel.

"Dr. Swan, what was the toughest case of your career?" the young journalist asked. A 20-year-old memory rose to the surface of Swan's mind. It was the memory of a soldier wounded so badly that Swan's colleagues thought him better off dead.

"What ever became of the guy?" asked McPherson after he had heard the story.

"He made it back to the States," said Swan. "That's all I know."

When Peter McPherson's article appeared, dozens of readers wrote letters to the editor, wanting to know what had become of the young soldier. McPherson called Dr. Swan and suggested they find out. Neither was

sure he would like what he found.

For two years the search became almost an obsession, facing many dead ends and bureaucratic runarounds. But on July 15, 1991, Dr. Swan finally learned that his former patient, Kenneth McGarity, was now living in Columbus, Georgia; that he had a wife and two daughters, had completed his high school education, attended Auburn University, and had learned to scuba dive.

"You must have the wrong guy," Swan said to the person at the Veterans Administration. "My patient had brain damage. He was a double amputee. How would he ever learn to scuba dive?"

"Doctor, this is your patient. If you want to call him, go ahead."

Even though Swan had been searching for Ken McGarity for two years, he was hesitant to call. Even if Ken McGarity was, miraculously, everything the VA said, he still had suffered unbelievably. Would he be hostile? Full of rage?

Finally, though, Swan felt compelled to call McGarity, the man who, according to so many people and human measures, should have died.

When Swan placed the call, an upbeat Southern male voice answered. It was Ken McGarity himself.

Swan explained about the story and his search. "I would like to meet you," he concluded.

"Fine," said Ken McGarity. "You can fill in a lot of holes for me, Dr. Swan. There's a lot of things about that day I would like to know."

So it was that on September 25, 1991, almost 23 years to the day since their fateful encounter in Pleiku, Dr. Swan and Ken McGarity met outside the McGarity home in Columbus, Georgia, accompanied by McPherson and a photographer.

When Ken McGarity extended his hand in greeting, Dr. Swan recognized the amputated right pinkie finger. In that instant, he felt a bond with this man and a healing affirmation that had been 23 years in the making. In the conversation that followed, he was able to offer Ken McGarity some reassuring answers to a host of troubling questions. One had to do with survivor's guilt: Maybe he should have been left to die, as so many had suggested. Perhaps someone else had needed medical attention more.

"No, no," Swan reassured him. Giving Ken the treatment he needed had not meant that he had denied treatment to anyone else.

Then Dr. Swan had his own troubling questions. Had it been worth it? Was Ken happy to be alive?

"I'll tell you," Ken said, "being blind in a wheelchair has its problems. I won't deny that, but really, it's not so bad, Dr. Swan. I would be dead if it weren't for you!"[2]

The publicity generated by Ken's meeting with Dr. Swan created a false image that Ken felt guilty about. Though Ken was indeed grateful to be alive, he was also struggling mightily with post-traumatic-stress disorder. He was separated from his wife and daughters because of the fear and rage that dominated his life.

Ken might be a hero to a nation trying to make up for its shabby treatment of Vietnam veterans, but he knew he was just a guy trying to be a decent husband and father. Yet he also believed that God had brought Dr. Swan back into his life to aid in the second part of his healing—his emotional and spiritual healing.

The publicity caused other vets to get in touch with him, to share war stories and their own problems as civilians. Ken realized he was not alone in his struggles. Others, many others, had suffered from post-traumatic stress disorder.

He was especially pleased to hear from guys in his old Ghostrider helicopter unit, particularly Otto Mertz, the soldier who had dragged him to safety in the midst of the firefight. When they met and renewed their friendship, Ken discovered that Otto was a strong Christian.

Through Otto's witness, Ken began to see that God had preserved his life and nurtured it all along. As Ken began to accept this loving God as the manager of his life, he also began another phase of his turnaround, not only in his behavior but in his affections as well. He no longer wanted to run from God; he wanted to run toward Him, into His embrace. While Ken had known God, even bargained with Him and called to Him, only through this meeting was Ken's spiritual healing complete. At long last Ken McGarity was at peace with God. He was finally on the road to a full recovery. How thankful he was that God, through Dr. Swan, hadn't left him to die that day at Pleiku.

What Ever Happened to Human Life?

Life is a miracle, a sacred gift from God. Nobody knows this better than Ken McGarity.

When Dr. Swan tracked down McGarity 20 years after their fateful encounter in Vietnam, admittedly he did not find his former patient living "happily ever after." Yet despite all his pain, suffering and handicaps, Ken McGarity is thankful to be alive. He knows how precious life is.

What is the meaning of human existence? Where did we come from? Why are we here? What is the value of human life? The most vexing cultural issues of our day—abortion, assisted suicide, euthanasia, genetic engineering—all turn on questions about what it means to be human, the value of human life, and how life should be protected. Which, in turn, center on the question of our origin.

Christians believe that God created human beings in His own image. And because human life bears this divine stamp, life is sacred, a gift from the Creator. He and He alone can set the boundaries of when we live and when we die. As we saw in earlier chapters, against this is the naturalistic belief that life arose from the primordial sea in a chance collision of chemicals, and through billions of years of chance mutations, this biological accident gave rise to the first humans. Millions of people today accept this basic presupposition that we are little more than grown-up germs.

These two worldviews are antithetical, and this antithesis lies at the very heart of our present cultural crisis. The question of where life comes from is not some academic argument for scientists to debate. Our understanding of the origin of life is intensely personal. It determines what we believe about human identity, what we value, and what we believe is the very reason for living. It determines who lives and who dies. This is why ethical questions surrounding human life have become the great defining debate of our age.

The Christian's commitment to life cannot be dismissed as some "love affair with the fetus," as critics charge, or as a desire to impose a repressive Victorian morality.[3] Rather, the Christian's driving conviction is based on biblical revelation, on the very nature of human origins existence.

Until recently, biblical views were also shared by a majority of nonbelievers, though perhaps inconsistently. That's why, confronted with a mangled soldier clinging to life, Dr. Kenneth Swan reacted instinctively. He did not consult some ethics book or fall on his knees and pray for guidance. Having been brought up in a culture steeped in the Judeo-Christian tradition that human life has intrinsic value because it was made in the image and likeness of God, he simply did what came naturally. He saved the man's life!

What has been a culture of life is today being overtaken by the culture of death, a naturalistic ethic sweeping across the entire spectrum, from the unborn to the old and infirm, from the deformed and disabled to the weak and defenseless. Relentlessly pursuing its own logic, this culture of death denies that the human species is superior to other biological species, and it ends by threatening life at every stage. It has advanced so far that assisted suicide (euthanasia) is now a protected constitutional right in one state, paid for by the state's Medicaid program, and infanticide is being openly advocated by respected professors and scientists, with hardly a ripple of public shock or dissent.

Surely this is hyperbole, you may say. Alarmist rhetoric. Well, let's take a look at how the most fundamental convictions upon which Western civilization rested for two millennia are being replaced by a naturalistic ethic of pragmatism and utilitarianism.

The Seismic Shift

The shift from a culture of life to a culture of death has been like a shift in the tectonic plates underlying the continents—as sudden as an earthquake, when measured against the long view of history. It occurred largely in the 1960s, although as with

so much else in American life, the fault lines were evident centuries earlier, in the Age of Reason and the Enlightenment.

The beginning point might be fixed in 1610, with René Descartes revolutionary idea that the human mind, not God, is the source of certainty. By establishing the human mind as the judge of all truth, his philosophy eventually rendered God irrelevant, and since traditional notions of morality and social order are largely derived from Christianity, these moral conventions likewise crumble when God is dismissed as irrelevant or nonexistent.[4] Thus the death of God means the death of morality. Friedrich Nietzsche pressed the idea to its logical conclusion—the loss of morality and meaning.[5]

This is exactly what the twentieth century has done. If we are not created by God—and therefore not bound by His laws—if we are simply the most advanced of the primates, why should we not do whatever we choose? Thus Sigmund Freud promised a utopia based on release of our impulses. In the 1960s, the Age of Aquarius, such views exploded into popular consciousness, aided by inhibition-freeing drugs. Sexual liberation would be the means to create a new, open, egalitarian society where "Nobody can tell us what to do with our bodies." As we have seen, sexual liberation took the place of the liberty provided through forgiveness of sin. In a complete reversal of biblical values, absolute freedom from biblical values became the new messiah, and biblical morality became the new worst sin.

Carry this view to its logical conclusion, and disposing of physical life is of no greater moral consequence than discarding an old set of ill-fitting clothes. Sexual acts between unmar-

ried people or partners of the same sex or even complete strangers have no moral significance.

The same logic is what caused the Supreme Court to decide in Roe v. Wade (1973) that a human fetus is not a person and can therefore legitimately be destroyed.[6] Justice Harry Blackmun, who wrote the majority opinion, acknowledged at the time that if a fetus were a person, then its right to life would be guaranteed under the Fourteenth Amendment (which instructs the states that they may not deprive "any person of life, liberty, or property"). In order to uphold the right to abortion, the Court had to argue that though the fetus is biologically human, it is not a legal person. What's more, if the justices acknowledged that the fetus changed from a nonperson to a person at any stage of pregnancy, then abortion would become an unlawful deprivation of life—in short, murder. Hence, the Court ruled that the fetus is a nonperson with no rights at all at any stage of pregnancy. Only the mother is a person, with a "right to privacy."

Roe v Wade was the leading edge of a powerful social movement, fueled by sexual politics, to free the individual from the yoke of allegedly repressive moral restraints. "Choice" over what to do with one's body became the defining value of the 1970s and 1980s—all the while ignoring the fact that choice in itself cannot possibly be a value and that value depends on what is chosen.

Abortion, you see, has always been about more than abortion. It is the wedge used to split open the historic Western commitment to the dignity of human life. In 1973, when pro-life proponents warned that Roe was taking us down a slippery slope to all manner of horrors, they were mocked as alarmists. Later events proved they were exactly on target.

In 1982, in Bloomington, Indiana, with the case of "Baby Doe," the relentless demand for choice crossed the great divide—from the living fetus in the womb to the living baby outside the womb—and America moved from abortion to infanticide. Baby Doe was born with a deformed esophagus, making it impossible for him to digest food. Doctors proposed a fairly simple operation, a procedure that had proven to be 90 percent successful, but the parents refused permission for the operation, even though they knew this meant certain death. Their own doctor concurred. The reason? Infant Doe was also born with Down's syndrome.[7]

Two Indiana courts declined to intervene, and six days later Baby Doe had starved to death. Columnist George Will, who himself has a Down's syndrome child, declared flatly, "The baby was killed because it was retarded."

In the controversy over Baby Doe, something shocking came to light: Handicapped infants were routinely being allowed to die. As early as 1975, a poll of pediatric surgeons revealed that 77 percent favored withholding food and treatment in the case of defective babies. And in an Oklahoma hospital it was discovered that the pediatric staff considered "quality of life" in deciding whether to treat handicapped children or let them die. Among their considerations of "quality" were race and family income.[8]

Even earlier, of course, the philosophical groundwork for eliminating defective babies was being laid by the abortion debate. In the 1960s, the American Medical Association (AMA) had passed a resolution endorsing abortion when "an infant [was] born with incapacitating physical deformity or mental deficiency."[9] Several states had also already passed laws allowing abortion in these cases. When such a law was passed in New York, a commentator at WCBS radio hailed it, saying, "Abortion … is one sensible method of dealing with such problems as over-population, illegitimacy, and possible birth defects."[10]

Joycelyn Elders, Arkansas State Health Director and later surgeon general of the United States, declared abortion has "an important and positive public health effect," reducing "the number of children afflicted with severe defects."[11] To support her position, Elders cited a study showing that the number of Down's syndrome children born in Washington State in 1976 was "sixty-four percent lower than it would have been without legal abortion."[12] What she failed to say is that most people with Down's syndrome are only moderately retarded and grow into adults capable of holding a job and living independently. If the birth parents cannot cope, there is a waiting list of couples eager to adopt these children. Yet today, they are being targeted for elimination.

Because people with Down's syndrome have an extra chromosome, the condition can be diagnosed before birth by amniocentesis. Insurance companies readily agree to pay for these tests; often, if the test is positive, the insurance companies also cover abortion. But the same companies will not pay the $100,000 or more that is required to sustain the first year of the baby's life. How many couples, facing such a choice, can withstand the economic pressure? Not many. Studies show that 90 percent choose abortion—often under pressure from doctors.[13]

For any "unwanted" or "defective" baby who may manage to slip through this front line of defense, there is always the ultimate solution. Francis Crick, who along with James Watson won the Nobel prize for the discovery of the double helix structure in DNA, advocates that all newborns be screened to determine who should live. All who fail to reach a certain level on the Apgar test, used to determine the health of newborns, would be euthanized.[14]

The rationale for all of this is a dualism between body and person. Rights belong only to persons; so if someone can be reduced to a nonperson, then he or she has no rights. Such is the ethical theory of Peter Singer, newly appointed Ira DeCamp Professor of Bioethics at Princeton, who openly advocates permitting parents to kill disabled babies on the basis that they are "nonpersons" until they are rational and self-conscious. As nonpersons, he says, they are "replaceable," like chickens or farm animals. And Singer does not stop there. He goes on to advocate killing incompetent persons of any age if their families decide their lives are "not worth living."[15] (This is the unspeakably inhumane brand of ethics that students in some of our nation's most prestigious schools are now learning. And what will happen when these elite students move into elite positions of power?)

The baby in the womb, having been reduced to the status of a nonperson, is then demonized in pro-choice literature as a hostile aggressor against the mother, and abortion is dressed up as self-defense. Northeastern University professor Eileen McDonagh claims that the fetus "massively intrudes on a woman's body and expropriates her liberty," justifying the "use of deadly force to stop it," just as in cases of "rape, kidnapping, or slavery."[16] Clearly, anyone who threatens our cherished right to do whatever we please with our bodies must be stopped, by whatever means necessary.

Many well-meaning Americans, including Christians, have bought into the "choice" argument. They don't see that abortion, infanticide, euthanasia, and genocide are all part of the same package. The logic that supports abortion as a "useful social policy" to prevent the birth of "defectives," or to reduce welfare and crime, applies with equal force at all stages of life. If the body is merely an instrument of the self, if it has no inherent dignity, then we are free to dispose of it at will—or others are free to dispose of it for us.

The abortion lobby does get it, however, which is why feminist organizations fight relentlessly to defend even partial-birth abortion—a gruesome procedure that the AMA has denounced and that even its practitioners have acknowledged is not medically necessary. It is why the abortion lobby fights so furiously against any diminution of abortion rights, even minor limits such as parental notification. Why do prochoicers oppose even modest limits? Because they understand that abortion represents a worldview conflict: God and the sanctity of life versus the individual's moral autonomy. They can give no quarter.

Opinion polls show consistent and growing public support for euthanasia—in the name of patients' rights and compassion, of course. Even Dr. Kevorkian, who puts his "patients" to death ignominiously in cheap trailers or motel rooms and then dumps the bodies at local hospitals, fails to arouse genuine public outcry.

The line between assisted suicide and euthanasia has become a legal fiction. Legislatures or courts may slow the process here or there, but the train is out of the station and roaring down the tracks. Even if euthanasia is not yet secure as a constitutional right (except in Oregon), its practice is on the increase.

In the end, these issues all hinge on the way a culture views human life. If human life bears the stamp of the divine Maker, it is infinitely precious, but if human life is simply a product of biology or nature, a utilitarian unit, then utilitarian values become the dominant determinant. Get the dying, the infirm, the disabled, the nonproductive, out of the way of the living.

Looking at life through the eyes of a helpless quadriplegic who requires vast sums of money and human resources for support, or through the eyes of a Ken McGarity, we see with laser-beam focus the deadly logic of a worldview that degrades life.[17]

The supremely tragic irony in all of this is that a supposedly exalted view of human reason has led to a degraded view of human life. When Descartes declared, "I think, therefore I am," he had no idea his slogan would lead to a culture in which what I am is determined by what other people think.

Brave New World?

Descartes also did not anticipate where this low view of human life would lead us. Aldous Huxley, in his strangely prophetic novel *Brave New World,* carried his family's utopian vision to its logical conclusion. The novel opens with a visit to a laboratory where rack upon rack of glass bottles clatter across conveyor belts. Each bottle contains a carefully fertilized human egg immersed in amni-

otic gel, predestined for a specific purpose, ranging from the alphas (the intellectuals) to the gammas (the manual laborers). Defects are eliminated, and most females are neutered.

This remarkable process creates a perfect species capable of living in complete harmony and stability, a species free of all antiquated encumbrances such as family and child rearing. To insure the unfettered pursuit of happiness, free sex is encouraged—the more the better—and an all-purpose drug is readily available. Life is perpetual bliss. When it becomes burdensome or inconvenient, it is gently and mercifully ended.

Huxley's vision was not some bizarre fantasy. All that he did was extrapolate from ideas then being soberly discussed among his friends in the intelligentsia. Eugenics—the idea of improving the human race through selective breeding—did not originate in Hitler's laboratories. It originated in the 1920s and 1930s among respectable and sophisticated men and women in places like London, Philadelphia, and New York.

On the horizon of today's brave new world looms the specter of genetic engineering, the ultimate attempt to create a race without defects. Hardly any obstacles remain in the path of this final expression of human autonomy; in fact we're nearly there.

Achieving *Brave New World* technology is only a matter of time. Research called EG—for extracorporeal gestation—is now underway at the Juntendo University in Tokyo and Temple University in Philadelphia and is intended to create an artificial womb for severely premature babies.[18] If the research is successful, the same technology will surely be developed further so the artificial womb can house a fertilized egg.

There is almost no stopping the technological imperative: If something can be done, it will be done. Then, with the role of biological parents rendered superfluous, humanity can take another important step along the road to total autonomy. Truly our capabilities have exceeded our ethical and moral grasp.

Though most Christian ethicists support assisted reproduction if used only to help restore natural function, the problem comes when we do things never done in nature—for example, genetic combinations impossible in nature. The technology of in vitro or in vivo fertilization also makes possible a host of morally dubious practices, such as the harvesting of fetal tissue for medical purposes, the disposal of fertilized eggs that are capable of becoming fetuses, and surrogate parenthood, which has already opened a Pandora's box. We hear of a woman who is impregnated by her son-in-law and gives birth to her daughter's child. Gay and lesbians mingle at gatherings they call "Sperm-Egg Mixers," where they examine one another with an eye toward selecting good genes. Two lesbians may contract with a gay man for his sperm for artificial insemination, or two men may contract with a lesbian whom they chose to be a surrogate mother.[19]

There is little left in our culture to restrain or even slow the process.[20] In Britain, a prestigious committee under the leadership of Dame Mary Warnock, professor of moral philosophy at Cambridge, was organized to provide moral guidance on these questions. But Dame Warnock herself says that in these issues "everyone has a right to judge for himself." And who could possibly object?

The answer, of course, is anyone who is truly human. Something within us stirs ceaselessly in search of meaning, purpose, and connection. Christians know this something as the soul, or the imago Dei—the image of God within us. Because of the doctrine of creation, we know life has worth. We know it is rooted in something beyond the test tube or colliding atoms, even as every voice around us says otherwise.

Discussion Questions

1. How does Ken McGarity's story illustrate the sacredness of every human life?

2. How does Ken's story illustrate how our society has adopted a view of life as cheap rather than sacred?

3. What practical difference has the naturalist worldview made in our society's view of life? What difference has it made in our laws?

4. What difference has your study of *How Now Shall We Live* made in how you view life?

5. How would you explain to a friend that worldview shapes the practical issues such as how we value life?

---

[1]This story is based not only on interviews with Ken and Theresa McGarity as well as with Dr. Kenneth Swan, but also on information found in the following sources: Peter MacPherson, "The War Surgeon's Dilemma: Confronting His Vietnam Past: Was the Life He Saved Worth Living?" *Washington Post,* 7 January 1992; Colonel Kenneth G. Swan, MC USAR, "Triage: The Path Revisited," *Military Medicine 161* (August 1996): 448-52; "Doubt Gone, Doctor Glad He Saved GI," *Chicago Tribune,* 28 November 1991; Joan Sanchez, "Army Doctor Tracks Down His Patient," *Los Angeles Times,* 8 December 1991.

[2]Dr. Kenneth Swan stayed in touch with Ken McGarity, and soon after their first meeting, Swan called with extraordinary news. He had arranged for McGarity to receive the medals he had never been awarded because of a mix-up in record keeping. On January 30, 1992, at Fort Benning, Georgia, Kenneth McGarity finally received his Purple Heart, an Air Medal, and four additional prestigious awards.

[3]Joycelyn Elders, former surgeon general, accused pro-lifers of carrying on a "love affair with the fetus" at an abortion rights rally in January 1992.

[4]Medieval philosophers had argued from the existence of God to the reality of the world. Descartes reversed that, and from then on philosophers argued from the certainty of self to the reality of God and the world. From human reason alone, philosophers would discover all truth. This was the birth of the autonomy of human reason.

[5]Friedrich Nietzsche, *The Gay Science,* trans. Walter Kaufmann (New York: Random, 1974), 125.

[6]Roe v. Wade, 410 US 113 (1973).

[7]Nearly a decade earlier, two eminent pediatricians at Yale-New Haven Hospital had supported the parents' right to let their severely handicapped children die in such cases and suggested that doctors present the option if parents don't bring it up themselves. See Raymond S. Duff and A.G. M. Campbell, "Moral and Ethical Dilemmas in the Special-Care Nursery," *New England Journal of Medicine 289,* no. 17 (October 25, 1973): 890-94.

[8]Richard A. Gross, Alan Cox, Ruth Tatyrek, Michael Polly, and William A. Barnes, "Early Management and Decision Making for the Treatment of Myelomeningocele," *Pediatrics 72,* no. 4 (October 4, 1983): 450-58.

[9]Tucker Carlson, "Eugenics, American Style," *The Weekly Standard 2,* no. 12 (December 2, 1996): 20.

[10]Nat Hentoff, "Abortion as Self-Defense," *Washington Post,* 1 February 1997.

[11]Carlson, "Eugenics, American Style," 20.

[12]Christopher Scanlan, "Elders: I'm Willing to Be a Lightning Rod," *Houston Chronicle,* 17 December 1992.

[13]Carlson, "Eugenics, American Style," 20.

[14]See C. Everett Koop, "Life and Death and the Handicapped Unborn," *Issues in Law & Medicine 5,* no. 1 (June 22, 1989): 101.

[15]As quoted in Cal Thomas, "Who Cares about Living When the Good Times Are Rolling," *Naples Daily News,* 16 July 1998.

[16]Eileen I. McDonagh, *Breaking the Abortion Deadlock: From Choice to Consent* (New York: Oxford University Press, 1996), 7.

[17]Tony Mauro, "Disabled Plan Protest against Assisted Suicide," *USA Today,* 6 January 1997.

[18]Eric Zorn, "'Brave New World' Awaits Debaters of Abortion Rights," *Chicago Tribune,* 9 March 1997.

[19]"Michael Has Four Parents: The Politics of Childbearing," *BreakPoint Commentary,* June 21, 1995.

[20]I strongly recommend reading Richard John Neuhaus, "The Return of Eugenics," *Commentary* (April 1988): 18-26.

God's Training Ground

The effects of the worldview war permeate society. In this unit you will examine naturalism's impact on the family.

We have seen that two worldviews—Christianity and naturalism—are at war in the world and in our culture. Both systems are essentially religious in nature. They represent the basic assumptions we make about where we came from, what's wrong with our world, and what needs to be done to fix it. Up until now, the war has been tragically one-sided. Our courts, and unfortunately, too many Christians have recognized only one of the worldviews as an expression of a religious belief. The result has been like a boxing match with one fighter's hands literally tied behind his back.

The effects of the worldview war can be seen in every area of society, but nowhere is the toll greater than in the family. In this unit we examine some of the results naturalism has brought about.

Attitudes Instilled in Children

Imagine your children bringing home a library book that assures them divorce is nothing serious, just a transition some families go through. Or don't imagine it. Go to the library yourself, and you'll find a rainbow of children's books that downplay the importance of an intact marriage.

"There are different kinds of daddies," one book for preschoolers reassures them. "Sometimes a daddy goes away like yours did. He may not see his children at all." In other words, divorce is just a normal variation on fatherhood. "Some kids know both their mom and their dad, and some kids don't," says another book. Still another treats divorce as an awkward moment that can be mastered by applying a few practical tips. "Living with one parent almost always means there will be less money. Be prepared to give up some things."[1] The message? That daddies who stay and daddies who leave are just "different kinds of daddies" and that divorce has no moral significance.

The message does not end with picture books for young children. When the Institute for American Values surveyed twenty of the most widely used college textbooks in undergraduate courses on marriage and family, it uncovered a shockingly negative outlook on the subject.[2] The textbooks emphasize problems such as domestic violence while downplaying the benefits of marriage. They warn women that marriage is likely to be psychologically stifling, and even physically threatening; one textbook

states boldly, "We do know ... that marriage has an adverse effect on women's mental health," an assertion that has no support in empirical data. In fact, most studies find that both men and women report higher levels of happiness when they are married.[3] Meanwhile, these volumes all but ignore the well-documented negative effects of divorce on children, only half even mentioning the fact that family breakdown correlates strongly with increased juvenile crime.

It would not have been surprising to find a few ideologically biased textbooks. What is disturbing is finding that virtually all the textbooks used by students across the nation are preaching the views of radical feminism and the sexual revolution to our nation's future teachers, guidance counselors, and case workers.

Out of sheer self-interest, if for no other reason, nearly every civilization has protected the family both legally and socially, for it is the institution that propagates the human race and civilizes children. Yet in postmodern America, the family is being assaulted on many fronts, from books to popular magazines, on television and in movies, through state and federal policies. This systematic deconstruction of the oldest, most basic social institution is a prime cause of the social chaos America has experienced in recent decades.

As we move out from the range of individuals and their choices, the first circle of influence is in the intimate relationships of the family. Nowhere is the clash of worldviews more pronounced than here. Nowhere are its effects more disastrous. Nowhere does it touch more deeply on the natural order that underlies all civilizations. And nowhere is it more evident that Christians must take a worldview approach if we are going to make a difference.

Many believers have become politically active over issues related to the family, yet our efforts are usually reactive rather than proactive, largely because we have failed to confront the underlying worldview assumptions.

Culture's View of the Family

Conflicting worldviews were displayed sharply when then-Vice President Dan Quayle delivered his infamous "Murphy Brown" speech in 1992, which evoked howls of ridicule from one end of the country to the other. Many Americans tuned in to the next season's opening show just to hear Candice Bergen's response. The star did not disappoint her audience. As Murphy Brown, she looked straight into the camera and lectured viewers that there is no normative definition of the family. All that matters, she intoned, is "commitment, love, and caring."

Shortly afterward, however, Bergen was interviewed in *TV Guide* and took quite a different line. "As far as my family values go," she said, "my child and my family have always been my top priority." Bergen even claimed that she had been one step ahead of

Dan Quayle, having warned the show's producers not to "send out the message … to young women especially, that we're encouraging them to be single mothers." She ended by declaring that "I myself … believe the ideal is that you have a two-parent family. I'm the last person to think fathers are obsolete."[4]

When speaking as cultural icon Murphy Brown, she insists there is no normative family structure. But as Candice Bergen, wife and mother, she enthusiastically supports the committed, two-parent family.

Double Messages

If we are to understand contemporary moral liberalism, we must dissect this puzzling inconsistency. We live in an age in which liberty has been defined as absolutely free choice. It doesn't matter what we choose; the dignity of the individual resides in the mere capacity to choose.

So we are perfectly free to favor marriage and traditional values, just as long as we don't deny others the right to choose other values. That is, as long as we don't claim that our choice is based on an objective, normative standard of truth that applies to everyone.

So Bergen feels perfectly free to reveal her own adherence to traditional ideals for the family because all she's doing is expressing her own private, personal, subjective opinion. But when Dan Quayle expresses identical ideals, he is savaged in the media and ridiculed by late-night comedians. Even Bergen condemned him as "arrogant," "aggressive," and "offensive"— even though she apparently holds precisely the same views.[5] Why? Because Quayle is presenting these views not as personal preferences but as objective moral truths.

This subtle distinction is at the heart of moral conflicts in our culture. As a result, we cannot determine people's worldview simply by asking about their position on particular moral questions: Are you for or against abortion? Are you for or against homosexual marriage? Instead, we must ask how they justify their views.

Many Americans retain traditional ideals but regard them as matters of personal choice, refusing to insist on them as objective, universal norms. The most familiar example is those who are "personally opposed" to abortion yet defend the right of others to make their own choice. In fact, many Americans practice exemplary ethical behavior, yet when asked to articulate objective principles to justify that behavior, they can offer nothing beyond, "It feels right for me."[6]

The distinction between personal beliefs and objective truth appears most glaringly when it comes to family and sexuality. People use the traditional terms *marriage* and *family,* but the words no longer muster a sense of objective obligation.

Many Americans no longer treat marriage as a moral commitment with its own definition and nature, a commitment that makes objective demands of us, regardless of what we might prefer. Instead, marriage is regarded as a social construction, as something one can define according to one's own preferences.

We must learn to cut through the rhetoric and get to the root of this conflict, which again hinges on our basic assumptions about creation, the fall, and redemption. The Christian worldview teaches that from the beginning, God created individuals in relationship. By creating human beings as male and female, God established the interrelatedness of human sexuality, the marital relationship, and the institution of the family, each with its own divinely-given moral norms. While there can be great variety in the cultural expression of these institutions, when we enter into the covenant of marriage and family, we submit to an objective and God-given structure.

During the Enlightenment, as we explained earlier, philosophers began rejecting the doctrine of creation and substituting the idea of a pre-social, pre-political "state of nature." In this primeval state, they believe individuals are autonomous, and social bonds are reduced to a matter of choice. The basic tenet of modern liberalism is, in the words of French philosopher Pierre Manent, that "no individual can have an obligation to which he has not consented."[7]

This radically changes one's view of marriage, for if it is not rooted in the way we were originally created, then it is something we can alter at our own will. What's more, all choices become morally equivalent, and there is no justification for favoring some choices over others.

If someone wants a traditional marriage, that's fine. If someone else wants a same-sex marriage or some other variant, well, that's fine too.

This moral equivalence has led to an aggressive defense of deviant practices. In Hollywood, for example, it's become normal to have children out of wedlock and to grow patchwork families from various couplings. For these people, foregoing marriage is not merely a matter of unrestrained sexual urges; it's an expression of genuine conviction, an assertion that cohabitation is as morally acceptable as marriage.

Inverse Moral Crusades

Film critic Michael Medved found out about this inverse moral crusade when he commended the film production work of a particular Hollywood couple, referring to them as "married." This was a natural assumption, since they had been together more than 15 years and had given birth to two children. Ah, but one can no longer assume such things, and Medved received an angry letter from a friend of the couple, saying that the two were certainly not married and that they would be "offended" to hear themselves described that way.[8]

Offended? Assuming that someone is married is now an insult? What we're seeing is that challenges to traditional morality are themselves treated as moral crusades. For if no choices are wrong, then no lifestyle may be criticized and one must never be made to feel guilty. Put in world-view terms, "sin" is hemming others in with oppressive rules and artificial moral codes; "redemption" means getting back to the freedom once enjoyed in the original "state of nature."

As political philosopher John Stuart Mill once wrote, "the mere example of nonconformity, the mere refusal to bend the knee to custom, is itself a service."[9] Now, there's a positive spin on immorality: If you deliberately reject moral and social rules, you're actually performing a service, helping to free people from the grip of oppressive moral traditions.

This is the philosophy of the "unencumbered self," says Harvard political philosopher Michael Sandel, a worldview that depicts the self as prior to all commitments or moral obligations. In traditional societies, a person's identity was found in and expressed through the social roles he or she played in the family, church, village,

trade, tribe, and ethnic group. Today, however, roles and responsibilities are regarded as separate from, even contradictory to, one's essential identity, one's core self. The self can either accept or reject them in the process of defining itself.[10]

This has intensely practical consequences. One of the themes of the feminist movement has been that women are stifled by the roles of wife and mother, and must discover their true self apart from these relationships. As a result, many women have rejected marriage and motherhood; some have resorted to abortion to avoid having children, or, if they do have children, the mothers use day care to avoid rearing them.

The blame for these trends, however, does not rest solely with feminism. One reason women found the theme of autonomy so persuasive is that it had already been adopted by men for nearly half a century.

In colonial times, manhood was defined in terms of responsibility for the family and the common good; today, "true" masculinity tends to be defined as individualistic, aggressive, and self-assertive.

This new image emerged at the end of the nineteenth century in cowboy and adventure fiction that "celebrated the man who had escaped the confines of domesticity."[11] By the 1950s, *Playboy* came on the scene, warning that marriage is a trap that will "crush man's adventurous, freedom-loving spirit."[12]

The roles of husband and father, instead of being God-ordained responsibilities that express a man's essential nature, became restricting conventions that contradict a man's true self. This bore deadly fruit as men deserted their family responsibilities, a trend so widespread today that the dominant social problem in America is male flight from the family.[13]

The notion of the "unencumbered self" has caused both men and women to view family relationships as arbitrary and confusing roles. That's why people like sexuality researcher Shere Hite can insist that "the breakdown of the family is a good thing," because it liberates us from restrictive roles and rules.[14]

This negative view of marriage has yielded consequences across the culture. If people dare to say marriage is superior to other arrangements, they are accused of "discrimination."

Elayne Bennett, founder of Best Friends, a program that teaches girls to delay sexual involvement until after high school, was once asked why she did not urge girls to delay sex until marriage. "If we talk about marriage," she said, "the schools won't let us in."[15]

Let that sink in for a moment: Many public schools today won't even consider a program that holds marriage up as an ideal. In addition, many public policies no longer protect marriage as a unique social good: In tax law, there's the marriage penalty; in business, there are spousal benefits for people who are not married; in the courts, there are rulings that put homosexual unions on the same level as marriage.[16] The family is treated as a loose collection of rights-bearing individuals who hook up with others in whatever ways they choose to for their own benefit.

Popular culture echoes this message. The same people who bring us heartwarming Hallmark family films also produced a wedding card that reads, "I can't promise you forever. But I can promise you today." Equally telling, a cartoon in a major magazine depicts a young man saying to his girlfriend, "It's only marriage I'm proposing, after all, not a lifetime commitment."

Acclaimed novelist Toni Morrison has said the nuclear family "is a paradigm that just doesn't work. … Why we are hanging on to it, I don't know."[17] And popular entertainment consistently portrays divorce and adultery as forms of liberation.

In the closing scene of the hit movie *Mrs. Doubtfire,* the central character reassures a young girl after her parents' break-up that after divorce some parents "get along much better … and they can become better people and much better mommies and daddies."[18]

How about a reality check here? Social science statistics show that divorced parents don't generally become "better mommies and daddies." Few fathers even see their children regularly, and mothers spend less time with their children, too, because of the emotional devastation they suffer and the increased responsibilities they bear. In fact, the negative consequences of divorce are being measured over and over again, and the findings are grim.[19]

Consider these statistics. Children in single-parent families are six times more likely to be poor, and half the single mothers in the United States live below the poverty line. Children of divorce suffer intense grief, which often lasts for many years. Even as young adults, they are nearly twice as likely to require psychological help.

Children from disrupted families have more academic and behavioral problems and are nearly twice as likely to drop out of high school.[20] Girls in single-parent homes are at much greater risk for precocious sexuality and are three times more likely to have a child out of wedlock.[21]

Crime and substance abuse are strongly linked to fatherless households. Studies show that 60 percent of rapists grew up in fatherless homes, as did 72 percent of adolescent murderers, and 70 percent of all long-term prison inmates. In fact, most social pathologies disrupting American life today can be traced to fatherlessness.[22]

Surprisingly, when divorced parents marry other people, their children are not any better off, and some studies actually show that the children develop increased pathologies. Preschool children in stepfamilies, for example, are 40 times more likely to suffer physical or sexual abuse.[23]

Adults are also profoundly harmed by divorce. A study that examined the impact of divorce 10 years after the divorce found that among two-thirds of divorced couples, one partner is still depressed and financially precarious. Among a quarter of all divorced couples, both former partners are worse off, suffering from loneliness and depression.[24]

Divorce affects even physical health. Children of divorce are more prone to illness, accidents, and suicide. Divorced men are twice as likely as married men to die from heart disease, stroke, hypertension, and cancer. They are four times more likely to die in auto accidents and suicide, and their odds are seven times higher for pneumonia and cirrhosis of the liver. Divorced women lose 50 percent more time to illness and injury each year than do married women, and they are two to three times as likely to die of all forms of cancer. Both divorced men and women are almost five times more likely to succumb to substance abuse.[25] The impact of divorce on health, says psychiatrist David Larson, "is like starting to smoke a pack of cigarettes a day."[26]

The effects don't stop with the families directly involved. When family breakdown becomes widespread, entire neighborhoods decay. Neighborhoods without fathers are often infected with crime and delinquency. They are often places where teachers cannot teach because misbehaving children disrupt classrooms. Moreover, children of divorce are much more likely to get divorced themselves as adults, so that the negative consequences pass on to the next generation. In this way, family breakdown affects the entire society.[27]

Generation Xers often sense these truths better than their baby-boomer parents do. Many have suffered through their parents' divorce(s) and typically say they desperately hope for a marriage that will endure while at the same time they are profoundly pessimistic about marriage. When grunge-rock star Kurt Cobain committed suicide, reporters digging into his private life discovered that when he was eight years old, his parents divorced, sending him into a sharp downward spiral. "It destroyed him," admits his mother, Wendy Cobain. "He changed completely." The experience was so painful that in a 1994 suicide attempt, Cobain had a note in his pocket that said, "I'd rather die than go through a divorce."[28]

The time is ripe for Christians to make a persuasive case for a biblical view of marriage and family, using statistics like these to frame a convincing argument that people are happier and healthier in stable families. And then we must learn how to model the biblical view before a watching world.

A Biblical View of the Family

What does the Christian worldview say about the family? The doctrine of creation tells us God made us with a definite nature (in his image) and gave us a definite task: to nurture and develop the powers of nature (fill the earth and subdue it) and to form families and create societies (be fruitful and increase in number).

The image of God is reflected, in part, in the differentiation of humanity into two sexes. "God created man in his own image … male and female he created them" (Gen. 1:27). The implication is that to be a husband or wife, a father or mother, is not an artificial or arbitrary role separate from our "true" self, a threat to authentic personhood. Instead, these relationships form an intrinsic part of our fundamental identity, of what makes us fully human. Liberation is not found by escaping these roles but by embracing them and carrying out our responsibilities in a manner faithful to God's ideals.

In other parts of Scripture, we learn that marriage is deep in spiritual symbolism and meaning—a mystical mirror of the relationship between God and His people. Ancient fertility religions often imagined God to be both male and female, and pagan theology was expressed in fertility celebrations of ritual fornication in temple prostitution. That's why, in the Old Testament, idolatry is often called fornication. In direct contrast to their pagan neighbors, the Bible writers saw in marriage, with the faithful love between husband and wife, an image of God's faithful love for His people. In the New Testament, Paul likened the relationship between a husband and a wife to the "profound mystery" of Christ's union with His bride, the church (see Eph. 5).

As husband and wife come together, they form a family, the core institution of human society—the training ground, in fact, for all other social institutions. Human sexuality is not designed merely as a source of pleasure or a means of expressing affection. It was designed as a powerful bond between husband and wife to form a secure, stable environment for raising vulnerable children to adulthood. Family life is the "first school" that prepares us to participate in the religious, civic, and political life of society, training us in the virtues that enable us to place the common good before our own private goals. Saying no to sex outside marriage means saying yes to this broader vision of marriage as the foundation of an enduring institution that not only meets personal needs but also ties us into a wider community through mutual obligations and benefits.

It's not enough to insist that sex outside marriage is sinful or that practicing homosexuality is wrong. We must learn to articulate in a positive way the overall biblical worldview that makes sense of these moral principles. We must explain what it means to live within an objective, created moral order instead of perpetuating the chaotic reign of the autonomous self.

Restoring the Family

How well has the church taught this biblical model and helped believers to live it? Sadly, many local churches' response to the decline of marriage has been helpless hand-wringing and haranguing against a decadent culture. Few clergy have known how to put the brakes on the destructive trends that have torn marriages apart at ever-increasing rates, even within their own congregations.

What are some of the most important principles that churches can teach families? For starters, believers should be encouraged to treat their own families as a ministry—a mission to the surrounding culture. Many friends of mine have this kind of vision for their families, and one family in particular has achieved bountiful success. As a young couple, Jack and Rhodora Donahue decided that their job as Christians was to produce a strong family. Today, they have 13 children and 75 grandchildren, and all are committed Christians. Some are clergy, some are involved in starting Christian schools, and most are active in lay ministries such as Young Life and Prison Fellowship. And the Donahues continue to educate their children and grandchildren, often holding dinner parties where they invite speakers to address topical issues, then spending the entire evening discussing related theological, philosophical, and moral questions.

As a stirring historical model, consider Jonathan Edwards, the Congregational pastor, scholar, and leader of the first Great Awakening. He and his wife, Sarah, reared 11 children, and by the year 1900, the family had 1400 descendants, among them 13 college presidents; 65 professors; 100 lawyers; 30 judges; 66 physicians; and 80 prominent public officials, including 3 governors, 3 senators, and a vice president of the United States. With families of such learning and distinction, it's no wonder the Puritans did so much to shape the American mind and character. If modern evangelicals hope to leave the same powerful legacy, we need to realize that the task of culture building requires a long-term commitment, and we must focus on nurturing godly families to influence future generations.[29]

Whether your family is small or large, whether your resources are extensive or sparse, every Christian par-

ent is called to make the home a ministry. This means educating our children in a biblical worldview and equipping them to have an impact on the world. In the long run, this is the best way that Christians can restore and redeem the surrounding culture.

Back in the 1970s, books touted divorce as liberation, with titles like *Divorce: The New Freedom* and *Creative Divorce*.[30] The common presumption was that divorce creates only temporary distress and that individuals soon bounce back and go on to form new and more "meaningful relationships." Divorce was even presented as a chance for inner growth and self-actualization. But the moral tides are turning, and people are showing a growing concern for the social cost of family breakdown, reflected in titles such as, *The Case against Divorce* by Diane Medved, *Divorce Busters* by Michele Weiner-Davis, and *Rethinking Divorce* by William Galston.[31]

There are even efforts underway to eliminate no-fault divorce, which gives all the legal power to those who walk away from their family commitments. Christians ought to line up behind efforts like these to build moral accountability back into family law.

The family is one arena where every Christian can and must be a redemptive force. Yet, as Christian parents work to incorporate biblical principles within their own families, they inevitably come up against the counterforce of public education. Nowhere has the secular worldview gained a firmer foothold than in our nation's schools. Since the education of our children shapes the future, Christians must actively begin to take our redemptive message directly into the nation's classrooms.

Discussion Questions

1. What are some reasons that well-meaning people might downplay the negative aspects of divorce?

2. What deeper worldview beliefs might cause the writers of materials on marriage and family to present a falsely negative view of marriage?

3. Put yourself in the place of the person with a secular worldview and a feminist ideology. Think in terms of the Marxist categories where oppression by men becomes the equivalent of the fall. How might you be on an "inverse moral crusade" against marriage?

4. How would you argue the case for a biblical view of marriage?

5. What can you do to strengthen marriage in your home, church, community, and nation?

[1] David Blankenhorn, "Where's Dad?" *Atlanta Journal and Constitution,* 19 March 1995; and Barbara Dafoe Whitehead, "Dan Quayle Was Right," *Atlantic Monthly* 271, no. 4 (April 1993): 47. We are not criticizing books that genuinely help children of divorce—only those that treat divorce as morally insignificant.
[2] See Norval D. Glenn, *Closed Hearts, Closed Minds: The Textbook Story of Marriage* (New York: The Institution for American Values, 1997).
[3] Ibid., 5.
[4] Candice Bergen, interviewed in "Candy Is Dandy, but Don't Mess with Murphy," *TV Guide* (September 19, 1992): 8.
[5] Ibid.
[6] See Robert N. Bellah, *Habits of the Heart: Individualism and Commitment in American Life* (Berkeley, Calif.: University of California, 1985).
[7] Pierre Manent, "Modern Individualism," *Crisis* (October 1995): 35.
[8] Michael Medved, "Hollywood Chic," *Washington Post* 4 October 1992.
[9] John Stuart Mill, On Liberty (Indianapolis: Hackett, 1978), 12.
[10] Michael J. Sandel, *Democracy's Discontent: America in Search of a Public Philosophy* (Cambridge Mass.: Belknap Press, 1996), 113.
[11] Steven Mintz and Susan Kellogg, *Domestic Revolutions: A Social History of American Family Life* (New York: Free Press, 1988), 117. For a discussion of these historical trends and a definition of masculinity and fatherhood, see Nancy R. Pearcey, "Rediscovering Parenthood in the Information Age," *The Family in America*

8, no. 3 (March 1994).

[12]Cited in Barbara Ehrenreich, *The Hearts of Men: American Dreams and the Flight from Commitment* (New York: Doubleday, 1983), 47. See also Pearcey, "Rediscovering Parenthood in the Information Age."

[13]David Blankenhorn, *Fatherless America: Confronting Our Most Urgent Social Problem* (New York: HarperPerennial, 1996).

[14]Shere Hite, "The Case against Family Values," *Washington Post,* 10 July 1994.

[15]Elayne Bennett, "If She's Facing Adolescent Girls Today," lecture given at the Heritage Foundation, February 1995).

[16]A recent Hawaii Supreme Court decision permitting gay "marriage" is often portrayed as simply opening up traditional marriage to gays. Rather than broaden traditional marriage, however, the decision denies the existence of traditional marriage altogether by redefining "marriage" purely in terms of legally protected economic benefits, leading to the logical conclusion that these benefits ought to be available to any and all people, regardless of gender or sexuality. In the same way, the legal definition of the family has been so watered down that it no longer bears any resemblance to traditional notions, as when a New Jersey judge said that six college kids on summer vacation constituted a family. See Gerard Bradley, "The New Constitutional Covenant," *World & I* (March 1994): 374.

[17]Bonnie Angelo and Toni Morrison, "The Pain of Being Black," *Time* (May 22, 1989), 120.

[18]As quoted in William R. Mattox, "Split Personality: Why Aren't Conservatives Talking about Divorce?" *Policy Review,* no. 73 (summer 1995): 50.

[19]Ibid.

[20]Whitehead, "Dan Quayle Was Right," 47.

[21]Michael McManus, "Voters Should Care about Divorce Reform," *Detroit News,* 19 September 1996.

[22]David Popenoe, *Life without Fathers: Compelling New Evidence That Fatherhood and Marriage Are Indispensible for the Good of Children and Society* (New York: Free Press, 1996), 63.

[23]Whitehead, "Dan Quayle Was Right," 47.

[24]Judith S. Wallerstein and Sandra Blakeslee, *Second Chances: Men, Women, and Children a Decade after Divorce* (New York: Ticknor & Fields, 1989), 21-31.

[25]James J. Lynch, *The Broken Heart: The Medical Consequences of Loneliness in America* (New York: Basic Books, 1977), 69-86, 87-90, 41-50, appendix B.

[26]David Larson, as quoted in Mattox, "Split Personality," 50.

[27]Allan Carlson is president of the Howard Center for the Family, Religion, and Society, which analyzes the status of the family today and disseminates research that empirically validates marriage as the foundation to a healthy society. These findings are published in *The Family in America,* available from The Howard Center for the Family, Religion, and Society, 934 North Main Street, Rockford, IL 61103, phone: (815) 964-5819.

[28]Karl Zinsmeister, "The Humble Generation," American Enterprise 9, no. 1 (January/February 1998): 4.

[29]Elisabeth D. Dodds, *Marriage to a Difficult Man: The "Uncommon Union" of Jonathan and Sarah Edwards* (Philadelphia: Westminster Press, 1971), chapter 14.

[30]Mel Krantzler, *Creative Divorce* (New York: M. Evans, 1973); and Esther Oshiver Fisher, *Divorce: The New Freedom* (New York: Harper & Row, 1974).

[31]Diane Medved, *The Case against Divorce* (New York: Ivy Books, 1990); Michele Weiner-Davis, *Divorce Busting: A Revolutionary and Rapid Program for Staying Together* (New York: Simon & Schuster, 1993); and William A. Galston, *Rethinking Divorce* (Minneapolis: Center for the American Experiment, 1996).

A Society that Works

For peace and harmony, we must have a shared sense of ethics.
In this unit you will consider worldview's impact on morality.

What does it take to achieve the good life, a life of virtue? Our Founding Fathers understood this is a crucial question for any society; virtue is essential to freedom. People who cannot restrain their own baser instincts and treat one another with civility are not capable of self-government. "Our Constitution was designed for a moral and religious people," said John Adams. "It is wholly inadequate for the government of any other."[1] Without virtue, a society can be ruled only by fear, a truth tyrants understand all too well.

How can we achieve the virtue necessary to maintain a good society and to preserve liberty? How do the worldview categories of creation, fall, and redemption help us analyze the false views we confront in our culture?

Sadly, in our relativistic age, many people, even Christians, have lost the ethical categories of right and wrong. A few years ago, a young acquaintance of mine, a member of a good church, raved about a four-week ethics course at Harvard Business School—a course that was started in response to the "Savings and Loans" scandals in the 1980s.

"What kind of ethics are they teaching?" I asked.

"Well, the professor really summed it up the last day when he said, 'Don't do anything that will get you in the newspapers. It's bad for business.'"

"But that's pure pragmatism!" I replied. "Don't get caught. Don't get the company in trouble. What's that got to do with ethics?"

"But isn't the point?" said the young man. "To stay out of trouble."

This perspective is quite common. I have no grounds for self-righteousness; when I was in politics I practiced similar principles. I wouldn't do anything I knew was illegal, but felt entitled to do to our opposition whatever they had done to us when they were in power (a sort of reverse Golden Rule). That's why the Watergate scandal was frequently defended with the excuse, "Everyone does it."

Americans make similar arguments when justifying their own choices. In some polls, close to 80 percent of the people say that they don't believe in moral absolutes; they believe right or wrong varies from situation to situation.[2] This is sheer relativism.

Relativism provides no foundation for safe and orderly society. If all people are free to choose for themselves what is right, how can a society agree on and enforce even minimal standards? If there is no ultimate moral law, what motivation is there to be virtuous? The result is the loss of community; if your neighbor had no clear definition of right and wrong, would you sleep well at night or let your children play in his yard?

Western history's moral consensus was largely informed by Judeo-Christian tradition. Enlightenment intellectuals began to argue that since God was no longer needed to explain Creation, he wasn't needed to establish moral laws. Reason alone would form the basis for morality. Since then, the great question facing Western society is posed by the great Russian novelist Fyodor Dostoevsky: "Can man be good without God?"[4] Can reason alone come up with a viable moral system?

The answer is no. This was illustrated quite forcefully some years ago by the fate of the Conference on Science, Philosophy, and Religion. In 1939, the last hopes for appeasing Hitler were shattered, and the world girded itself for another world war. Realizing that the Western world's moral resolve must be reinforced, Louis Finkelstein, chancellor of the Jewish Theological Seminary in New York, planned for a conference where the greatest scholars from every discipline would draw on their collective wisdom to devise a universal code of ethics to provide the moral foundation for democracy. The conference was announced in June 1940 in a statement signed by 79 leading intellectuals, including Albert Einstein. The New York Times printed the announcement on page one, breathlessly hailing it as "an intellectual declaration of independence ... a new social contract ... a new declaration of the rights of man."[3]

The goal was to synthesize Judeo-Christian ethics, Enlightenment humanism, and modern science to create a new foundation for democratic societies. Yet, before the opening gun, battle lines were drawn between traditionalists and modernists. For traditionalists, Mortimer Adler, editor of the Great Books series, declared, "We have more to fear from our professors than from Hitler," referring to intellectuals who had abandoned historically accepted moral truths. His adversary, Sidney Hook, responded that Adler was promoting a "new medievalism." "The only absolute is science," Hook contended, and called for a pragmatic approach to morality. The modernists contended that all values are relative—except the value of tolerance.[4]

Notwithstanding the difficulties of the first meeting, hopes ran high for the second conference. It wasn't until the third conference that the optimistic fervor began to subside as the debate came to a stalemate over which morality to adopt. The country's editorialists reduced expectations with headlines such as, "Scholars Confess They Are Confused."[5]

The Conference met through and after the war years. By 1948, reports Fred Beuttler of the University of Illinois, "the biggest fear of most academic intellectuals was dogmatism and indoctrination." The relativists had carried the day. "All absolutist thinking," they said, "has totalitarian potential." By the early 1960s the conference disbanded. The goal of defining "cultural universals" had proved impossible.[6]

Think of it: For two decades some of the world's greatest minds engaged in stimulating debate and produced ... nothing. Why? Because they disagreed about the proper starting point of ethical knowledge.

Traditionalists, such as Adler, understood that to have objective, universal ethical principles, there must be an absolute source, a transcendent authority. The modernists started with the assumption that morality is merely a human invention that can be altered to meet changing circumstances in an evolving world. The two sides started with conflicting worldviews and merely played out logical consequences of their starting points.

Louis Finkelstein's endeavor focuses the failure of efforts to discover ethical rules by reason alone. Today ethics has degenerated into relativism, with individuals carving out their own private truths to live by. In the words of Father Richard John Neuhaus, we are "herds of independent minds marching towards moral oblivion with Frank Sinatra's witless boast on our lips, 'I Did It My Way.' "[7]

This climate considers offensive for Western civilization, under the influence of the Judeo-Christian tradition, might enjoy any moral advantage or that its historic beliefs might be drawn on to arrest our moral free-fall. When one of the Bass brothers of Texas gave $20 million to his alma mater, Yale University, stipulating that the grant be used for the study of Western civilization, the university hemmed and hawed. The faculty wanted a multicultural curriculum, not one that favored Western tradition, so they delayed until Lee Bass asked that his gift be returned.[8]

It has become nearly impossible to teach traditional precepts of right and wrong in our public schools, leading to disastrous consequences. "For generations," writes theologian Michael Novak, "the primary task explicitly assigned public schools was character formation."[9] That is no longer the case.

Don't educators understand where this kind of value-free teaching leads? A nation without virtue cannot govern itself. "Our people are losing virtue," Novak says bluntly. "That is why we have been losing self-government."[10] If we can't govern ourselves, we invite others to govern us. Virtue's death threatens our liberty.

At root, this great struggle is between worldviews, and it poses the question: *How now shall we live?* By the Judeo-Christian tradition or by the moral nihilism of today's relativistic, individualistic culture?

Becoming Moral Persons

Virtuous society can be created only by virtuous people, wherein each individual's conscience guards the person's behavior and holds him or her accountable. Without conscience, a society can be held in check only through coercion. Yet even coercion ultimately fails, for there is no police force large enough to keep an eye on every individual. "In an America in which virtue is exalted, there will be 270 million policemen," says Michael Novak, referring to individual conscience, but "in an America which mocks virtue, you can't hire enough."[11]

The emphasis on social justice at the expense of private virtue is not only mistaken but downright dangerous. People without personal morality inevitably fail in their efforts to create public morality. "There is no social sin without personal sin," writes Georgetown professor James Schall. "Our youth today are almost invariably taught they must change the world, not their souls. So they change the world, and it becomes worse."[12] Moral crusaders with zeal but no ethical understanding are likely to give us solutions that are worse than the problem.

When we focus young people's moral attention solely on public issues and causes, they fail to treat the personal realm as morally serious. Some years ago, Christina Hoff Sommers wrote an article entitled "Ethics without Virtue," in which she attacked higher education for teaching ethics as social justice rather than as individual decency and honesty. One colleague complained that she was promoting bourgeois morality and ignoring the real issues of oppression of women, evils of multinational corporations, and exploitation of the environment. But at the end of the semester, the same teacher came to Sommers' office, horrified that more than half her students had plagiarized their take-home exam. They had cheated in an ethics course!

"What are you going to do?" Sommers asked. Sheepishly, she asked for a copy of Sommers' article on the importance of individual virtue.[13]

Christianity gives absolute moral law that allows us to judge between right and wrong. Try asking your secular friends how they decide what they ought to do, what ethical principles to follow. On what authority do they rely? Without moral absolutes, there is no real basis for ethics.

An absolute moral law doesn't confine people in a straitjacket of Victorian prudery. People will always debate the boundaries of moral law and its varied applications, but the very idea of right and wrong makes sense only if there is a final standard, a measuring rod, by which we can make moral judgments.

Only the Christian worldview offers redemption from sin, giving power to overcome the most powerful obstacle to becoming virtuous: the rebellious human will. Morality is not just about intellectual acknowledgment of ultimate standards, of what ought to be; it is also about developing virtue—the full range of habits and dispositions that constitute good character. We must not only assent mentally to principles; we must become people who are just, courageous, patient, kind, loyal, loving, persistent, and devoted to duty. Only the Christian worldview tells us how to develop virtuous character, to become moral persons.

In the movie adaptation of Tolstoy's *War and Peace,* the central character Pierre asks dolefully, "Why is it that I know what is right, but do what is wrong?" That is the human dilemma. We may know the right thing, but that is no guarantee that we will do it. the Old Testament prophet Jeremiah laments, "The heart is deceitful above all things and beyond cure. Who can understand it?" (Jer. 17:9). The apostle Paul put it: "I know that nothing good lives in me, that is, in my sinful nature. For I have the desire to do what is good, but I cannot carry it out. For what I do is not the good I want to do; no, the evil I do not want to do—this I keep on doing" (Rom. 7:18-19).

Even if Louis Finkelstein's grand vision had succeeded and a universal code of morality had been agreed on, would people have been able to live by it? Could they have become moral persons? The optimist says yes, but both Scripture and empirical evidence say otherwise. The secular view of ethics offers no salvation, no power to change the human heart.

I testify to this from personal experience. I was reared in a good family. My father, whom I idolized, drilled into me principles of duty, honor, and honesty. I remember sitting with him on Sunday afternoons, listening to him lecture on the evils of cheating or stealing.

When President Nixon asked me to leave my lucrative law practice to serve as his special counsel, I saw it as my duty to do so, even though it meant a drastic pay cut. To guard against temptation, or even the appearance of impropriety, I put my law firm investment and all other assets into a blind trust and vowed never even to see former law partners or clients (who might seek government favors). I was determined: No one would corrupt me. Yet, I went to prison for obstruction of justice.

What happened? I didn't understand the deceptiveness of the human heart. We humans have an infinite capacity for self-rationalization; we can justify anything, which is what I did.

C. S. Lewis explained the dilemma in my favorite of his essays, "Men without Chests." To be moral, the "head," the seat of reason, must rule the "stomach," or the passions. But it can do this only through the "chest," which in Lewis's analogy represents the will, the moral imagination. Modern rationalism has reduced morality to simple understanding, Lewis wrote; it has focused on moral reasoning while ignoring the role of the will and moral imagination; it has robbed us of our "chests." And then we wonder why morality is declining. In Lewis's unforgettable words, "We make men without chests and expect of them virtue and enterprise. We laugh at honor and are shocked to find traitors in our midst. We castrate and bid the geldings be fruitful."[14]

Moral reasoning and intellectual knowledge aren't enough. A human can fulfill the moral law only if the will is transformed. "For what the law was powerless to do in that it was weakened by the sinful nature, God did by sending his own Son in the likeness of sinful man to be a sin offering," wrote the apostle Paul. "And so he condemned sin in sinful man, in order that the righteous requirements of the law might be fully met in us" (Rom. 8:3). When we turn to God, the Holy Spirit empowers us to do what we can't do on our own. The essence of *conversion* is the will is turned around, transformed. At Christianity's heart is a supernatural transforming power that enables us to know what is right and also to do it—to become virtuous.

Our most intractable social problems such as crime can only be solved by the practice of virtuous behavior. Sociologists and policy experts endlessly debate, *"What causes crime?"* Michael Novak notes, even if we uncovered the answer to that question, how would it help us? It would merely enable us to produce more crime. We really need to know how to produce virtue. Society should concentrate on encouraging virtuous behavior, and then crime will begin to fall.[15]

Societies positively encourage virtuous behavior through custom and convention and negatively through social stigmas, taboos, and shame. Negatives are difficult to exert in a culture where moral stigmas aren't permitted for fear of damaging one's self-esteem, but Christians can argue for the right of a healthy society to express moral disapproval of socially harmful behavior.

We can't rely on law alone; not all immoral actions should be made illegal. Many times, right behavior is better enforced by an informal social consensus that defines certain behavior as unacceptable or worthy of contempt. Campaigns against drunk driving or drug abuse are often more effective than laws against them. If we abandon such social conventions, we invite the imposition of more laws, which, in the absence of support, have to be enforced with ever increasing severity.

The Good Life

What does it take to create the good life? A firm sense of right and wrong, and a determination to order one's life accordingly because it is what fits with our created nature and makes us happiest and most fulfilled—not out of a grim sense of duty. When persons act in accord with their true nature, they feel a sense of harmony, contentment, and joy. This is happiness, the fruit of virtue. In fact, ancient philosophers defined happiness as something one achieves only at the end of life, after spending a whole lifetime in character training.[16]

The American founders had this definition in mind when they declared that we have an inalienable right to life, liberty, and the pursuit of happiness. The last phrase did not mean a right to hedonistic pleasure, as many people believe today, but a life spent ordering our appetites and desires to the truth of who we are, producing happy individuals and a harmonious society.[17]

When we know the secret to true happiness, we will seek virtue in every area of life, even those typically thought to be purely technical, scientific, or utilitarian. Then we will make the astonishing discovery that the Christian worldview is vital for our economic well-being and gives genuine meaning even to our work.

A Biblical View of Work

The Bible may not endorse a particular economic theory, but it lays out a basic blueprint for a free, prosperous, and just society. Biblical principles inspired the development of our system of democratic capitalism, which triumphed dramatically in the closing decades of the twentieth century. Other nations are casting off socialism and embracing Western models of economic freedom. In the West, liberal and leftist political parties scramble toward the political center. Even fervent socialist sympathizers have conceded that free-market system is better at lifting people from poverty and recognizing human dignity.

Ironically, the Soviet system's collapse and Marxism's discredit make it more important for us to understand the undergirding principles of the Western free-market system. In the past, Americans have had before them a clear and menacing contrast between the free world and two regimes of terror: Nazism and Communism.

Whatever our own system's failures, it was obvious to all but the willfully blind it was immeasurably superior to the alternatives.[18] We can no longer simply point to that stark contrast; we must formulate a positive defense of the principles undergirding a free society. We must articulate biblical principles that support economic freedom and a sense of vocation.

A Christian worldview perspective on work and economic development clearly follows basic contours of the categories of creation, fall, and redemption. In the Book of Genesis, we learn human beings were made in God's image, to reflect His character; therefore, we are called to reflect His creative activity through our own creativity—by cultivating the world, drawing out its potential, and giving it shape and form. All work has dignity as an expression of the divine image.

When God placed the first couple in the Garden of Eden, He gave the first job description: work the earth and take care of it (Gen. 2:15). Even in Paradise, in the ideal state of innocence, work was the natural activity of human beings. Theologian T. M. Moore wrote, "Labor and economic development, using minds and hands in a communal effort, are thus part of the original mandate from God."[19]

Scripture is never romantic or naïve about the human condition. The world God created was soon marred by the Fall, and work is now under a "curse," as theologians put it. Because of the Fall, making a living and raising a family are fraught with pain and difficulty. Understanding this, we can be realistic about the agony of life in a broken world.

The sorrow sin injected into creation does not cancel out the way we were originally made or the mandate to work. Redemption enables us to restore the original meaning and purpose of work, giving us the power to carry out the task we were created for, to develop culture and civilization. In our work, we cooperate with God in the task of redemption, helping free the world from the effects of the Fall.

The Bible gives underlying principles of economics, ranging from private property to commerce to economic justice. It speaks clearly to the first requirement of economic liberty, the protection of private ownership of goods and property.

As shown in the Ten Commandments, Scripture recognizes and defends private property. The moral principle in the eighth forbids stealing, and the tenth forbids coveting. Mosaic law required those who stole another's property to make restitution (Ex. 22).

The Bible says interesting things about wealth and does not treat its accumulation as evil. Abraham and Solomon were wealthy. Sometimes wealth is a reward for spiritual faithfulness, as when God restored Job's property to twice what he had before disaster struck (Job 42:10-12). Scripture does warn against seeking wealth as an end in itself or using oppression and cruelty as means for amassing it. Paul called the love of money "a root of all kinds of evils," and Old Testament prophets warned wealth easily leads to spiritual complacency and disobedience to God. The right to private property does not mean we have the right to do whatever we please with our possessions.

Ultimately, we don't own anything; we are stewards of the things God entrusted to us. God owns all things: "the earth is the Lord's, and everything in it" (Ps. 24:1). We are to use our economic resources and labor as He commands, according to His law of justice and mercy. That's why Scripture calls for just scales and balances (Prov. 11:1; 20:23; Amos 8:5) and warns of God's judgment against oppressors who take advantage of the needy or who withhold wages (Amos 5:11-12; 8:5-6; Lev. 19:13). Scripture condemns those who manipulate the economy for sinful purposes, whether by hoarding or other wickedness such as greed, indolence, and deception (Prov. 3:27-28; 11:26; Jas. 5:1-6).

The underlying principle is that private property is a gift from God to be used to establish social justice and to care for the poor and disadvantaged. Repentant thieves were told to steal no more but work with their hands so that they would "have something to share with those in need" (Eph. 4:28).

Few themes in Scripture sound more loudly or clearly than God's commandments to care for the less fortunate. "Learn to do right!" God thunders. "Seek justice, encourage the oppressed. Defend the cause of the fatherless, plead the case of the widow" (Isa. 1:17). Through Isaiah, God announces that a true fast is not empty religious ritual but "to share your food with the hungry and to provide the poor wanderer with shelter—when you see the naked, to clothe him, and not to turn away from your own flesh and blood" (Isa. 58:7). Jesus deepens our sense of responsibility by telling us that in helping the poor, hungry, naked, sick, and imprisoned, we are actually serving him (Matt. 25:31-46).

The poor are never passive recipients of charity; the able-bodied must work. This is best embodied in Old Testament laws requiring landowners to leave generous margins unharvested around their fields so the poor could glean enough to live on (Lev. 19:9-10; Deut. 24:20-22). In the New Testament, Paul chastised those who refused to work, urging they "settle down and earn the bread they eat" (2 Thess. 3:12). The poor are to retain dignity as competent and responsible people capable of helping themselves.

These directives aren't for the state or even the church; they are given to private individuals and are to be carried out as private acts of generosity and compassion. Only the truly destitute, usually lumped under the category of "widows and orphans," are to be cared for by the church as a whole.

The Value of Work

Turning to the testimony of history, we can trace a steady development in the dignity accorded to the individual and to economic vocation. The early church was forced to define a biblical view of work and economic development in contrast to the views inherited from Greek culture which equated the material world with evil and disorder. Greeks denigrated anything related to material things, including manual labor. Working with one's hands was relegated to slaves and artisans, whose labor freed up the intellectual elite for the "nobler" pursuit of culture and philosophy.

Against this backdrop, the early church defended a high view of the material world as God's creation. "There has never been room in the Hebrew or Christian tradition for the idea that the material world is something to be escaped from and that work in it is degrading. Material things are to be used to the glory of God and for the good of men," writes British philosopher Mary Hesse. As a result, "in western Europe in the Christian era, there was never the same derogation of manual work. There was no slave class to do the work, and craftsmen were respected."[20]

Nevertheless, many theologians influenced by Greek philosophy often drew a distinction between sacred and secular realms. Full-time religious workers, devoted "to the service of God alone," embody the "perfect form of the Christian life," wrote Eusebius in the fourth century, whereas farmers and traders may achieve only "a kind of secondary grade of piety."[21]

Thomas Aquinas challenged this by stressing created world's value, causing the Scholastics to explore topics now a part of economics, such as property, trade, prices, and wealth creation. This exploration culminated in the work of Spain's sixteenth-century School of Salamanca, praised by economist Joseph Schumpeter as the "founders" of scientific economics.[22]

Reformers likewise protested the dichotomy between the sacred and secular and its implicit devaluation of creation. When we carry out our vocation in obedience to God, wrote Martin Luther, God Himself works through us to His purposes. This partnership with God includes all legitimate forms of work, not just spiritual vocations. Luther rejected the notion that monks and clergy engaged in holier work than shopkeepers and housewives, "Seemingly secular works are a worship of God and an obedience well pleasing to God."[23]

Division into sacred and secular made secular work second-best and held secular workers to a lower standard of devotion and spirituality. The Reformation challenged that, insisting no believer is exempt from the highest spiritual standards. Looking through a biblical lens, Luther wrote, we see that "the entire world [is] full of service to God, not only the churches but also the home, the kitchen, the cellar, the workshop, and the field of the townsfolk and farmers."[24]

Drawing from passages such as Jesus' talents parable in Matthew 25, the Reformation cast aside a common medieval belief that making a profit is immoral. "One of the simplest lessons from the parable," writes Father Robert Sirico, "is that it is not immoral to profit from our resources, wit, and labor." After all, profit's alternative is loss; and loss due to lack of initiative "does not constitute good stewardship."[25] God expects us to use our talents—our abilities and our money—productively to serve others.

These beliefs about the value of work and entrepreneurial talent shaped what became known as the Protestant work ethic which then became the driving force behind the industrial revolution and raised the standard of living immeasurably for vast numbers of societies.[26] Work ethic's impact is a great example of the way a Christian worldview can revolutionize a culture.

Today the practical and moral superiority of free-market economics is universally accepted throughout the Christian church—except in outposts of Marxism hidden away in academia and mainline church bureaucracies.[27]

A variety of secular views of work emerged after the enlightenment in opposition to the Christian view. Rejection of the biblical doctrine of creation led to rejection of its doctrine of human nature (its anthropology).

No longer were humans seen as the God's handiwork, living to love God and serve their neighbor; instead, they were part of nature, driven by self-interest and expediency. Protestant work ethic was separated from stewardship and service, degraded into a creed of personal success.

Adam Smith, founder of capitalism, defined work solely as a means of fulfilling one's self-interest. No one acts out of benevolence, but only out of enlightened concern for personal advancement: "It is not from the benevolence of the butcher, the brewer, or the baker, that we expect our dinner, but from their regard to their own interest. We address ourselves, not to their humanity but to their self-love."[28]

Both classical and Christian ethics had regarded self-interest as a vice to be overcome for the common good, but Smith contended that self-interest was good for society. His theory of capitalism turned an attitude once thought to be evil into a virtue. "The paradox," writes theologian Michael Novak, "consisted in ... [getting rid of hunger and poverty] by placing less stress on moral purposes" and greater stress on rational self-interest.[29]

For Smith, economy was an amoral, autonomous mechanism, grinding along apart from the moral influence of law, church, or family. He urged the best thing for the economy was for everyone to stand out of its way and give free reign to "the invisible hand," which ensured supply and demand would always balance. This vision of self-regulating production and exchange was a secularization of the Christian providence, replacing it with an interlocking order of nature.

Focusing on self-interest proved very effective, for in a fallen world, it is one of the strongest forms of motivation. But instead of raising the moral bar, challenging people to go beyond self-interest, Smith's system seemed to accommodate our sinful state. The system demanded the very impulses Christianity had traditionally renounced as immoral: self-interest instead of concern for the common good, personal ambition instead of altruism, and drive for personal gain instead of self-sacrifice and charity. It also seemed to glorify those impulses by treating them as the driving force for a healthy economy, thus paving the way for a new ethic of ambition, aggression, and self-advancement.

Moreover, Smith was mistaken in thinking that an autonomous free market would operate most beneficently. Quite the opposite. As the early days of industrialism proved, an autonomous, secularized capitalism exploits both workers and the environment, creating new forms of slavery in what poet William Blake called the "dark, satanic mills."

Capitalism is astonishingly efficient at generating new wealth, but it operates beneficently only when the market is shaped by moral forces coming from both the law and the culture—derived ultimately from religion.

How to bring these moral forces to bear on our economy is the major issue facing Christians in this area.

How do we transform secularized, demoralized capitalism into a morally responsible free-market system?

Most important, economy is not an autonomous mechanism. It depends on laws to maintain sound currency, protect private property, enforce contracts, and control corruption. Government acts as a referee, making sure everyone follows the rules and plays fair. Business transactions can't be carried out in a society where people can't trust one another, where graft and corruption are the rule, where contracts are made to be broken.

Humane capitalism depends on sound moral culture; a free market readily caters to moral choices we make, supplying what consumers want, from Bibles to porn. Only virtuous citizenry refuse to manufacture or to buy immoral and destructive products. Morality in the marketplace depends on individual economic actors. The Christian's role is indispensable; we alone have the resources to help create a healthy moral climate.

Entrepreneurship requires the practice of moral virtues. Those who invest their time and money in enterprises where rewards are not immediate must practice hard work, self-sacrifice, and delayed gratification, says Novak.[30] They must also cultivate sensitivity and courtesy to others, because if you don't please the customer, you're out of business.

Economic success depends on morality—strange as that may sound to some economic conservatives. I am sometimes told by members of Congress that they struggle to hold together religious conservatives and corporate interests. My response is that these two groups are allies, not enemies. "Businesses are plants that do not grow in just any soil," Michael Novak writes. They thrive best in a

culture that is both politically free and morally virtuous. Novak uses the image of a three-legged stool: A healthy democracy comprises political liberty, economic freedom, and moral responsibility. Weaken any leg, and the stool topples over.[31]

As world societies break the chains of communism and socialism, it is imperative that Christians make a case for the moral and spiritual basis of a free economy. If a thoroughly secular capitalism is adopted, it will lead to new forms of slavery, not to freedom. Capitalism provides the best opportunity for economic growth and human freedom only if tempered by compassion and social justice.

Today, Christians have the opportunity to make the case that work is truly fulfilling only when firmly tied to its moral and spiritual moorings. It is time for the church to reclaim this crucial part of life, restoring a biblical understanding of work and economics. A biblical theology of work should be a frequent subject for sermons, just as it was during the Reformation, when establishing one's vocation was considered a crucial element in discipleship.[32] Churches should organize classes on business ethics and biblical work principles for those in the workplace.[33] Finally, they should set up programs to help the able-bodied poor become self-sufficient instead of dependent on government welfare.

Only the church can impart the work ethic and sense of purpose that lift people from poverty. When Allen-Edmonds Shoe Company set up a factory in inner-city Milwaukee, president John Stollenwerk contacted pastors at neighborhood churches. When asked why he had not contacted local federal and state job-training programs to recruit new employees, Stollenwerk replied, "It just never

A Society that Works

195

occurred to us." Government training may impart skills, he explained, but they can't provide moral habits of reliability, hard work, and commitment to family that make good workers. Churches, on the other hand, impart precisely these fundamental values.[34]

Contemporary concerns over economic issues reflect a profound confusion in secular society—whether it is welfare reform, tensions over work and family commitments, or the relationship of morality to economic policy. Only Christianity holds the key to this dilemma. Only the Christian worldview provides the moral foundation essential to preserving free economic systems; only the Christian worldview provides a high view of work that gives meaning and dignity to human labor. Once again we see that Christianity offers the truth about reality, providing a road map to find our way amidst the confusions and perplexities of everyday life.

Christianity gives us the basic presuppositions needed to run a nation through just and fair-minded laws, and to foster a political system that is both free and well ordered.

Discussion Questions

1. How do you respond to the statement that good ethics means "staying out of trouble"?

2. Why could the conference on science, philosophy, and religion come up with no standard of right and wrong?

3. Why is tolerance the only absolute for modernists?

4. How does the death of virtue threaten our liberty as a people?

5. What practical steps can our society take to encourage virtue?

6. What is distinctive about the Christian view of work? How does it differ from the views in society?

[1]From President John Adams's October 11, 1798, address to the military, as quoted in *The Works of John Adams—Second President of the United States,* Charles Francis Adams, ed., vol. 9 (Boston: Little, Brown & Co., 1854), 229.

[2]Princeton Religious Research Council, *Emerging Trends,* February, 1992.

[3]"79 Leaders Unite to Aid Democracy," *New York Times,* 1 June 1940.

[4]Fred W. Beuttler, "For the World at Large: Intergroup Activities at the Jewish Theological Seminary," in *Tradition Renewed: A History of the Jewish Theological Seminary—Beyond the Academy,* vol. 2 (New York: The Seminary, 1997), 667. See also Sidney Hook's address reprinted in the *New Republic,* 2 (October 28, 1940): 684.

[5]"Scholars Confess They Are Confused," *New York Times,* 1 September 1942.

[6]Beuttler, "For the World at Large," 667. We are indebted to Beuttler, who performed a great service in studying the history of the conference. He discovered a revealing historical footnote. In 1956, Nelson Rockefeller launched a special-studies project to define national goals for America's future. Rockefeller engaged young Harvard professor Henry Kissinger to staff the project. Kissinger shrewdly saw that the effort would have to have a moral framework for national purpose. He called in Finkelstein, then head of the Institute of Ethics at the New York Seminary, for advice, specifically in formulating a moral justification for using limited nuclear weapons. Kissinger asked, What are we "willing to die for in terms of values"? The Institute, under Finkelstein's direction, began extensive discussions, but soon broke down, just as the conference had earlier. Panelists dodged Kissinger's questions as he pushed them to deal with the role of religion and natural law. The panel eventually gave up trying to reach a consensus, in effect telling Rockefeller and Kissinger that they could only help them clarify their values.

[7]Richard John Neuhaus, "The Truth about Freedom," *Wall Street Journal,* 8 October 1993.

[8]Dan Shine, "Yale OKs Return of Gift to Billionaire Lee Bass: Clash over $20 Million for Program," *Dallas Morning News,* 15 March 1995.

[9]Michael Novak, *Character and Crime: An Inquiry into the Causes of the Virtue of Nations* (Notre Dame, Ind.: Brownson Institute, 1986), 107.

[10]Michael Novak, "The Conservative Momentum" (speech given at the Center for the American Experiment, March 24, 1993).

[11]Michael Novak, "The Causes of Virtue" (speech given in Washington, D.C., January 31, 1994, reprinted by Prison Fellowship in *Sources,* no. 7 [1994]).

[12]James Schall, "Personal Sin and Social Sin," *Crisis* (June 1997): 57.

[13]Christina Hoff Sommers, "Teaching the Virtues," *Chicago Tribune,* 12 September 1993.

[14]C.S. Lewis, *The Abolition of Man* (New York: Macmillan, 1947), 35.

[15]Michael Novak, *Character and Crime,* 38. Novak draws a significant parallel with economics. For centuries people sought the cause of poverty. But the most profound change for the economic betterment of the world came about when the 18th-century economist Adam Smith reversed that question, asking instead, What is the cause of wealth? See Adam Smith, *The Wealth of Nations: An Inquiry into the Nature and Cause of* (New York: Modern Library, 1994).

[16]Deal W. Hudson, *Happiness and the Limits of Satisfaction* (Lanham, Md.: Rowman & Littlefield, 1996).

[17]Ibid.

[18]Richard John Neuhaus, *Doing Well and Doing Good: The Challenge to the Christian Capitalist* (New York: Doubleday, 1992).

[19]Theologian T. M. Moore in a memo entitled "Economic Aspects of the Biblical Worldview" (August 12, 1998).

[20]Mary Hesse, *Science and the Human Imagination: Aspects of the History and Logic of Physical Science* (New York: Philosophical Library, 1955), 263.

[21]Eusebius, as quoted in Leland Ryken, *Work and Leisure: In Christian Perspective* (Portland, Ore.: Multnomah, 1987), 66.

[22]Robert A. Sirico, "The Late-Scholastic and Austrian Link to Modern Catholic Economic Thought," *Markets and Morality 1,* no. 2 (October 1988): 122-29.

[23]Martin Luther, as quoted in Ryken, *Work and Leisure,* 95, 97. Applies to all forms of work, not just paid: All our tasks and duties, including those as parents or as citizens, Luther regarded as a call from God.

[24]Luther as quoted in Ryken, 135.

[25]Robert A. Sirico, "The Parable of the Talents," *Freeman 44,* no. 7 (July 1994): 354.

[26]See Chuck Colson and Jack Eckerd, *Why America Doesn't Work* (Dallas: Word, 1991).

[27]Although the Catholic hierarchy showed little sympathy for free-market economics, it was given a ringing endorsement by Pope John Paul II in his encyclical *Centessimus Annus* (May 16, 1991), 1-23.

[28]Adam Smith, *The Wealth of Nations* (New York: Modern Library, 1994), 15

[29]Michael Novak, *The Spirit of Democratic Capitalism* (New York: Simon & Schuster, 1982), 79.

[30]Michael Novak, *Business as a Calling: Work and the Examined Life* (New York: Free Press, 1996).

[31]Michael Novak, "Profits with Honor," *Policy Review* (May/June 1996), 50. Also "Sweet Vindication: Award of 1994 Templeton Prize to Michael Novak for Progress in Religion," *National Review 46,* no. 6 (April 4, 1994), 22; and Walter Isaacson, "Exalting the City of Man," *Time* (May 10, 1982): 38.

[32]Os Guinness, *The Call: Finding and Fulfilling the Central Purpose of Life* (Nashville: Word, 1998), chapter 4.

[33]See Chuck Colson and Jack Eckerd, *Why America Doesn't Work* (Dallas, Word, 1991).

[34]John Stollenwerk, as quoted in Spencer Abraham and Dan Coats, "Hard-Working Churches," *American Enterprise 8,* no. 4 (July/August 1997): 13.

Creating a Just Society

In this final unit you will explore the relationship between God's law and man's law. How can you contribute to a just society?

Birmingham, Alabama, 1963, just days before Easter weekend, nine years since Rosa Parks had refused to sit in the back of the bus in Selma, Alabama, and nearly as long since the Freedom Riders made their harrowing journeys on Greyhound and Trailway buses to challenge segregated seating. Martin Luther King, Jr.; Ralph Abernathy; Andrew Young; and others in the Southern Christian Leader-ship Conference (SCLC) gathered in downtown Gaston Hotel to make their most significant strategy decision yet.

They had launched a civil rights campaign in Birmingham, and it was taking off. Thousands of young people joined their elders in peaceful marches. Their boycott of downtown stores was also making an impact. The strategy of nonviolent resistance was working: They were overflowing the jails, making it impossible to suppress the movement by sheer force.

This much progress in Birmingham was remarkable—a city so racist that the authorities had shut down parks and baseball leagues rather than integrate them. A city whose leaders had declared that blood would flow in the streets before they complied with the Supreme Court's decision to integrate;

where serving food to whites and blacks at the same lunch counter was still illegal; where 17 bombings of black churches and homes of civil rights leaders remained unsolved; a city in which racist terrorists castrated a man and left him on a deserted road.

Birmingham officials decided to fight King and his collaborators. The officials were plotting tactics that had been used successfully a year earlier in Albany, Georgia. Birmingham leaders had a federal judge to issue a restraining order against King and other leaders of the movement who had announced plans to march on Good Friday. If the leaders obeyed the restraining order, as they had in Albany, they would miss the march. Without leadership, past movements lost momentum and fizzled. Yet if King and his followers disobeyed the order, they would be defying a federal court, taking civil disobedience to new levels. Was that morally justifiable?

King's advisers urged him to forgo the march so he could raise money to bail the other marchers out of jail, but how could he ask others to sit in prison unless he was willing to join them? Besides, his pledge to march had been made repeatedly in public rallies. If he didn't show up, support-

ers would be demoralized; enemies would think he had backed down.

What to do? King went into one of the bedrooms to pray through his decision. When he reemerged after more than an hour, he was wearing a pair of overalls he had bought to wear to jail.

"I'm going to march," he said. "We can't know what lies ahead.We just have to fulfill our promises as best we can. We're in God's hands now."

"Son," said his father, Dr. Martin Luther King, Sr., "I've never gone against any of your decisions. But this time I think you'd better stay home. I wouldn't disobey that injunction."

The agony of the decision seized King once more. He thought for a moment, then said,"No. I'm determined."

"All right then," his father nodded.[1]

A photographer caught King's arrest—the great civil rights leader in handcuffs, glancing back toward his supporters, his face haunted. Inside the jail, he was locked in solitary confinement in a room the size of a monk's cell, narrow and windowless. Imprisonment was made even more bitter when his lawyers brought in a copy of the *Birmingham News* containing a statement signed by eight white clergymen criticizing his strategy of civil disobedience.

Suddenly, King had an inspiration to compose a rebuttal to those clergy in an open letter–a defense of the civil rights movement that would appeal to the conscience of all America. On toilet paper scraps and writing paper later smuggled out page by page, King wrote a lyrical epistle on why it is sometimes justifiable to break the law.

The civil rights movement, he acknowledged, gained much of its leverage from urging obedience to the Supreme Court's 1954 decision outlawing segregation in public schools. Thus, "at first glance it may seem rather paradoxical for us consciously to break laws. One may well ask: 'How can you advocate breaking some laws and obeying others?' The answer lies in the fact that there are two types of laws: just and unjust. One has not only a legal but a moral responsibility to obey just laws. Conversely, one has a moral responsibility to disobey unjust laws. I would agree with St. Augustine that 'an unjust law is no law at all.'

"Now, what is the difference between the two? ... A just law is a man-made code that squares with the moral law or the law of God. An unjust law is out of harmony with the moral law. To put it in the terms of St. Thomas Aquinas: An unjust law is a human law that is not rooted in eternal law and natural law."[2]

Civil disobedience's tradition, King reiterated, goes back to Old Testament times–to Shadrach, Meshach, and Abednego, three young Jewish men who for the conscience's sake disobeyed laws of Babylonian monarch Nebuchadnezzar; back to reformer Martin Luther, who declared, "Here I stand; I can do no other. God help me. Amen." Back to John Bunyan, imprisoned for his beliefs: "I will stay in jail to the end of my days before I make a butchery of my conscience"; and Thomas Jefferson, who justified the American Revolution: "We hold these truths to be self-evident, that all men are created equal."

King always remembered his incarceration as the moment his beliefs were put to the severest test, and his "Letter from Birmingham Jail" became one of his greatest testaments of faith.

A great burden lifted from his mind when he learned money had been quickly raised to secure the release of all civil rights workers. Surprised and relieved, he became "aware of a feeling that had been present all along below the surface of consciousness"–a feeling that "I had never been truly in solitary confinement; God's companionship does not stop at the door of a jail cell. I don't know whether the sun was shining at that moment. But I know that once again I could see the light."[3]

Christianity's Contributions to Law

Martin Luther King, Jr. secured his place in American history when the populist movement he led convinced the nation to affirm that the principles of the Declaration of Independence apply to all Americans, but just as important as his crusade's success is its principle. That principle is the most fundamental basis for our republican form of government: government is not simply a social contract between the people and those who govern, but a social contract made under the authority of a higher law.

The greatest moral struggle in our nation's history–the campaign to end slavery–turned on the same principle. Abolitionists denounced the fugitive-slave bill by which Congress required people to return escaped slaves as contrary to a "higher law," even though it carried out an express provision of the Constitution.[4] Lincoln employed the same argument opposing the Supreme Court decision condoning slavery.[5] He wrote passionately about "the duty of nations as well as of men to own their dependence upon the overruling power of God." Only his conviction about our obligation to submit to a higher authority could have steeled this humble country lawyer to oppose slavery when it was a legally established institution.[6]

The most significant moral debate of our own day–the depate over abortion and related life issues–is fueled by the same conviction. The pro-life movement refuses to accept current abortion law on the grounds that no human law is valid as long as it is contrary to a higher law.

Understanding of a transcendent law above human law is critical to the preservation of liberty and justice. The Declaration of Independence states, there exist certain "inalienable rights" that are beyond government's authority to either grant or deny; it may only recognize them as pre-existing. If the government confers these rights, then it can also take them away. Any group out of favor can be crushed by the self-interest of the majority or the naked force of the state.

Princeton's Robert George made the point in a civil liberties course by reading to students the opening words of the Declaration of Independence: "We hold these truths to be self-evident, that all men are created equal, that they are endowed by their Creator with certain unalienable rights." He looked out at the sea of students in the packed lecture hall and said: "These are the foundational words of the American doctrine of civil liberties, and in light of the content of that doctrine as expressed in the Declaration, perhaps it wouldn't be inappropriate to begin our deliberations by offering thanksgiving to the Creator who endowed us with these rights. So let us in silence, each according to his own tradition and in his own way, give thanks to the Creator for our precious rights and liberties." And then added, impishly, "Those of you who are not believers might take this opportunity to reflect in silence upon the source of our most important rights and liberties, which I believe you too cherish." When he looked up again, he saw two hundred fifty undergraduates with their heads bowed—and to the side, a handful of pale and horrified teaching assistants.[7]

The idea of a transcendent law has deep historical roots, as even a cursory survey makes clear. In ancient Jewish culture, the law (Torah) was revered as divine revelation. Among the ancient Greeks, Plato and Aristotle contended that human justice is defined by higher truths, or ideals, accessible to human reason and knowable through natural law—the moral principles that are in tune with our nature as human beings. The Romans likewise appealed to an eternal source of law, as reflected in Cicero's statement that "Law is not the product of human thought, nor is it any enactment of peoples, but something eternal which rules the whole universe."[8] After Constantine declared Christianity the official religion of the Roman Empire in A.D. 341, Western law was largely shaped by the Christian conception of law, based on the doctrine of creation. Theologians such as Augustine and Aquinas contended human law must reflect the moral order created by God—knowable by believer and nonbeliever alike since it is the "law written on the heart." A law that does not reflect this natural law, as King was to write from the jail, is an unjust law—which is no

law at all. Western political tradition has generally assumed that in order to be valid, human laws must be grounded in the natural law by which God orders His creation, which is in turn a participation in his eternal law.[9]

The Reformation heritage passed on a balanced view of the state as ordained by God but limited by other divinely ordained social institutions. The state's function is to restrain the force of sin unleashed by the Fall. Genesis 3:24 tells us God stationed angels and a flaming sword to guard the tree of life—the first cops on the beat. By preserving social order, the state allows liberty to flourish; the liberty of other sections of society in turn limits the state. Their liberty is, as Kuyper wrote, "the God-ordained means to bridle the authority" of the state, which could otherwise degenerate into despotism. In this balanced conception we see roots the American Founders called "ordered liberty."[10]

Christianity also contributed the notion of separation of powers, based on the doctrine of the Fall. The Founders realized that everyone is prone to sin, and it is a mistake to entrust too much power to any individual or group. So, they established three branches of government—judicial, legislative, and executive—based on the biblical teaching that God is our judge, lawgiver, and king (Isa. 33:22). The Founders also established a federal system, in which state governments were to keep a check on the national government. This is why the Consti-tution originally reserved to the states the right to appoint senators; and even the election of the president was made the task of electors appointed by the states (the electoral college). The states were to have real power, not function merely as administrative units of the national government.

Finally, the Founders built a system that to protect against direct democracy—against any system where "the voice of the people is the voice of God." Such democracies, James Madison warned, "have ever been spectacles of turbulence and contention."[11] Hence the Founders built a republican system, where the will of the people is sifted through elected representatives, intended to be persons of virtue and concern for the common good, capable of rising above the passions of the moment. At the same time, the representatives remain accountable to the people, achieving a marvelous balance.

Ingenious! I never cease to marvel at the plan and to be grateful for this historical expression of a Christian worldview. For more than two centuries, the American experiment has provided a dramatic illustration of the way biblical principles successfully sustain both order and liberty.[12] Yet in recent decades, those principles have come under withering assault from increasingly aggressive forces of modern secularism. So much so that the rule of law and the very character of our political order is now threatened.

Biblical Foundation Crumbles

The erosion of the biblical foundation of our government began, as great cultural changes so often do, with intellectuals. The idea that human (or positive) law must reflect a higher law was seriously challenged in the latter part of the nineteenth century—especially after the work of Charles Darwin. His theory of evolution implied that there is no created moral order that functions as the basis for law; rather, life is the result of a process of trial and error, with new structures being preserved if they help the organism get what it needs to survive. This new view, appearing with the imprimatur of science, seemed to suggest that truth itself was found by a process of trial and error—the "true" idea being the one that works best at getting the results desired. Thus was born the philosophy of *pragmatism.*

Pragmatism was formulated when prominent university professors organized the Cambridge Metaphysical Club. These men—Oliver Wendell Holmes, Charles Pierce, and William James—defined truth as the hypothesis that works best. Or, as James put it, "Truth is the cash value of an idea."[13]

What pragmatism meant for law was stated baldly by Oliver Wendell Holmes in 1897 when he advised law school students to put aside notions of morality and look instead at the law as a science—the science of state coercion.[14] His crassest summary of what this means is captured in his famous dictum that law is the "majority vote of that nation that can lick all others."[15] In other words, without divine law as the final moral authority, the law is reduced to sheer force.

More recently, the authority law received another blow at the hands of deconstructionism, which began as a method of literary criticism but is now applied to all types of texts, including legal texts. According to deconstructionism, language does not reveal meaning (which would imply that there is a transcendent realm of truth); rather, language is a social construction. Text reflects several and often conflicting social and cultural forces, aimed ultimately at enhancing some social group's power. Interpretation does not mean identifying what the author meant but "unmasking" the underlying power relationships.[16]

In recent years, these radical views of the law have begun to filter down to shape actual court decisions, initially in cases involving religious rights. There was no anti-Christian conspiracy at work here, contrary to what many Christian's belief; rather, religious cases were the most obvious target because they most clearly relied on what now had to be discredited—the authority of a higher law.

The courts moved swiftly and dramatically. As recently as 1952, Justice William O. Douglas had described America as a "religious people whose institutions presuppose a supreme being" and urged that the state should therefore "accommodate the public service to their needs."[17] Douglas was not defending any particular religion but simply stating that religion is good for people and that the state ought to respect it. Only two decades later, in 1973, the Court breezed right past the people's deepest religious and moral concerns to "discover" in the Constitution an implied right to "privacy" protecting a woman's right to abortion (Roe v. Wade). In one swoop, the Court sought to extinguish a political debate then being carried out in 50 state legislatures regarding a sensitive moral question—the legal status of the early stages of human life. It was an act of judicial pride that could only call into question the law's authority, thereby assuring that the abortion debate would continue and grow more angry. Which, of course, it has done.

Roe v. Wade was only the first in a swelling stream of cases involving prayer, religious displays, and sexual rights in which judges usurped the legislative process and showed an increasing hostility to religious and moral traditions that have historically informed American law. In some cases judges actually ruled that religious motivation behind a law serves to disqualify it: in 1987 the Supreme Court struck down a Louisiana statute mandating teaching creation alongside evolution, because the Court decided that the legislature's claimed secular purpose of academic freedom was a "sham," covering what was really an attempt to promote biblical religion.[18] This is a stunning turnaround. Biblical principles once considered the authority undergirding law, now disqualify it.

One destructive recent decision was the 1992 case *Casey v. Planned Parenthood.*[19] While upholding some modest state restrictions on abortion, the Court sought to place the right to abortion created in *Roe vs. Wade* on firmer constitutional ground. It abandoned the old tactic of justifying abortion by implied right to "privacy" lurking in the "penumbras" of the 14th Amendment and went straight for the explicit right of "liberty."[20] The Court then chastised pro-life supporters for having the effrontery to challenge their decisions. In essence, the Court admonished them to be quiet and go home. So 20 years after having summarily overridden the democratic debate about abortion in 1973, the Court decreed that even to challenge abortion is an affront to the rule of law.[21]

Justice Kennedy then defined the "liberty" of the 14th Amendment in breathtakingly sweeping terms: "At the heart of liberty," he wrote, "is the right to define one's own concept of existence, of meaning, of the universe, and of the mystery of human life." In short, the Court placed the isolated individual, constructing his or her own sense of meaning, at the center of gravity for constitutional law. Collective self-government by the people by a common moral code was rejected as "majoritarian intolerance."[22]

Indeed, the Court has rejected belief in transcendent ethic as "intolerance," thereby rejecting the idea of a higher law above the Court. In 1992's *Lee v. Weisman,* the Court decreed that even an innocuous, to-whom-it-may-concern prayer offered by a rabbi at a junior high school commencement was unconstitutional because it infringed on a fifteen-year-old's right not to have to listen respectfully to religious expression with which she disagreed.[23] What was considered a mark of civility a generation ago was transformed into a constitutional grievance. More disturbing, the religious expression the Court disallowed covered not just the traditional faiths, but any "shared conviction that there is an ethic and a morality which transcend human invention."[24] The Court said that no transcendent morality is to be permitted in the public square, only the postmodernist view that regards morality as a "human invention."

If no appeal to transcendent authority is permitted, then the justices themselves become the supreme authority. In the 1995 case of *Romer v. Evans* the justices struck down a referendum, democratically enacted by the citizens of Colorado, barring special civil rights protections and preferences based on "sexual orientation." Admittedly the referendum was not carefully drafted, but Justice Kennedy, writing for the majority, completely discounted the voters' stated purpose, presuming to have an uncanny ability to know their minds better than they did. "Laws of the kind before us," he wrote, "raise the inevitable inference that the disadvantage imposed is born of animosity toward the class of persons affected."[25] In a single disdainful sentence, a basic moral position long shared by Christians, Jews, Muslims, and people of other faiths—and a position democratically enacted into law—was reduced to nothing more than personal "animosity." The justices did

not merely disagree with the biblical ethic; they didn't even recognize it as an ethic. They dismissed it as bigotry.

The same attitude soon filtered down to lower levels of the judiciary. Writing for the Ninth Circuit Court of Appeals in 1996 and overturning a state referendum banning assisted suicide, Judge Stephen Reinhardt slammed the courthouse door on people "with strong moral or religious convictions." He wrote: "They are not free to force their views, their religious convictions, or their philosophies on all other members of a democratic society."[26] Yet what is the democratic process but an attempt by like-minded citizens to join together and pass laws in conformity with their best judgment of right and wrong? And on what basis can a judge say that all citizens are free to participate in this process except those "with strong moral and religious convictions"?

This judicial *coup d' etat* culminated in the 1997 decision *Boerne v. Flores,* the first challenge to the Religious Freedom Restoration Act (RFRA) of 1993, which reestablished a strict standard for protecting free religious exercise. Significantly, RFRA passed unanimously in the House, had only three dissenting votes in the Senate, and was enthusiastically signed by President Clinton. If ever a piece of legislation reflected the will of the people, it was RFRA.[27] Nevertheless, in *Boerne* the Supreme Court declared RFRA unconstitutional on the grounds that the express authority of Congress to enforce the basic civil rights guaranteed by the Fourteenth Amendment is not "substantive" but "remedial." In other words, Congress cannot use its power to expand constitutional protections except for the sake of rectifying violations of rights that the Supreme Court

itself has deigned to recognize. Two major trends by activist courts converged in this case: one against the transcendent right of religious liberty and the other against self-government. Not only was the free exercise clause emasculated, but a vote reflecting the nearly unanimous will of the American people was overruled.

The result of these trends is that today the courts, unrestrained by higher law and disdainful of majority will, are the dominant force in American politics. As law professor Russell Hittinger writes, the Court has laid down a "new covenant" by which it agrees to give citizens the right to decide for themselves the meaning of life, to decide what is right and wrong, to do as they please. In exchange for this guarantee, the Court asks only that the people accept the Court's assumption of ultimate power.[28] Or as Notre Dame's Gerard Bradley puts it, the Court has said: "We will be your Court, and you will be our people."[29]

This new covenant with the Court is inherently unstable and will give way in time to either anarchy or sheer power. Imbalance of power among the three branches of government has always been the great vulnerability of the American system. From time to time, the scales have tilted precariously; but providentially, each time the balance has been restored. Until now. Judicial imperialism now threatens to destroy the delicate balance that guarantees our liberty. The late historian Russell Kirk once warned that the Supreme Court's "power to do mischief would become almost infinite" were it to become the dominant force in American public life, for it would "abolish America's democracy."[30] Precisely. This is why it is so urgent for Christians with a biblical worldview of law and justice to alert our neighbors to the serious threat facing our system of government.

Law's Moral Basis Declines

The Christian understanding of law as based on a higher moral law has parallels in most historical civilizations. C. S. Lewis pointed out that all major religions and moral systems assume the existence of an objective morality (which he called *the Way* or *the Tao).*[31] We all sense there must be some ultimate moral justification for the law, something that makes it right. Otherwise, any law can be shot down with the defiant expression "sez who?" So argued the late Arthur Leff of Yale Law School in a 1979 speech. Unless there is a God who is Goodness and Justice, Leff said, there can be no ultimate moral basis for the law. For if there is no God, nothing can take His place. No human standard—no person, no group of people, no document—is immune to challenge.[32]

Leff deftly captured the consequences of a secular worldview. Once the Enlightenment began to deny the reality of divine creation and revelation, the basis of law was eroded. Enlightenment thinkers assumed they would find an alternative basis in human reason and experience, but Leff points out moral beliefs of groups or individuals are open to challenge. The logical conclusion of all efforts to ground the law in something less than God's transcendent law is moral skepticism—the great "sez who?" The consequences shake the foundations of our government and society today.

First, the loss of moral authority in the law removes restraints on individual behavior. Americans seem oblivious to connections between the loss of moral authority in law and the resulting social chaos: crime, corruption, and the loss of civic duty. I discovered just how oblivious when I was talked about criminal justice with a group of newspaper editors in the Midwest.

Getting acquainted over lunch, a senior editor assured me of his paper's commitment to religious liberty, "We led the campaign to take the Ten Commandments off classroom walls."

"Why did you do that?" I asked.

"We must be sensitive to all faiths," he said confidently.

"But Christians, Jews, and Muslims all believe in the Ten Commandments. Even Buddhists and Hindus don't object to them," I responded.

"Separation of church and state," he said.

"Of course," I nodded. "But the Decalogue and the Lex Divina are the historical roots of our legal system. That's why Moses is among the great lawgivers whose faces are represented in the fresco adorning the walls of the House of Representatives chamber."

"Tolerance, sir. Times have changed. We must recognize that." He drew himself up in his chair, a solid pillar of the community.

After our meal, I spoke on justice reform; many took notes as I reeled off the chilling statistics.

"Have you seen the Josephson Institute report? Two-thirds of all kids cheat in school," the senior editor interrupted. "And almost half admit that they steal," he frowned. "What can we do about it?"

"Hmmm," I said in mock puzzlement. "Maybe we should put a sign on the wall that says 'You shall not steal!'"

The postmodernist impasse is that we want freedom from rules and transcendent moral principles, but we hate the moral chaos that ensues.

Second, the loss of moral authority in the law means government is reduced to utilitarian procedures. Aristotle said that at the heart of politics is the question, *How shall we order our lives together?* The question presupposes some common good around which we should order our lives, a moral imperative proper to government. Today, as the logic of *Casey v. Planned Parenthood* suggests, government's task is to protect individual autonomy—the people's right to do whatever they choose. In the Court's new vision, writes Bradley, good government is secured by the liberation of the atomistic individual from the constraints of the common morality of the traditional religions.[33] As a result, government has no positive moral task but acts as little more than a traffic cop, keeping people from bumping into each other as they do their own thing. Harvard professor Michael Sandel says, The government has become a "procedural republic," its laws nothing more than procedures for helping people get what they want.[34]

Third, the loss of a moral basis for law means we can no longer engage in moral debate. If politics is only about who gets what, then it becomes a shouting match, with endless bickering over competing demands for rights—settled ultimately by the loudest voice or the most votes. Issues are settled not by principle but by power. In these circumstances, individuals feel increasingly helpless and eventually give up on the political system—a dangerous trend in a democratic society which depends on the participation of informed and active citizenry.[35]

Finally, the loss of moral authority in law means we have forfeited the rule of law and reverted to arbitrary human rule. The rule of law can't survive unless there is an unchanging and transcendent standard against which we can measure human laws. Otherwise, the law is whatever lawmakers or judges say it is—which can only result, eventually, in the collapse of free government.[36] Postmodernist assault on objective moral truth put us on the road to tyranny.

Yet we must not give up hope, for Christian truth still offers us a way out of the postmodernist impasse. Christians everywhere can help revitalize our political culture and reestablish the rule of law by advancing a biblical view of law and politics.

Restoring Politics and Law

How should Christians work to renew political and legal structures? If we learned anything in recent decades, it is that we should not roll out heavy-handed political movements that recklessly toss around "God-and-country" cliches and scare off our secular neighbors. Our goal is not to grab power and impose our views. Instead, we should act through principled persuasion and responsible participation.

Persuasion means our first task is apologetics—striving to convince our neighbors the Christian worldview provides the best way to order society. We can assume most of our neighbors do not understand the necessity of even something so basic as the rule of law. When I was in school, that was covered in the first civics lesson; today, civics courses are more likely to address the exploitation of Native Americans by European settlers.

We also need to press home the importance of the idea of the common good. Take the illustration of a stoplight: For the public good, all people are required to stop at stoplights; otherwise, there would be chaos and death on the streets. This law applies to Christians, agnostics, Hindus, and New Age proponents alike; whether or not they are offended by the law, they must obey it for the public good.

We need to apply the same reasoning to other laws, such as those recognizing marriage only between two persons of the opposite sex. Protecting heterosexual marriage is in the interest of society. It recognizes a social pattern that every civilized society has adopted in order to propagate the human race and rear children. Christians can argue that such laws do not impose a religious belief but are based on rational moral principles and historical evidence showing that protection of the family promotes the public interest. Decisions such as *Casey v. Planned Parenthood* and *Romer v. Evans* are disastrous, for they make determination of the public good impossible. Finally, we can argue that the Christian worldview provides the most reliable standard for determining the public good and encouraging responsible personal behavior.

Perhaps the toughest sell is persuading people they ought to govern their personal behavior for the public good. Individualism has grown so rampant that most people think society exists to serve them, that they do not owe anything to society. We can argue that unless individuals voluntarily restrain their behavior for the common good, government will have to restrain them by coercive measures—at the cost of our liberty.

Witness the coercion that already characterizes efforts to maintain political correctness. As people disregard the voluntary restraints of civility and social convention (the outdated customs of courtesy), the state begins to micromanage behavior by passing increasingly oppressive laws. For example, we see the often ridiculous attempts to define what is or what is not sexual harassment. For example, Antioch College has published a code requiring students to give and get verbal consent at each stage of escalating passion.[37] Even more absurd, a six-year-old child was penalized by his public school teacher for planting a friendly kiss on the cheek of another six-year-old, and the principal handed the miscreant's mother a copy of the school's sexual harassment policy.[38] And a Kansas bank was fined because it did not have Braille instructions on the ATM machine in its *drive-through* banking lanes.[39]

We may dismiss such things as signs of temporary national insanity, but they are not illogical. They are the inevitable consequence of the loss of voluntary restraints. At one time, hurling a racial epithet would have been considered a lack of civility and would have been suppressed through disapproval and ostracism; today, in the absence of such social sanctions, it has to be an actionable hate crime. At one time, well-behaved young men did not "take advantage" of the "fairer sex"; today, in the absence of such social conventions, women must be protected by laws against sexual harassment. We have been "freed" from rules of courtesy and morality only to be hemmed in by rules imposed by law. To reverse this erosion of freedom, we must make the case that self-government in the political sense depends on self-government in the personal sense—that is, governing our own speech and behavior by the norms of civility and respect.

Commitment to a Higher Law

The Bible is not a political document, yet it has profound political consequences that are important to the general welfare of all citizens. Those who say Jesus and the apostles ignored politics miss the political implications of the maxim, "Give to Caesar what is Caesar's, and to God what is God's" (Matt. 22:21). The first-century church knew exactly what Jesus' words meant—and it was because of a political act (they would not say "Caesar is Lord") that they were crucified, tortured, and thrown to the lions.

What is the fundamental scriptural teaching on the state? We are to live in submission to the state. For our benefit God has appointed kings and rulers to carry out the ordained duties of the state: to restrain evil, to preserve order, and to promote justice. Thus, we are to "honor the king" and to submit ourselves "to the governing authorities, for … the authorities that exist have been established by God" (see, for example, Dan. 2:21; Rom. 13:1-7; Titus 3:1; 1 Pet. 2:13-14,17).

Some people have interpreted these passages as an absolute grant of authority, meaning that government is to be obeyed at all times and in all circumstances, but the injunction to obey is conditioned on the assumption that officials and magistrates are carrying out the purposes for which God has ordained government (in Romans 13:4 the magistrate is called "God's servant"). Thus rulers act contrary to their delegation of authority. Iif they do not act as God's servants, then Christians are not bound to obey them; believers may be morally obligated to resist. For example, if the state prohibits the preaching of the gospel, it is clearly acting contrary to the commandments of the One who granted government its authority in the first place. If the state practices injustice, such as massacring Jews or engaging in systematic tyranny, it loses its claim to divine authority.

Christianity has historically proven to be the most dependable defender of human liberty. The commitment to a higher law means Christians have been on the front lines resisting laws or actions contrary to that law.

Christian conviction gives a basis for resistance to unjust earthly authority. Those who died to defend liberty predominantly feature believers.

Tyrants recognize this all too clearly. The Chinese government persecutes religious believers fiercely, jailing pastors, burning churches, outlawing home meetings not because they are atheists and want to stamp out religion, but because they cannot tolerate anyone who worships a King who stands above the kings of this world. That higher allegiance gives a basis for demanding freedom and rights from the earthly king.[40]

Living Out Our Convictions

We must learn to articulate these principles in making a case for a Christian view of politics, engaging in "backyard apologetics" over the barbecue grill with friends. Though our beliefs derive from Scripture, we must also translate them into terms nonbelievers can understand. For example, when we work to change abortion laws, we must appeal to divine revelation and also point out that the most fundamental duty of government is to defend the defenseless. When opposing legalization of assisted suicide and eugenics, we can note the purpose of government is to prevent the private use of lethal force. (Government wields the sword's power precisely so individuals won't.) We must advance public and persuasive arguments that appeal to reason and evidence.[41]

We must also make the case by the way we live. Others will see the truth of what we believe most clearly if we live out our convictions as responsible citizens in our communities.

First, we live out our convictions when we are good citizens. The most basic requirement of society is that its citizens behave responsibly, obey the law, and carry out their civic duties. Christians should be model citizens because we do out of love for God what others do because they are forced by law. We vote, pay taxes, care for our neighborhoods, and live peaceably with others. We honor and obey leaders and civil magistrates; we pray for those in authority. We can support those who protect religious liberty such as the Beckett Fund, the American Center for Law and Justice (ACLJ), the Rutherford Institute, and the Alliance Defense League.[42]

Second, we live out our convictions when we do our civic duty in every walk of life. When Alexis de Tocqueville came to this country in the early 19th century, he was startled by the extent to which citizens helped their neighbors, organizing all manner of voluntary associations to meet social needs and carry out projects for the common good. "There aren't ten men in all of France who do what ordinary Americans do every day as a matter of course," he said.[43] Most of the associations that so impressed the French statesman were founded and run by Christians, following the command to love our neighbors.

Third, we live out our convictions when we are engaged in politics. Christians should exercise diligently the opportunities available for shaping the political process. As already noted, this begins with voting; beyond that, it includes joining civic groups and political organizations, and perhaps even running for public office. As we do so, we must be ever vigilant to keep our priorities in order, not compromising our commitment to Christ or putting partisan agendas first. Christian organizations active in politics need to set distinctively Christian goals and be uncompromising in biblical fidelity, never allowing themselves to be in the hip pocket of any political party. This is a narrow line to walk, but it can be done.

Christians can and should seek political office, without compromising and without fitting into common stereotypes. I know scores of men and women who do this successfully in the national and state legislatures.

Fourth, we live out our convictions when we as the church act as the conscience of society, as a restraining influence against the misuse of governing authority. Corporately, the church must zealously guard its independence, keep its prophetic voice sharp, and resist the allure of worldly power. It should hold government morally accountable to live up to its delegated authority from God (along with holding all other spheres of society accountable to fulfill the functions ordained to them by God).

This is not to say that Christians go about "imposing" their beliefs on an unwilling populace. Whenever the church speaks to public issues, we're sure to hear some secularists muttering darkly that what Christians really want is a theocracy, where they are in charge. That is not true. Historically, it was Christians who first formulated the principle of separation of church and state, for we recognize that God has ordained government as a separate institution with its own distinctive purposes. Government is a civil function, not a church function. Christians have often been the staunchest defenders of religious liberty for all faiths. One need only compare Western polity, shaped historically by Christianity, with an Islamic polity, which recognizes no distinction between church and state, and which often mercilessly oppresses and persecutes religious minorities.[44]

In addressing the state, we must do so not on the basis of power, as special interests do, but on the basis of principle. This is a crucial distinction, yet it is one that secular politicians and journalists frequently miss. For example, in early 1998 Jim Dobson met with Republican congressional leaders in Washington to confront them on failing to promote the social issues they had promised to support. For Dobson, this was a matter of principle, and it was a valid one. Yet journalists interpreted Dobson's action as a power play, warning in apocalyptic tones that religious conservatives were "marching on Washington" and "demanding their due." Newspaper articles described Christians as a powerful voting bloc that had delivered 45 percent of the vote in the 1994 Republican sweep of Congress and warned that they were now demanding "their place at the table." Christians were depicted in the same terms used for a labor union or any other special-interest group.[45]

Just as any other citizens, we have a right to a place at the table, and yes, we do have political clout, but only because millions of Americans share our moral concerns. Yet these facts are not the basis of our political stance. We contend for certain truths in the political arena because they are crucial to liberty and public justice—and we would do so whether we had 45 percent of the vote or 5 percent.

So our message is not, We put you in office, now pay up. Rather, we are saying, This should be done because it is right, because it is a principle that undergirds any well-ordered civil society, and because it is a proper duty of the state ordained by God.

All this can be summed up by saying we should exhibit the best of Christian patriotism, always holding dear our own land and nation while always holding it up against the standard of divine justice.

Discussion Questions

1. What difference separates laws into the categories of just and unjust?
2. How is the understanding of a transcendent law above human law critical to the preservation of liberty and justice?
3. How did the Reformation view of the state as ordained by God but limited by the other divinely ordained social institutions contribute to American democracy?
4. How does deconstructionism effectively render the law useless?
5. How can Christians work to renew our political and legal structures?

[1] Taken largely from Stephen B. Oates, *Let the Trumpet Sound: A Life of Martin Luther King, Jr.* (New York: HarperPerennial, 1994).
[2] Martin Luther King Jr., *Why We Can't Wait* (New York: Harper & Row, 1964), 84-85.
[3] Ibid., 75.
[4] Russell Hittinger, *Introduction to Rights and Duties: Reflections on Our Conservative Constitution by Russell Kirk* (Dallas: Spence, 1997), xxvii.
[5] The decision was *Dred Scott v. Sandford,* 60 US 393 (1857).
[6] Abraham Lincoln, "Proclamation for Appointing a National Fast Day: (March 20, 1863), as quoted in Mark Noll, *One Nation Under God?: Christian Faith and Political Action in America* (San Francisco: Harper San Francisco, 1988), 98.
[7] Robert P. George, *A Preserving Grace: Protestants, Catholics, and Natural Law,* ed. Michael Cromartie (Washington, D.C.: Ethics and Public Policy Center; Grand Rapids: Eerdmans, 1997), 94.
[8] Marcus Tullius Cicero, *The Great Legal Philosophers: Selected Readings in Jurisprudence,* ed., Clarence Morris (Philadelphia: University of Pennsylvania Press, 1971), 50.
[9] See Willmoore Kendall, *The Conservative Affirmation in America* (Chicago: Henry Regnery, 1963), chap. 5. The church played a major role in making this tradition explicit. In the 11th century, Pope Gregory VII set out to reform the primitive tribal societies of Europe with laws drawn from Scripture. The first German law book (1220) stated that "God is Himself law; and therefore law is dear to Him." (H. J. Berman, "Religious Foundations of Law in the West: An Historical Perspective," *Journal of Law and Religion* 1, no. 1 [summer 1983]: 3-43).
[10] Abraham Kuyper, *Christianity: A Total World and Life System* (Marlborough, N.H.:

Plymouth Rock Foundation, 1996), 46. "Calvin personally preferred a republic," in which there would be cooperation between the spheres of society "under mutual control." He also considered it most ideal "where the people themselves choose their own magistrate," and admonished people to take seriously their responsibility to choose their leaders: "see to it that ye do not forfeit this favor by electing to the positions of highest honor, rascals and enemies of God" (49-50).

[11]James Madison, "Federalist No. 10," *New York Packet,* 23 November 1787.

[12]Historians say some Founders were Enlightenment deists, including Jefferson and Madison. Yet both agreed that the rule of law is rooted in a higher law, objectively true and binding—what Jefferson called "the law of nature and nature's God. Among the Founders, a minority held the Lockean idea of individuals with natural rights based in their personhood coming together and entering a political contract, by which they consent to be governed. The majority held a political contract is made in the context of a higher law and that the contract reflects the natural order of things ordained by God.

[13]William James, as quoted in R.C. Sproul, *Lifeviews: Understanding the Ideas That Shape Society Today* (Old Tapan, N.J.: Revell, 1986), 89.

[14]Phillip E. Johnson, *Reason in the Balance: The Case against Naturalism in Science, Law, and Education* (Downers Grove, Ill.: InterVarsity Press, 1995), chapter 7.

[15]Oliver Wendell Holmes, "Natural Law," *Harvard Law Review,* 30-32 (1918).

[16]Gene Edward Veith, *Postmodern Times: A Christian Guide to Contemporary Thought and Culture* (Wheaton, Ill.: Crossway, 1994).

[17]William Orville Douglas, Zorach v. Clauson, 343 US 306 (1952). See also Richard John Neuhaus, *The Naked Public Square* (Grand Rapids: Eerdmans, 1995), introduction and chapter 3.

[18]*Edwards v. Aguillard,* 482 US 578 (1987).

[19]*Planned Parenthood v. Casey,* 505 US 833 (1992).

[20]The Court could not have been unaware that only once in American history (a contract case) had the Court ever reversed a right protected by the 14th Amendment.

[21]The Court followed *Casey* with unusually harsh decisions, such as pro-lifers may not demonstrate within a bubble zone surrounding an abortion clinic, though pro-choicers may *(Madsen v. Women's Health Center, Inc.,* 512 US 753 [1994]).

[22]Gerard V. Bradley, "The New Constitutional Covenant," *World & I* (March 1994): 361. The Court was talking about the liberty of whether to define oneself as a mother. This definition of liberty could undercut all law. All laws restrain someone's behavior, and all behavior expresses in some way a worldview, a belief about the meaning of existence and the universe.

[23]*Lee v. Weisman,* 505 US 577 (1992).

[24]Ibid.

[25]*Romer v. Evans,* 517 US 620 (1996).

[26]*Compassion in Dying v. Washington,* 79 F 3d 790 (9th Cir 1996). More frightening is the argument the justices used to reach their decision. *Compassion in Dying v. Washington,* the infamous assisted suicide case of 1997, reached the Supreme Court when appellate courts overturned a referendum passed by the Washington State voters banning assisted suicide. Since the appellate courts had reversed the referendum based on the Supreme Court's decision in *Planned Parenthood v. Casey,* which defined liberty as the right to decide for one's self the meaning of life, to be consistent the Supreme Court should have affirmed the lower court, but even the insulated Supreme Court judges weren't ready to face the degree of moral outrage this might have triggered. (Justices do read newspapers and polls.) So what did they do? Examine the Constitution or law? Research legislative history? No, they wrote in their opinion that America hasn't had enough experience with assisted suicide to know whether we are ready for it. They were not speaking in juridical terms but using the language of social scientists. This decision was not based on principled opposition but on the sociological fact that America might not be ready to face it. Their only moral concern was reduced to pure pragmatism: Let's see how things work out. Let's see indeed.

[27]*Boerne v. Flores,* 521 US 507 (1997); *Employment Division v. Smith,* 494 US 872 (1990). City authorities objected to the expansion of a growing Catholic parish in Boerne, Texas, contending the church was an historic monument and its quaint charm was important to an area being redeveloped for tourism. A line was drawn: Was the church a tourist museum or a worship sanctuary? The answer the Court handed down was that tourism was more important.

[28]In the *Casey* case, the Court referred to the Constitution as a covenant. See Russell Hittinger, "A Crisis of Legitimacy," *Loyola Law Review* 44 (1998): 83.

[29]Bradley, "The New Constitutional Covenant," 374.

[30]Russell Kirk, "The 'Original Intent' Controversy," *The Heritage Foundation Report,* no. 138, (October 15, 1987).

[31]See C. S. Lewis, *The Abolition of Man* (New York: Touchstone, 1975) and *Mere Christianity* (New York: Touchstone, 1996).

[32]Arthur Leff, "Unspeakable Ethics, Unnatural Law," *Duke Law Journal* (speech given at Duke University Law School on April 2, 1979): 1229.

[33]Bradley, "The New Constitutional Covenant," 359.

[34]Michael Sandel, *Democracy's Discontent: America in Search of a Public Philosophy* (Boston: Harvard University Press, 1996).

[35]A 1996 Gallup survey of American political culture reports 32 percent of Americans have "a great deal of confidence" in the federal government generally, 13 percent in the presidency and 5 percent in the Congress (comparable figures for 1966 were 41 percent for the president, 42 percent for Congress); 80 percent believe "our country is run by a close network of special interests, public officials and the media." Only one in five is satisfied with political debate quality. One-fourth believe their government works against interests of the citizenry; three-quarters believe it's run by a "few big interests looking out for themselves"; and one in five believes the people who run our nation's institutions are "involved in a conspiracy!" See James Hunter, *The State of Disunion: 1996 Survey of American Political Culture,* vol. 2 (Ivy, Va.: In Medias Res Educational Foundation, 1996).

[36]Pope John Paul II said, "Moral relativism is incompatible with democracy;" rights cannot exist apart from a moral law (speech to U.S. Bishops at the Vatican, October 1998).

[37]Clarence Page, "On Today's Campus: Consent for a Kiss Is Romance 101," *Orlando Sentinel,* 16 September 1993. See also Martin Gross, *The End of Sanity: Social and Cultural Madness in America* (New York: Avon Books, 1998); and James Hannah, "Applications Up after College Enacts Sex Rules for Every Step of the Way," *Rocky Mountain News,* 15 January 1995.

[38]Meg Greenfield, "Sexual Harrasser?" *Washington Post,* 30 September 1996.

[39]George F. Will, "The Popcorn Board Lives!" *Newsweek* (October 13, 1997): 88.

[40]In late 1997, Chinese president Jiang Zemin defended his government's persecution of Christians on the grounds that he could not permit them to incite movements for freedom in China as they did in Eastern Europe. See Diane Knippers, "How to Pressure China," *Christianity Today* (July 14, 1997): 52.

[41]See Robert P. George, "God's Reasons," (speech given at 1998 American Political Science Association Convention; published by Prison Fellowship, Reston, Virginia). Five colleagues and I, all critics of judicial overreach, wrote on the crisis in the law in a symposium that proved to be enormously controversial. See "The End of Democracy?" *First Things* (November 1996): 18-42. It was reported that this material was read by supreme court justices as they debated the recent assisted-suicide cases.

[42]Becket Fund for Religious Liberty, 2000 Pennsylvania Ave., NW, Suite 3580, Washington, D.C. 20006, (202) 955-0095; American Center for Law and Justice, P.O. Box 64429, Virginia Beach, VA 23467, (757) 226-2489; The Rutherford Institute, P.O. Box 7482, Charlottesville, VA 22906, (804) 978-3888; Alliance Defense Fund, 7819 East Greenway Rd., Suite 8, Scottsdale, AZ 85260, (602) 953-1200.

[43]Alexis de Tocqueville, *Democracy in America* (New Rochelle, N.Y.: Arlington House, 1966), 114. For additional material on social ministries run by Christians in the nineteenth century, see Gertrude Himmelfarb, *Victorian Minds* (Chicago: I.R. Dee, 1995); and Marvin N. Olasky, *The Tragedy of American Compassion* (Washington, D.C.: Regnery Gateway, 1992).

[44]Institutional separation does not mean that religious truth must never influence public policy, however, which is where the Christian conception of separation of church and state differs from the liberal conception.

[45]One of the many examples was Andrew Marshall, "Christians Out to Reclaim GOP Agenda," *Arizona Republic,* 5 July 1998.